A Field Guide to Sailboats of North America

Second Edition

A Field Guide to

Sailboats

of North America

Richard M. Sherwood

Second Edition

Houghton Mifflin Company · Boston · New York

For information about permission to reproduce selections from
this book, write to Permissions, Houghton Mifflin Company,
215 Park Avenue South, New York, New York 10003

For information about this and other Houghton Mifflin
trade and reference books and multimedia products, visit
The Bookstore at Houghton Mifflin on the World Wide Web at
http://www.hmco.com/trade/.

Library of Congress Cataloging in Publication Data
Sherwood, Richard M.
    A field guide to sailboats of North America / Richard M. Sherwood.
— 2nd ed.
        p.   cm.
    Includes index.
    ISBN 0-395-65240-5. — ISBN 0-395-65239-1 (pbk.)
    1. Sailboats — Handbooks, manuals, etc.   I. Title.
VM351.S483   1994
623.8'223 — dc20

Printed in the United States of America

QUM   12 11 10 9 8 7 6 5 4 3

Contents

Preface

Twenty years ago it was possible to identify just about every class of sailboat normally encountered. There were far fewer classes than there are today, and they were well known.

In the late 1950s the FRP (fiber-reinforced plastic) "chopper" gun was devised. This gun feeds resin, catalyst, and fiberglass strands through a mixing nozzle. If the mixture is sprayed onto a mold, a duplicate is obtained. I had occasion to see such a gun at that time. The workers were bringing in wheelbarrows, boats, birdbaths, and any other objects that caught their fancy, and happily making their personal copies. About the same time, FRP was used for the first production boats. The process required only a male or female mold, a limited investment in equipment, and semiskilled labor either to lay up by hand or to spray the fiberglass. The result, when capably done, was extremely resistant to corrosion and was lightweight. It could be colored. The immense market for production fiberglass boats soon followed.

Now there are literally thousands of different class or production boats. Recognition is difficult. Class identification marks are very helpful, but they are not always used. And, of course, sometimes the sails are down. This book has been written to help both new and experienced sailors identify boats by pinpointing distinguishing features. Forty-three new boats have been added for this second edition, as well as a new chapter on choosing boats.

In order to compile the information in this book, I sent hundreds of letters of inquiry to manufacturers. Almost all of the manufacturers are in the United States and Canada, but inquiries were also sent to England for certain sailboats exported to the United States. Class associations, or at least those that are members of the United States Sailing Association (formerly the United States Yacht Racing Union), were also contacted. I am grateful to those who replied.

As anyone who has written away for information knows, the results obtained vary widely in both quality and quantity. I felt that certain statistical information on each boat was important, but it was not always forthcoming. In some cases, second and third letters, telephone calls, and even visits proved useless.

There are some very good and well-known boats that unfortunately could not be included in this book because complete information on them could not be obtained.

My selection of boats for this guide is based on several criteria. Some classes simply have to be included; Olympic classes are a good example. Some types are historic. Some are very popular. Some are unusual. However, it was necessary to put a limit on the number of boats. Boats for which information was so scanty as to be worthless were excluded. For example, some manufacturers do not like to release underwater profiles. Also, very small boats have received little consideration; and boats longer than 45 feet overall have received none. Further restrictions have been necessary, and these I must admit were personal choices. While the primary purpose of this book is sailboat identification, a second is to present interesting designs and diversity of types.

The book is in two sections. The first section contains one-designs, small boats, and other boats (generally less than 20 feet) that have no inboard engine. Cruising boats and auxiliaries are in the second section. In both sections, boats are arranged by length overall (LOA). If a boat has a bowsprit, I have used length on deck (LOD), and not the length including the bowsprit.

In the drawing of each boat, short arrows are used to highlight notable identification features — which are also listed briefly at the beginning of the boat's description.

A word about the second edition of the book. It has been interesting to note the changes that have occurred in the industry. A number of very fine manufacturers are no longer in business. There are few production boats over 40 feet — most of these boats are custom built. I found no yawls or ketches in my search, although these rigs are often available upon request as conversions from sloops. Finally, there seems to be a significant concentration of new small boats in the 13 foot to 18 foot range, many small cruisers from 22 feet to 28 feet long, and lots of cruisers from 32 feet to 36 feet in length. This is apparently downsizing in response to cost and to demand.

My deepest thanks go to Kevin Delapenta, who did all of the drawings of the new boats.

I hope this book is helpful. I will welcome information on any boat.

Richard M. Sherwood

Introduction

This section discusses the features of a boat that are most helpful for identification. As sailing has its own language, many other terms are defined in the glossary.

Class Identification

In most cases, the designer, manufacturer, or class association concerned with a small one-design boat has designed a class emblem, or logo. This usually appears on the mainsail. It is certainly the most simple and accurate means of identifying a boat. A number of these are reproduced on the endpapers of this book. Look through them to find the logo of an individual boat, note the name, then use the alphabetical index to find the boat.

A list of class associations belonging to the United States Sailing Association appears in the Appendix. This list was current as of 1993.

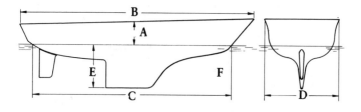

A. freeboard

B. length overall (LOA)

C. length on the waterline (LWL)

D. beam (maximum)

E. draft

F. forefoot

General Dimensions

Length overall (LOA) is the length of the boat from the farthest point forward on the bow to a similar point on the stern.

Length on the waterline (LWL) is measured with the boat upright. Freeboard is the height of the rail above water, and it usually changes along the length of the boat. Draft is the maximum depth of the boat under the water. Beam is the width of the boat and may be measured on deck, at the waterline, or elsewhere. The dimension given for beam in the statistics in this book is the maximum beam, wherever it may occur.

Hull Sections

round bilge   hard chine   modern dinghy

bulb keel   fin keel   integral keel

Hulls

Most of the boats in this book are of recent design. While a few classes date to 1900 and several to 1920 and 1930, the majority were designed after World War II. Early in this century hulls tended to be quite narrow and deep, with full-length keels and rudders attached directly to the keel. (There were many deviations, however; the Star is a notable example.) Largely because of the influence of the racing rating rules, boat design has changed. The rules have changed frequently. Following each change, designs were modified to obtain the most favorable rating. Displacement, or weight, was reduced until the "ultra-light" displacement boats appeared. Displacement, however, gives a sailboat stability. Some substitute was required, and since the beam of a boat also adds stability, beam has often been increased.

Except for planing hulls, the waterline of a boat has a distinct effect on speed. The longer the waterline, the faster the boat. The most recent designs have eliminated the long overhangs that were common in the early part of the century, and waterline length now approaches overall length in many classes, particularly among the smaller boats.

The friction between the boat and the water causes drag. If the area of hull in the water ("wetted surface") is small, friction is minimized. Long, deep keels with large surface areas have given way to short, narrow keels. Rudders have moved far aft, where they exert a very quick and positive control.

Most of these changes are under water and are not ordinarily seen. The aspects of modern design that are most often visible include sharp, drawn out bows, beam well aft, and reverse transoms, as well as the wide beam and short overhangs mentioned above.

Most boats are not designed solely for racing. In order to sell to both racing and cruising markets, production boats are a compromise. Some emphasize racing, some cruising or day sailing. But most still represent compromises, because if they were designed solely as racers or as cruisers the potential market would be limited. Some of the smaller boats are exceptions, however, as are maxi boats designed solely for racing.

Hull Cross-Sections

When a boat heels, the wind is spilled from the sails. Pressure on the sails is reduced, and often the boat sails more slowly. Too much heel may lead to a capsize. Hull shape can reduce heel by incorporating a keel or centerboard and/or by greater width.

Weight in the bottom of the boat tends to keep it upright. The lower the weight, the better. Weight is often designed into a keel, below the actual hull. In small boats it is placed in a centerboard. However, heavy boats are slow in light airs and won't accelerate quickly. Deep projections limit where boats can go without running aground. The goal is to have as much weight as possible as low as possible, but not too much weight, and not too low.

(The centerboard or keel also projects below the hull for a second purpose: It plays a vital role when the boat is sailing across the wind or upwind. That component of the apparent wind which pushes the boat sideways makes it skid, which is of no use. The pressure of the water against the keel or centerboard resists that force, and the boat moves forward.)

Narrow boats are tippy; wide boats are not. A designer can add stability by making the boat wider so that as it starts to heel, buoyancy is increased. Furthermore, under the present

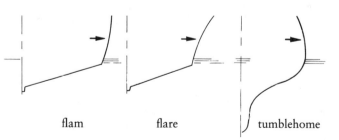

flam   flare   tumblehome

Hull Sections

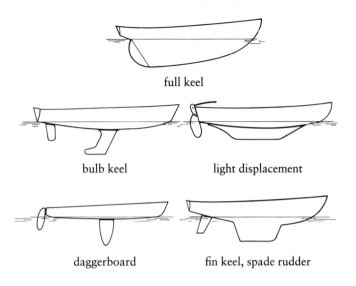

full keel

bulb keel

light displacement

daggerboard

fin keel, spade rudder

Hull Profiles

racing rules, wide beam is not penalized; that is, increasing the beam does not increase the rating as fast as increasing some other dimension, such as waterline length. But very wide-beam boats have a lot of resistance at speeds below planing speed, or in rough water. So beam is also a compromise.

Dinghies most often are round-bottom, round-bilge, or hard-chine, or have the exaggerated flare of a modern dinghy such as the International 505. An alternative to flare is flam, where the hull's sides have a convex instead of a concave curve, but where the beam at the deck is still wider than at the waterline. Another possibility is tumblehome. Here the curve is convex but the maximum beam is at the water. Flam is preferred today for most boats. Tumblehome reduces reserve buoyancy when the boat is heeled; and flare can cause tripping, turbulence, and drag. Flare, however, is frequently used at the bow, where the concave shape of the hull throws water down and out, keeping the boat drier.

Other cross-sections most commonly seen on larger boats are the bulb keel, an obvious attempt to place weight low; the fin keel, with the ballast of the keel attached to the hull; and the integral keel.

Hull Profiles

Underwater shapes shown include a traditional hull whose full keel has an attached rudder; a bulb-keel boat; a small light-displacement keel cruiser; a dinghy with a daggerboard; and a modern high-performance racing boat with a fin keel and a spade rudder supported by a skeg.

Sheer

The line of the deck is termed sheer. While sheer may have some effect upon boat performance, it is usually chosen for appearance. Reverse sheer, for example, gives the maximum freeboard at the middle of the boat and increases stability as the boat heels; but because of its bulky appearance it is uncommon. Straight sheer is unusual. The most common is the conventional hollow sheer, with freeboard decreasing from the bow going aft, and at some point increasing towards the stern. Variations are common. One is powderhorn or coble sheer, in which the sheer at the bow is reverse and the sheer aft is conventional.

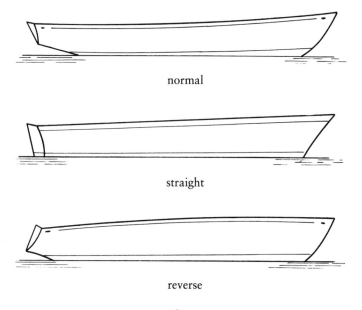

normal

straight

reverse

Sheer

Bows

The basic bow shapes are cruiser; plumb; spoon; a longer spoon with a "chin"; and clipper. Plumb bows are often found on catboats and are frequently used for small one-design racing boats. Cruiser and spoon bows are the most common and are found on all types. Recently the spoon has evolved into a nearly straight line above the water. Traditional clipper bows are usually found on cruising boats. Below the bow and underwater is the forefoot, which may be full or cut away. In small boats and in auxiliaries with fin keels the forefoot is almost totally cut away.

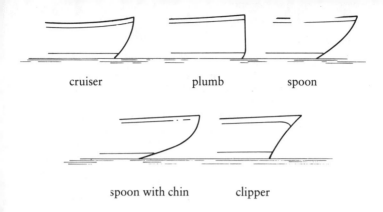

cruiser   plumb   spoon

spoon with chin   clipper

Bows

Sterns

Older and more traditional designs employ long counters that overhang the water. The transom may be vertical, angled aft, or reversed. Double-ended boats have pointed or "canoe" sterns that may or may not have the rudder mounted on the transom. Modern designs tend to have fairly wide sterns, which develop from long, flat sections below the waterline leading to the stern.

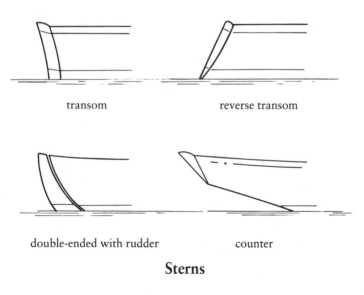

transom   reverse transom

double-ended with rudder   counter

Sterns

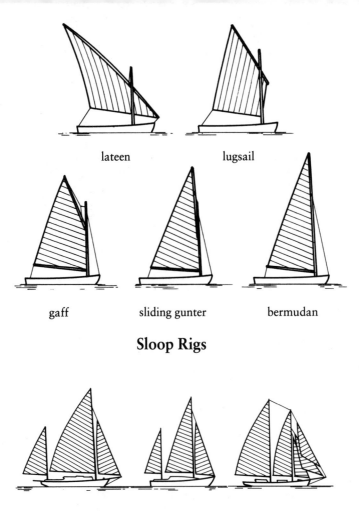

lateen

lugsail

gaff

sliding gunter

bermudan

Sloop Rigs

yawl

ketch

Schooner

Rigs

Although Marconi or Bermuda rigs are the most common sloop rigs, lateen, gaff, gunter, and sliding gunter are not uncommon. Ketch, yawl, and schooner rigs are most often used for cruisers.

The aspect ratio of a boat helps to describe the boat's appearance. A high aspect ratio is the equivalent of a tall rig. The aspect ratio most often used by sailors is obtained by dividing the length of the mainsail's luff by the length of its foot. (In aerodynamics a different proportion is used, and the length of the luff is divided by the area of the sail.) Tall, narrow sails have high aspect ratios and tend to be most efficient going upwind. Low-aspect-ratio rigs are lower, broader, and more efficient off the wind.

In a masthead rig the forestay runs to the peak of the mast and the jib usually fills the entire foretriangle. There are also partial rigs. In a ⅞ rig, for example, the stay runs to the point ⅞ of the way up the mast.

Rudders

Rudders may be keel-mounted, balanced, semibalanced, skeg-mounted, or mounted on the transom. A rudder shape typical of a catboat is also shown. Like a boat's rig, the rudder has an aspect ratio. For the rudder it is the depth of the rudder divided by the chord, or fore-and-aft dimension. A Beetle Cat's rudder has a low aspect ratio; the Soling's is high.

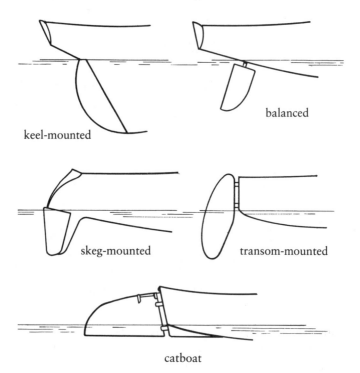

keel-mounted

balanced

skeg-mounted

transom-mounted

catboat

Rudders

Statistical Data

For the most part, the statistics given for each boat are self-explanatory. Statistics have been obtained almost entirely from manufacturers' literature. Certain notes follow that may be helpful.

Length: Overall length (LOA) is used for all small boats; for cruisers, length on the waterline (LWL) is also given. Both small and large boats appear in order of LOA, from shortest to longest.

Beam: Unless otherwise noted, beam listed is the maximum.

Draft: Where variable, as for centerboard boats, board condition is noted. Cruisers are very often available with several keel configurations, and therefore, several drafts.

Weight/Displacement: Weight is given for small one-designs, displacement for cruisers.

Sail area: If the information was available, area is given by sail; i.e., main, jib, mizzen, etc. Where no sails are specified, the sail area is for the sails shown. In some instances, the following symbols — for measurements used to obtain the rated sail areas — appear.

    I: The measured height of the foretriangle, from deck to the truck (top) of the mast.

    J: The measured foretriangle base, from the forestay to the mast.

    P: The measured luff of the mainsail, from head to tack.

    E: The measured foot of the mainsail, from tack to clew.

Hull: If sandwich construction is noted, it is for the hull. Sandwich construction is very commonly used for decks.

Spars: Finish is not always noted. Wood and aluminum spars should always be finished. When aluminum is anodized the thin oxide film normally present, which gives aluminum its resistance to corrosion, is artificially increased in thickness. The result is an improvement in weathering characteristics and a uniform silver color. The coating may be dyed, perhaps gold, but this is unusual. Hard-coated aluminum is anodized in a modified process. The resulting oxide coating is denser and thicker than normal anodic coatings, and it also has a typical integral color, usually either bronze or black.

Racing Crew: Used only for small one-designs, or for boats whose class rules limit crew. Comfortable capacity for day sailing is almost always higher.

First Built: "Modern" design is not always recent, and an older design may be modern indeed. Sources sometimes disagree by one or two years (and in some cases no date is available). The date used is considered the most authoritative. This entry is not given for cruisers.

No. Built: Always approximate, and given for one-designs only. This information gives some idea of the boat's popularity. Frequently this figure is considered confidential by the manufacturer and is therefore not available. In some instances an estimated figure is given.

Berths: Infrequently, this figure had to be assumed.

Engine: Where possible, the type and horsepower are given.

Fuel: The type and tank capacity are given.

Head: "Standard" indicates a marine head conforming to environmental regulations.

Galley: The number of burners and the type of fuel are given.

Water: Tank capacity is given.

Rating: One-design boats may race level, or "head to head"; but when boats from different classes race against each other, more even competition is possible if a handicapping system is used. The total time for each boat is adjusted and the winner determined after the handicap is applied. In the United States, the rating and handicap are based on systems resulting in a time-over-distance correction.

IOR *(International Offshore Rule):* This rule was adopted in 1970 by the International Yacht Racing Union and is not a measurement, although it is given in linear feet. The IOR evolved from the rule of the Cruising Club of America and the British Royal Ocean Racing Club. If shown, it has been provided by the manufacturer.

D-PN *(Portsmouth Number):* The Portsmouth yardstick is a widely used method of rating different classes sailing the same course. The numbers represent the length of time boats take to sail a common but unspecified distance. They are useful for comparing boats. A smaller number indicates a faster boat. Portsmouth numbers used here were taken from the 1993 compilation of Portsmouth numbers by the United States Sailing Association. Portsmouth numbers may be corrected into handicaps for different wind strengths, but here only the primary number has been given. When "suspect" is used it is not a criticism, but indicates that the rating has been derived from fairly limited data. Additional race results may, in the near future, result in a nonsuspect rating that shows little or no change.

PHRF *(Performance Handicap Racing Fleets):* This is the most popular handicapping system for cruisers and is based upon estimates of potential speed. The handicaps are given in seconds per nautical mile; a higher PHRF rating indicates a slower boat. Normally they are given for various geographic areas with differing climatic conditions. In an attempt to smooth out the wide geographic variations that are listed, I have averaged the handicaps.

No rating shown: Ratings are frequently not available, but this should never condemn the boat. In some instances the manufacturer, the class, and the owners have no interest in racing. Also, ratings are based upon measurements, racing experience, or a combination of factors; and newer boats may not have had sufficient time or use to obtain a rating.

Choosing a Boat

Like most decisions, choosing a boat consists primarily of evaluating priorities. Most are subjective, and many are likely to change over time. The boat for a single or young married couple may not be suitable for a couple with small children, or for an older couple whose sailing interests have probably changed with the years. There are, however, certain important areas to consider and to weigh in terms of their relative importance. Well over 1,000 kinds of boats are manufactured and sold in the United States, and while there are certain similarities in types, the sheer volume means that you have many choices.

Race, Day Sail or Cruise

Probably the most important single factor to determine is if you wish to day sail, cruise, or race. You may wish to do more than one. Boat design and construction involves compromise — if it did not, there would be only a few types of boats. To generalize, speed is achieved at the expense of comfort. Weight is the enemy of speed, but weight is important to stability. Most items of comfort, such as galleys, bunks, and heads, add weight. High-speed planing dinghies don't have galleys, bunks, or heads. Ultra-light displacement boats may, but they are kept to a minimum. Twelve meters don't have engines, nor do the newest types of Americas Cup boats. Motors add weight. Tall, fast rigs put the center of pressure on the sails up high, which reduces stability. Adding weight, in the form of ballast or a keel, helps the stability but reduces speed. Boats with a wide beam have more room below for amenities, and stability is increased. Wetted surface, however, is increased, and so is drag. Any designer who solves all of these problems in a single boat will become very wealthy.

Within the categories of racing, day sailing, and cruising there are further subdivisions. Race big boats or small? Sail with calm deliberation or constant activity? Harbor races, where wind and waves are minimized? Short races or day-long? Overnight? Where will you day sail? Lake? Bay? Ocean? If you cruise will you anchor, moor, or use a slip? If you sail at night, you will either require a larger crew or lose sleep.

When you decide to race, day sail, or cruise, you are apt to be deciding on both the size and type of design you want, but this is not at all absolute. Racing boats begin at about 10 feet and, for economic reasons, top off at about 70 feet. Over 40 feet they are almost always custom designed. Boats may be sailed in very short races, around the harbor, or in very long races, around the world. Day sailing may be on "board" boats — 12 feet long — or on cruisers, where size may be almost anything. I've "day sailed" on a 110-foot ketch with a paid crew of four, and two diesel engines. The boat only cruised to and from the Mediterranean each fall and winter — and the owner wasn't aboard. Cruising may be overnight or extended for months. Crew may vary from one to many. A cruiser with a small crew requires a much simpler rig than one with lots of available manpower.

Your Interests

If you have been sailing for any length of time and have experience in a variety of boats, you have probably developed a particular liking for certain sailing activities. Almost everyone likes to be the helmsman. How about sail tending, piloting or navigating, or maintenance? Succcessful racing requires a thorough knowledge of the rules. If you enjoy maintaining a boat, you may well have developed a special liking for work on the hull, on the rigging, the engine, or even on the electronic equipment common to large boats. Generally, the larger the boat and the more complex the rigging, the more requirement for maintenance. If you don't enjoy maintaining a boat, you either need to pay someone to do it for you, or let it slide. That is all right, but racing will require maintenance, and if you cruise deep water or sail hard, lack of maintenance can be dangerous.

Do you want to sail to relax, to compete, or to learn? Do you wish to work hard and to constantly change your position or that of the sails? Is the type and variety of food important, and will you want to socialize? Again, there are many degrees within these categories. Racing may involve riding a trapeze, constantly trimming sails, and giving 100 percent of your attention to the race, the boat, and your competitors. But racing may be simply sitting in a boat and providing verbal guidance to junior sailors, who are learning by doing all the work. I remember with great pleasure racing with two young sons in catboats. The races were each about 400 yards long. First prize was a lollipop. (We were known to barge at the start, but the captain was only eight years old.) Racing in small boats is very different than in cruisers, even though the rules may be the same. Small boats don't usually have galleys or heads, so food may consist of sandwiches, and the head may be a bucket, or behind the sail to leeward. Big boats take a certain amount of muscle, even if there are lots of winches.

Location

Where you will sail and how the boat will be kept have a great deal to do with the type of boat you choose. It's hard to find an area without at least a few sailboats. Inland sailing on lakes and rivers takes place all over the United States. There are scows in Colorado on Grand Lake. There are lots of boats on Lake Mead, in Nevada. Many people sail on the Allegheny River north of Pittsburgh. If you want to sail on lakes, you may want to consider a boat that is reasonably small — say under 30 feet — with a shallower draft than a boat for use on the ocean. Lakes have marinas, and perhaps only one. The opportunities for cruising are more limited than on the ocean. There just aren't as many possible destinations. But some lakes are large, and extended cruises are possible. You may cruise for weeks in the northern Great Lakes. On big lakes, keel boats with considerable draft are common.

The winds inland are different from those on the ocean. Ocean winds tend to be more constant, and from a few limited directions. The winds on Buzzards Bay, in Massachusetts, for example, tend to be from the southwest. It is normal for the winds to be light in the morning and then to pickup around noon. Increases of wind during the day are also common inland, but the winds are more erratic, both in speed and in direction. If you wish to race, or to sail hard, you must pay more attention to wind direction. Races are often won or lost because of wind shifts. Winds on the West Coast are most often from the west, and the coast is behind you. You will beat offshore, and then, going up and down the coast, sail reaches. Not much chance for downwind. If you cruise "down east" in Maine, you will sail broad reaches, or downwind. Sailing home will probably be a beat, and plans for a cruise to Maine had better allow more time for the trip back.

How do you plan to keep your boat? Some common possibilities are to dry sail the boat, to moor it, to cartop, to trailer, or to keep it in a slip. How close are you to sailing areas? Cartopping and trailering enable you to sail in many areas, but the size of the boat will be somewhat restricted, you must allow time for travel, there must be a way to get the boat into the water, and the tow vehicle must be able to pull the trailer.

Moorings are safe, and the boat is ready to sail when kept this way, but there may be problems. You must get to the boat from the shore, either with launch service or your own smaller boat. And you need to transport any crew or supplies. Moorings cost money, and the boat is susceptible to storm damage. Moorings are more crowded each year, with new locations very far out, behind breakwaters, and worse, behind draw bridges that only operate at certain times. Dedicated sailors in Duxbury, Massachusetts, pay close attention to the tide, as the harbor, excellent for sailing half the time, is dry the rest of the time, and so are the boats. Slips alleviate many of the problems of moorings, but they are expensive.

In conjunction with the question of where to keep the boat is the question of winter storage and maintenance. If you like to do your own work, having the boat in the garage or backyard during the fall or winter is convenient and less expensive. Again, while 30 – 40-foot boats are sometimes stored this way, there is a practical limit on size. Boat yards are convenient, but they may not allow you to work on the boat, reserving that privilege for boat yard employees. Yards are also expensive. Worse, they are busy and may not take your boat in the fall or put it in the water just when you wish.

Options to Ownership

It is possible to sail often without owning a boat. One possibility is to join a sailing club. When you do, you'll probably pay a membership fee, plus a set hourly or daily fee when you use a boat. The club may have several types of boats, but they are apt to be simple rigs, unsuited for serious racing, and with sizes generally under 30 feet. Bigger, more complicated boats are harder to maintain, so they aren't as available in a club setting. Sailing clubs provide a wonderful way to learn to sail — almost all offer instruction. If you want to simply get aboard and go sailing, clubs have a lot to offer, without the responsibilities of ownership.

Crewing will get you aboard at almost no cost except for appropriate clothing. The owner provides the boat, the equipment, and probably the lunch. Many owners of big boats want and need crew, and if you can provide some expertise and muscle, they will take you. It helps to have desirable personality traits. (This goes two ways. Some captains are so laid back that you will be bored. Others are direct descendents of Captain Bligh.) Racing skippers must have knowledgeable, dependable crew. The key is dependability. You must show up at the proper time, and you must, therefore, gear your schedule to that of the boat. If you don't, you will lose your value as crew. Also, crewing on racers is best if you are an experienced sailor. Long distance cruising requires crew, and there are always advertisements in boating magazines. Crew for these boats is sometimes even paid. Compatibility and knowledge are crucial, as is the ability to be away from home or work for extended periods.

Chartering a boat has many advantages. Usually depending upon size, they may be chartered for the day, week, or month. Cruisers are available fully staffed, and with or without food and other provisions. If the boat comes with a captain, you may work or not, as you wish.

Charters can also be "bareboat" — without captain or crew. Possibly the best thing about chartering is that, in addition to relieving you of ownership responsibilities and costs, it enables you to visit various sailing locations. In the U.S., charters are available in many different locations, and especially in those famous for cruising, such as Maine, Puget Sound, Buzzards and

Narragansett bays, the Chesapeake, Florida, and the Virgin Islands. The Windward and Leeward Islands of the Caribbean are famous for cruising, as are Scandanavia, Great Britain, and the Mediterranean. The sailing magazines list many charters, and local advertisements and bulletin boards at yacht clubs and boat yards frequently list shorter charters. These local sources are best for smaller boats.

Small Boats

Small boats sometimes are not. Many are over 20 feet in length, and there are a number at 30 feet. For this discussion, however, small boats are those with minimum cabin facilities. They generally don't have any type of cabin, but if they do, it is often for storage. Bunks are uncommon. If there is a head, it may be the portable type. There may be room to store a cooler, but it usually is not built in. Typically, the bow may have a small covered deck, usually extending aft of the mast (and helping to support it), and then a large or small cockpit. Lack of comfort is the primary distinction, as many small boats have very sophisticated rigging and controls.

Small boat design usually concentrates on a single aspect of sailing, although the boats may often be used for several purposes. The majority of small boats are designed either for racing or for day sailing. Racing boats come in a wide variety of sizes, shapes, and complexity. Masts are stayed or unstayed. There are keel, centerboard, and daggerboard models available. It is not uncommon for a design to be available either with a centerboard or a keel. Some classes are strictly regulated, with rules governing every aspect of design and fit out. The intention is usually to keep each boat so similar that racing is decided solely by the skill of the crew, and not because time and money has been spent on maintenance, rigging, and sails. However, there are racing classes in which rig tuning and innovation is encouraged.

If you wish to race, other factors must be considered. Is there a local, active fleet of boats racing the classes in which you are interested? Do you have national or international ambitions? Do you have to be agile or strong? Do you wish to work hard, fly spinnakers, make constant adjustments, or simply tack with self-tending sails?

Boats designed for day sailing are usually less complex in design than racers. Rigging, in particular, is simpler, so that less attention is needed for minor changes or adjustments while sailing. Day sailers may be more comfortable than racing boats.

Cruisers

Cruisers are not necessarily large. They start at about 19 feet, and for purposes of this book, end up at about 45 feet. However, lots of people camp out in small boats. Boom tents are available, and camping gear designed for the mountains works perfectly well on a boat. There has been a great deal of interest in smaller cruisers, ranging from about 21 feet to 28 feet. Some have an astonishing amount of comfort in a small space, with standard heads, real galleys, and as many as four bunks. Some have cabin heaters. In general, they are sloop rigged and are designed to be sailed by two people. To fit comfort into the cabin, the cockpit is sometimes very small.

To reduce congestion in the cabin, centerboards are less common than keel or swing keel boats, and rigging tends to be simple. Because the crew is apt to be small, large genoa jibs are not often used. Inboard engines are uncommon, but batteries are normal, as are outboard engines. Don't discount these boats — they have been cruised for long distances, even across oceans.

Cruisers with standing headroom and comfortable arrangements for four tend to be 30 feet and over. Many sleep six or even more. They sometimes have two private cabins. Rigs may be more complex, and the number and size of sails available increases. There are many variables in cabin arrangements and equipment. Heads may be standard or portable, but the former is more common. There is usually a holding tank. The galley is two- or four-burner. There is probably an engine, and with engines comes the possibility of mechanical refrigeration instead of ice, and pressure instead of hand-pumped water. Space may be given to a navigation station, with a power panel to service electronic aids.

Hull shapes may be of any type. Older designs, more suited for cruising, are displacement hulls, often with a keel that is full length, or perhaps cut away at the bow. Such hulls often have the rudder fastened to the keel. Newer designs, and particularly those designed for racing, usually have a much shorter keel, with the rudder mounted separately, well aft of the keel. The rudder is apt to be balanced, or more often, mounted on a skeg. The keel itself may be just about anything — spade, bulb, fin, or winged. Centerboards become less common as boats become larger. Older designs may exhibit overhanging bows and sterns. New designs tend to have wider beams, with the sections becoming flat towards the stern. But you will see just about anything.

Most boats designed for racing have sloop, or sometimes, cutter rigs, but there have been some very famous yawls and ketches that were successfully raced. Cutters are helpful, as crew size may be reduced, and the number of sail combinations is increased. Yawls, ketches, and schooners also have this advantage; however, as they are two-masted, rigging is more complex, the sail inventory is increased, and so are both first cost and maintenance.

When racing becomes very serious, many of the below-decks features for comfort are minimized. Bunks give way to sail stowage, and the remaining bunks may have to be shared. Hulls are lighter, and the cost and number of sails increases. If you wish to race cruisers, you should consider the crew size required, the type and number of meals to be served, navigation requirements, and the number of nights away from port. In extreme cases there will be *no* bunks, *no* enclosed head, and *very little* provision for meals.

Even a casual investigation will indicate that most cruisers are a compromise, suitable either for racing or cruising, but with a leaning towards one or the other.

Finances

Most of the following list applies to owning a boat. As mentioned, crewing involves very little cost. Chartering involves a set, known cost, plus the expense of getting to the boat, and perhaps of purchasing food. A hard, realistic analysis of possible costs is critical if you don't want unpleasant surprises in the future.

Purchase price After negotiation, purchase price is a known. Not known, and very important to determine in advance are down payment, financing, principal, interest, and the loan period.

Taxes Possibilities include sales, excise, and registration taxes.

Insurance If you keep the boat at home, you may not even want insurance. However, marine insurance should clearly be considered.

Fitting out Don't discount this. Be very clear on what is provided with the boat. Sails are often extra. You will have to provide most of the safety equipment, and except for basic instrumentation such as wind direction and boat speed indicators, you will probably have to provide all of the electronics. How about extra lines, tools, anchors, spare tools and equipment, pots and pans, foul weather gear, or "critical" additions to the cabin? List what you want to have, and obtain pricing. Fitting out may cost nothing, or it may run to 15-20 percent additional.

Annual maintenance The best source for this is the experience of others. Eventually, you will replace sails and rigging. How often and how hard the boat is sailed becomes important, as does your does your ability and desire to do your own maintenance.

Hauling and storage Even if the boat is in the water for the entire year, it will be necessary to haul or beach it for maintenance. Storage at home is free, but you may have to pay to get the boat there. And you may need a cradle and/or a trailer. Find out the cost of hauling, transportation, and boat yard storage if they may apply. In cold climates you may wish to cocoon the boat for the winter, and motors should certainly be prepared for a long period of inactivity. It is more and more common to see boats hauled and stored still fully rigged, but the risk of damage needs to be considered.

Moorings If the boat is to be kept moored, find out how much it costs. It is usually a monthly or seasonal charge.

Electronics Some boats have none, and some have lots. You may not need all that you want, or you may be deeply interested in the refinements that electronics can provide. Navigational requirements for cruising and sophisticated gear for racing will cost the most and are particularly applicable for bigger boats.

Boat Types

A brief discussion of the most common types of boats follows. Remember that there are no absolutes about boats — but there are certain general characteristics.

Catboats

Catboats have a single sail — but not all boats with a single sail are catboats. Most board boats and many dinghies have single sails. Cat masts are stepped well forward. The sail is apt to be large and gaff-rigged on most production boats. This keeps the center of effort lower, adding to stability. Also adding to stability is the wide beam catboats tend to have. There are, however, a number of newer designs in which this is not the case. The mast is often unstayed, or with just a forestay. Because the sail is so big, it may be hard to handle, and the boat may have a weather helm, which tends to point into the wind if the tiller is unattended. Cockpits tend to be large. It is unusual to find a cat over 25 feet long. With no foresails, going to windward is not easily done, but with the large main, performance downwind is good.

Sloops

Nowadays, this is the most common rig. The two basic varieties are the fractional rig, with the forestay running to a point partway up the mast, and the masthead rig, with the forestay to the top of the mast. The former has smaller headsails — the height of the sails is limited by the stay. A wide variety of foresail sizes is available, and they have an influence on both the power of the sail and the size of the crew. A self-tending jib, for example, does not extend aft of the mast. It swings by itself to the other side of the boat when the sheet is loosened and the boat is tacked. A big genoa, on the other hand, may need a crew member to lead the sail forward in order to clear the mast when the boat is tacked. Since the genoa is so large, a winch may be required to control the sheet.

The mainsail may be large or small, set high off the deck or low, have a curved roach or not.

Rigging varies widely. The mast may be unstayed, but side and forestays are common. Backstays are often to the stern, but may be split or single. Running backstays run from the top of the mast to the sides of the boat, well aft. They must be adjusted when the boat is running downwind so that the boom can swing out without hitting the stay.

Cutters

Cutters have the mast stepped more towards the middle of the boat than sloops. Because of this, there is more of a balance between the forces exerted by the main and the headsails. Cutters often have two headsails, and when they do, there are two stays forward of the mast. They have a greater variety of sail combinations, which can be helpful in heavy weather. Because the sails are apt to be smaller, they are easier to handle, which may result in a need for a smaller crew. Cutters don't normally point as high as sloops.

Ketch

Ketches have two masts. There are several traditional methods to tell a ketch from a yawl. Perhaps the easiest is that a ketch has the aft mizzenmast stepped in front of the steering position. Because of this, the mizzenmast is almost always taller than that of a yawl, and the mizzen sail proportionately larger. The ketch may or may not have two headsails. One is usual. Main and mizzen sails are probably "jib-headed," or Marconi, and not gaff-rigged. Lots of sail variations are possible. Ketches are good upwind, but the aft sail tends to blanket the main going downwind. Like the yawl or schooner, the two-masted ketch has more rigging and therefore more maintenance requirements than a sloop. Any two-masted boat smaller than 25 feet is rare.

Yawl

Like ketches, yawls are two-masted, and they are similar in appearance. On yawls, however, the aft, or mizzenmast, is stepped aft of the position of the helmsman. To provide a location to sheet the mizzen sail, there is often a short boomkin extending aft of the transom. The mizzenmast, and therefore the mizzen sail, is proportionately smaller in the yawl than the ketch. Since the sail is smaller, it contributes less towards powering the boat. However, like the ketch, the yawl has a number of sail combinations used as the wind increases, with the most common being a jib and the mizzen, with no mainsail. Yawls usually don't point quite as well as sloops because the mizzen contributes very little and may be backwinded by the main. Blanketing of the main downwind is similar to the ketch, but not as severe. Most yawls and ketches are variations of sloop designs, and if new, must be custom ordered.

Schooners

Schooners may be as small as 25 feet, but most are over 30 feet. The foremast is shorter than the mainmast, which is aft. Older rigs have gaffs on both the fore and mainmasts. The other most common arrangement is marconi rigging on the main mast, and staysails set on the foremast. Lots of sail combinations, even including square-rigged topsails on the foremast, are seen. With a number of sails, the options for reducing sail for heavy weather are varied. Schooners tend to sail best on a reach or a broad reach. They are seldom raced.

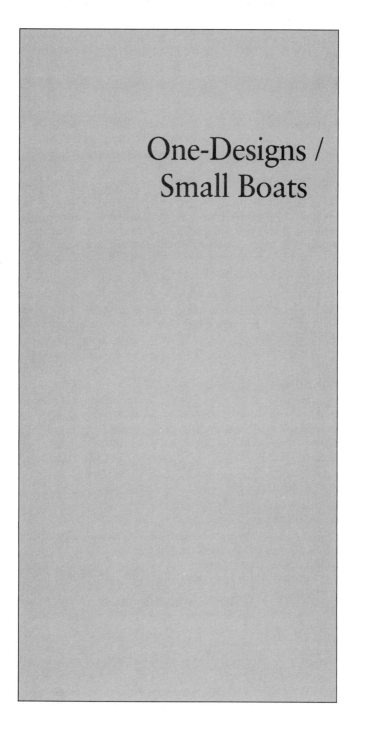

One-Designs /
Small Boats

Cape Cod Frosty

Length: 6 ft.4 in.
Beam: 2 ft. 9¼ in
Draft: 3 ft.
Weight: 34 lbs.
Sail area: 25 sq. ft.
Hull: Wood

Spars: Wood or aluminum
Racing crew: 1
Rating: None
First built: 1984
No. built: 1,000
Designer: Thomas Leach

Tiny. Unstayed mast.

The designer says that you "wear" this boat — and that you can build it for under $300. The boat is built using stitch-glue epoxy techniques. Frosty originated on Cape Cod, as a small, inexpensive boat for frost-biting races. There are no frames or chines, and only one bulkhead. This is the world's smallest racing class — and all boats are equally slow. But when you put your big boat up for the winter, you may still compete, and perhaps on a more friendly level. Class rules require flotation, and weight correction is required to bring the combined weight of the boat and crew to 214 pounds, for which water-filled plastic jugs are used. However, if you wish you may add a vang, Cunningham, more blocks, a traveler, etc.

Optimist

Length: 7 ft. 9 in.
Beam: 3 ft. 8 in.
Draft: 2 ft. 9 in.
Weight: 77 lbs. (FRP hull)
Sail area: 35 sq. ft.
Hull: Wood or FRP
Spars: Wood or aluminum

Racing crew: 1
Rating: D-PN 138.0 suspect
First built: 1947
No. built: 500,000 + world
Designer: Clark Mills, modified
   by Axel Damgard

Pram bow. Spritsail. No stays.

With the Mirror Dinghy, the Optimist is the most widely used junior training and racing pram. The Optimist is IYRU controlled, and it reached international status in 1973. There are class associations in 43 countries. There are many home-built boats in plywood, but the most recent races have been won by fiberglass boats. Flotation is required by class rules.

Cape Cod Frosty

Optimist

Shrimp

Length: 9 ft. 7 in.
Beam: 4 ft. 10 in.
Draft: 2 ft. 6 in.
Weight: 120 lbs.
Sail area: 50 sq. ft.
Hull: FRP
Spars: Aluminum

Racing crew: 2
Rating: None
First built: 1972
No. built: 340
Designers: Hubert Vandestadt
and Fraser McGruer

Gunter rig.

A tender, rowboat, outboard, and small training dinghy, the Shrimp has an unusual gunter rig that helps in trailering or car-topping because the spars are short. If Shrimp is to be used as a tender, the bow eye is relocated for better towing. The rudder and centerboard kick up. There are foam-filled buoyancy tanks. The sail is loose-footed.

International Moth

Length: 11 ft. maximum
Beam: 7 ft. 4 in. maximum
Draft: Varies
Weight: Varies; very light
Sail area: 85 sq. ft. maximum
Hull: Open

Spars: Open
Racing crew: 1
Rating: D-PN 106.9
First built: 1928
No. built: 10,000 world,
4,120 U. S.

Designer: Individually designed. Evolved from designs by Len Morris (Australia) and Captain Joel Van Sant (USA) in 1928-1929.

Identification is difficult because almost any hull shape except multihull is allowed in this open developmental class. Single-hander.

This is a boat for nonconformists. Build one. If you don't like the way it sails, redesign it and build another. The Moth is under IYRU control. It issues building permits and also controls one-design fleets. In the development class new designs, construction, and materials are encouraged. Hull designs are often skiff or scow, and there has been a tendency to add wings for hiking leverage. The wings extend the beam, which now averages about 3 feet 10 inches. Weight may be very low and appears to average 50-60 pounds. In addition to the U. S., there are International Moth Class Associations in Europe, New Zealand, Japan, and Colombia.

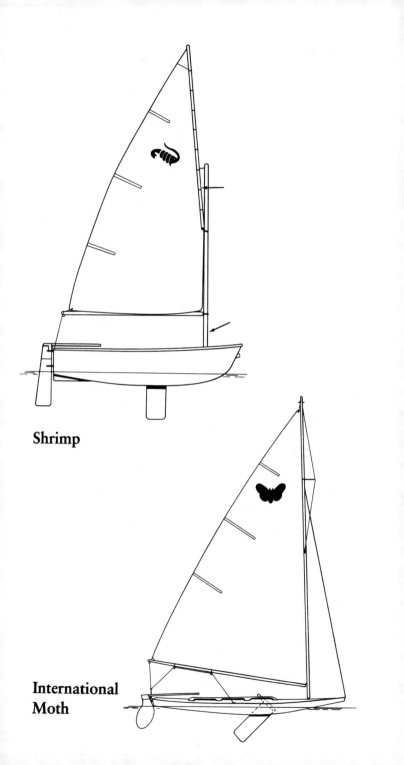

Shrimp

**International
Moth**

Sundancer

Length: 11 ft.
Beam: 3 ft. 6 in.
Draft: 2 ft. 3 in. (scaled)
Weight: 52 lbs. (hull only)
Sail area: 60 sq. ft.
Hull: Cryolac, foam core

Spars: Aluminum
Racing crew: 350 lbs. maximum
Rating: D-PN 128.0
First built: 1982
No. built: 1,000
Designer: Ray Kosteneuli

Sleeved sail. Cat rig, loose-footed. Unusual foredeck. Unstayed mast. Yellow hull.

The Sundancer is very light and easily cartopped. Oarlocks are provided. Boom vang. Wood trim. The mast is unstayed, and the loose-footed main is sleeved. There are 14 inches of freeboard.

Europe Dinghy

Length: 11 ft
Beam: 4 ft. 5 in.
Draft: very little
Weight: 66 lbs.
Sail area: 75 sq. ft.
Hull: PVC foam and FRP

Spars: Aluminum or carbon fiber
Racing crew: 1
Rating: Olympic class for
   women. D-PN 86.0
First built: 1960
Designer: Alois Roland

Unstayed mast. Little freeboard . Since Olympic, probably has "U. S." sail number. Kickup rudder.

The Europe Dinghy was designated international status in 1976, and the Olympic Dinghy for women in 1989. The boat is little and light and is well suited for crews ranging in weight from 100 to 160 pounds. The hull is PVC foam cored, with FRP skins. The rudder kicks up. There is a vang, and both it and the mainsheet lead to sail controls located on both sides of the hull. The spars are aluminum or carbon fiber. Seating is on the deck, so there is a long extension for the tiller. Flotation is positive.

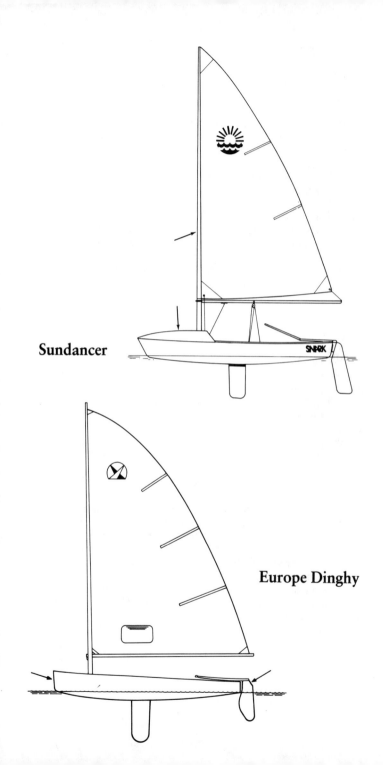

Sundancer

Europe Dinghy

Blue Crab

Length: 11 ft.1 in.
Beam: 5 ft. 2 in.
Draft: 2 ft. 9 in.
Weight: 205 lbs.
Sail area: Main, 65 sq. ft.;
jib, 23 sq. ft.
Hull: FRP

Spars: Aluminum
Racing crew: 2
Rating: D-PN 110.8 suspect
First built: 1972
No. built: 800
Designer: Harry R. Sindle

Shrouds aft of mast. Loose-footed main. Traveler quite high above transom.

Blue Crab is a beginner's boat. It is dry and easily rigged, and it can be sailed by one person. For its size, it is a light boat and may be cartopped or trailered. Capacity is three adults. The transom is reinforced, so additional brackets are not required for an outboard. Blue Crab may be rowed; when not sailing, it has a capacity of five adults.

Skunk

Length: 11 ft. 1 in
Beam: 5 ft. 5 in.
Draft: 2 ft. 6 in.
Weight: 190 lbs.
Sail area: Main, 50 sq. ft.;
jib, 38 sq. ft.
Hull: FRP

Spars: Aluminum
Racing crew: 2 or 3
Rating: None
First built: 1966
No. built: 1,050
Designers: Hubert Vandestadt
and Fraser McGruer

Gunter rig. Recessed foredeck. Bigger than Shrimp, and has jib.

Skunk is a light, easily transported boat. Because of the gunter rig, all spars will fit inside the boat. There are no stays. The Super Skunk is Marconi rigged and has an extra 10 square feet of mainsail. Besides sailing, the Skunk may be used for fishing, as an outboard, or as a rowboat. The transom is reinforced and there is a motor clamp pad. There are oarlocks and a skeg. The recommended maximum horsepower is five. The mahogany rudder and the fiberglass centerboard kick up. There is storage under the foredeck.

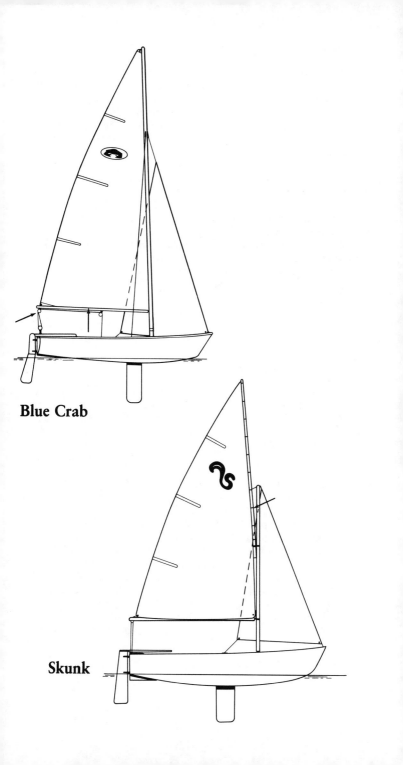

Blue Crab

Skunk

Sandpiper 100

Length: 11 ft. 4 in.
Beam: 4 ft. 10 in.
Draft: Not avail.
Weight: 110 lbs. (hull only)
Sail area: Main, 80 sq. ft.;
jib, 20 sq. ft.
Hull: Cryolac, foam core

Spars: Anodized aluminum
Racing crew: 580 lbs. maximum
Rating: D-PN 112.0
First built: 1970
No. built: Not avail.
Designer: A. Kostanecki

Jib halyard runs to mast head. Mast set well forward. Loose-footed main.

Sandpiper is an auxiliary boat capable of being used for sailing, for rowing, or with an outboard. (Maximum four horsepower). There is an aluminum mounting plate for the outboard and removable oarlocks. The rudder kicks up and there is a hiking stick on the tiller. The hull material, Cryolac, is uncommon in sailboats, although recently it has begun to be used in the manufacture of canoes.

International Penguin

Length: 11 ft. 5 in.
Beam: 4 ft. 8¾ in.
Draft: 3 ft. 9 in.
Weight: 180 lbs.
Sail area: 72 sq. ft.
Hull: Plywood or FRP

Spars: Spruce or aluminum
Racing crew: 1 or 2
Rating: D-PN 112.4
First built. 1938
No. built: 7,000+
Designer: Philip L. Rhodes

Hard chine. Cat. Loose-footed sail. Plumb bow. Racing boats have window. Stayed mast. Possible hood over fore portion.

The Penguin, very actively raced in the East, is not necessarily simple. The drawing shows a shock cord to the forestay, a mast-turning handle below it, and a spray hood lowest of all. There is a boom vang and also a Cunningham. There are both down- and outhauls, and lever stay adjustment. Stay tangs allow for mast rotation, and the mast itself is bendy. There are active racing fleets in New England, Long Island Sound, and New Jersey. In addition to professionally built boats, many Penguins are built at home.

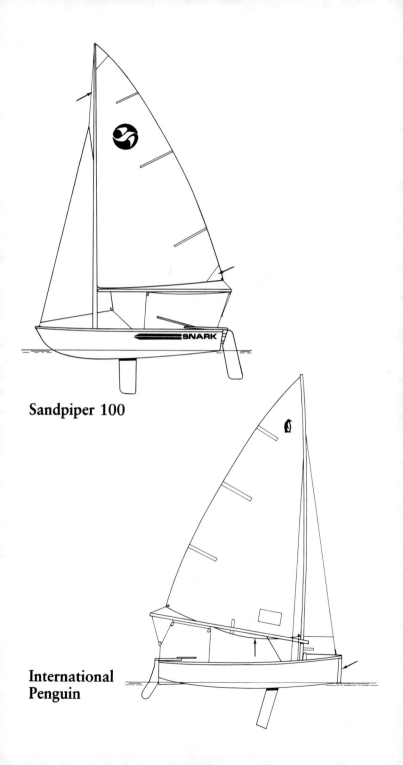

Sandpiper 100

International Penguin

Fatty Knees

Length: 11 ft. 6 in.
Beam: 4 ft.
Draft: 5 ft. CB down
Weight: 130 lbs.
Sail Area: 55 sq. ft.
Hull: FRP, Airex PVC foam
Spars: Mast, aluminum; boom, fir

Racing crew: not applicable
Rating: Not applicable
First built: 1905
No. built: not known
Designer: Nathaniel Herreshoff/
　　Lyle Hess

Lapstrake. Sailing or rowing. Vertical bow.

Lyle Hess has taken a lapstrake design originated by Nathaniel Herreshoff in 1905 and updated it, retaining the lapstrake in FRP. The molded lapstrake adds a great deal of rigidity. Wood trim is teak. There is a storage compartment in the bow, and two rowing positions. Options include tanbark sails, oars, a teak floor, and a pad to mount an outboard. There is a great deal of positive flotation — photographs show an adult rowing a load of eight children, and there is a lot of freeboard left. A deep skeg helps to maintain tracking, and while sailing, there is a daggerboard.

Interclub Dinghy

Length: 11 ft. 6 in.
Beam: 4 ft. 7 in.
Draft: 3 ft. 2 in.
Weight: 250 lbs.
Sail area: 72 sq. ft
Hull: FRP
Spars: Aluminum

Racing crew: 1 or 2
Rating: None
First built: 1920
No. built: 1,200
Designer: Sparkman and
　　Stephens

Sailing dinghy with forestay. Sail loose-footed. Vertical bow.

Originally built for dinghy racing fleets in western Long Island Sound. The forestay is adjustable, and there is a two-to-one Cunningham and a ten-to-one vang. The outhaul is internal. The boat may be purchased without rudder, tiller, centerboard and spars, and they may be purchased separately, with the spars available as blanks. An optional dolly is also available for sailing the boat from the beach.

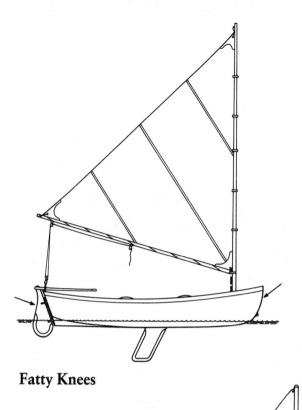

Fatty Knees

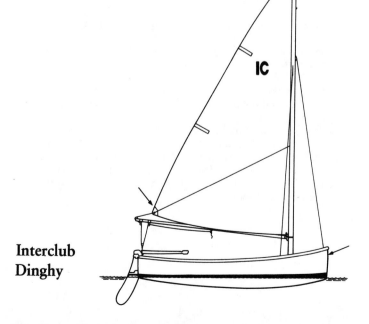

Interclub Dinghy

Echo

Length: 11 ft. 10 in.
Beam: 4 ft. 11 in.
Draft: 2 ft.
Weight: 140 lbs.
Sail area: Main and jib,
   92 sq. ft. total
Hull: FRP

Spars: Aluminum
Racing crew: 2
Rating: None
First built: Not avail.
No. built: Not avail.
Designer: Not known

Significant sheer. Vertical stern. Mid-boom sheeting. Single shroud, no jumper.

A straightforward beginner's boat, the Echo has been designed for versatility and may also be rowed or powered (with a maximum of five-horsepower outboard). Oarlock sockets are built in, and there is a pad for the motor. A rowing seat runs athwartship. The rudder and daggerboard are mahogany. The former kicks up. The mast is two-piece for cartopping. There is a storage compartment and an optional whisker pole.

Butterfly

Length: 12 ft.
Beam: 4 ft. 6 in.
Draft: 1 ft. 3 in. (hull only)
Weight: 137 lbs. (hull only)
Sail area: 75 sq. ft.
Hull: FRP

Spars: Aluminum
Racing crew: 1 or 2
Rating: D-PN 108.4
First built: 1960
No. built: 8,600
Designer: John Barnett

Reverse sheer of both top of deck and gunwale. No jib, but forestay and shrouds. Considerable roach to sail.

Butterfly is designed as a cartopper, so in addition to the normal one-piece anodized rotating mast, a two-piece mast is offered. Two people or three good friends is reasonable capacity. Sail control has a fixed outhaul, but there is a boom vang and a downhaul. Stays are adjustable. The boat is unsinkable, with foam flotation. Rudder kicks up and there is a snubber for the mahogany daggerboard. Handrails are mahogany, and there is a vinyl rub-rail. The main runs up the mast on a track, but it is sleeved over the boom.

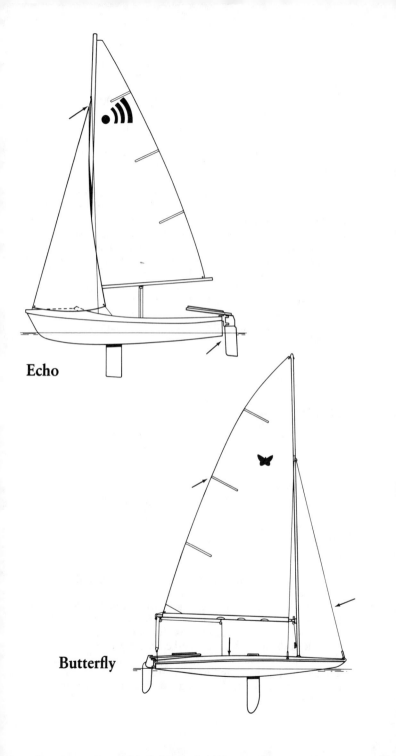

Echo

Butterfly

Byte

Length: 12 ft.	*Spars:* Aluminum
Beam: 4 ft. 3 in.	*Racing crew:* 1
Draft: Not given	*Rating:* None
Weight: 100 lbs.	*First built:* 1990
Sail area: 58 sq. ft.	*No. built:* 910
Hull: FRP	*Designer:* Ian Bruce

Raked, unstayed mast. Small version of the Laser. Mid-boom sheeting.

The Byte is a modification of the Laser and was designed by the original builder of that boat. The redesign is intended to make the boat more suitable for younger and lighter sailers — those weighing from 80 to 140 pounds. The Laser daggerboard and rudder may be used. The two-piece anodized aluminum mast has a zippered luff sleeved over the mast, so that the mast can be erected and the sail sleeved and zippered over it. There is a halyard. Two small adults will fit in the cockpit, or perhaps a coach and a student. Clearly, the boat is intended to be sailed by one. The sail sheets to a traveler in the middle of the cockpit.
The boat is now produced in Canada and Britain, and it is exported to the United States.

Howmar Twelve

Length: 12 ft. 2 in	*Spars:* Anodized aluminum
Beam: 5 ft.	*Racing crew:* 2
Draft: 2 ft. 6 in.	*Rating:* None
Weight: 160 lbs.	*First built:* 1981
Sail area: Main, 60 sq. ft.; jib, 30	*No. built:* 200
sq. ft.; spinnaker, 86 sq. ft.	*Designer:* Sparkman and
Hull: FRP	Stephens

Straight bow. Jib window. Loose-footed. Distinct sheer forward of mast.

Roomy for its size, the Howmar Twelve is a racer, a trainer, and day sailer. The hull's light weight makes for easy cartopping. The boat has internal seating, is self-bailing, and has foam flotation. There is a dry storage locker under the forward seat. Capacity is 480 pounds. The main is loose-footed and has an adjustable outhaul. Both rudder and centerboard are polyurethane. Options include a vang, hinged mast step, hiking straps, and a mounting block for an outboard. The sharp bow cuts through waves, and with its broad aft lines, the Howmar Twelve will plane.

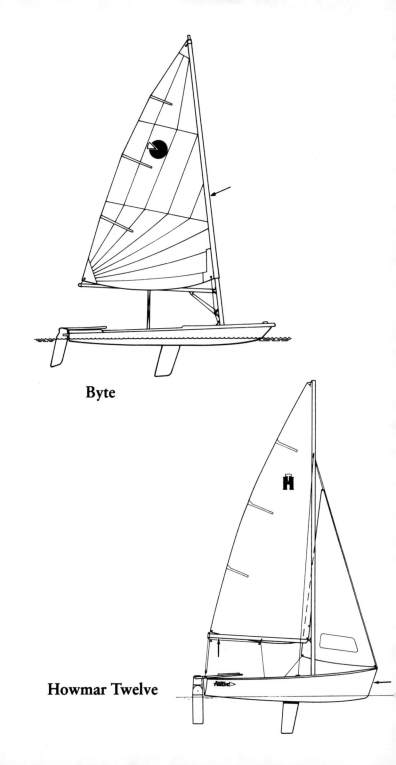

Byte

Howmar Twelve

Beetle Cat

Length: 12 ft. 4 in.
Beam: 6 ft.
Draft: 2 ft.
Weight: 450 lbs
Sail area: 100 sq. ft. approx.
Hull: Oak, cedar

Spars: Fir
Racing crew: 2
Rating: D-PN 103.8
First built: 1921, approx.
No. built: 3,000 est.
Designer: The Beetle family

Gaff-rigged cat. Wood hull and spars. Main sheeted to elevated rod traveler on transom. Typical Cape Cod rudder. Note bow.

Look for the Beetle Cat on the south and east of Cape Cod, in Buzzards Bay, and in Narragansett Bay. There are also fleets on Long Island. Competition, especially for juniors, is stiff. The Beetle is an excellent, stable training boat. Since 1946 the boat has been built (in wood only) by the Concordia Company. Fastenings are bronze, and the deck is canvas-covered. There are no seats--in light air one sits on the sole; in stronger winds, on the gunwale. The boat is offered complete, although sidestays and a clew outhaul are optional.

Widgeon

Length: 12 ft. 4 in
Beam: 5 ft.
Draft: 3 ft. 6 in.
Weight: 318 lbs.
Sail area: Main and jib,
    90 sq. ft. total
Hull: FRP

Spars: Aluminum
Racing crew: 2
Rating: D-PN 122.6
First built: 1964
No. built: 5,040
Designer: Robert Baker

Bow almost plumb. Note sheer line. Loose-footed main. Bow-eye.

Widgeon is light and responsive and accelerates quickly. It is raced, but probably the primary use has been as a trainer. The transom has been designed to carry an outboard with a recommended maximum of four horsepower. The mast is sealed, and there is foam flotation, so the boat is self-rescuing. There is a bow eye for mooring and trailering. Some of the options available include an outhaul and boom vang, compartment doors for the bow stowage, and a tiller extension. The centerboard is fiberglass and weighs 15 pounds. The rudder kicks up. There is seating for four.

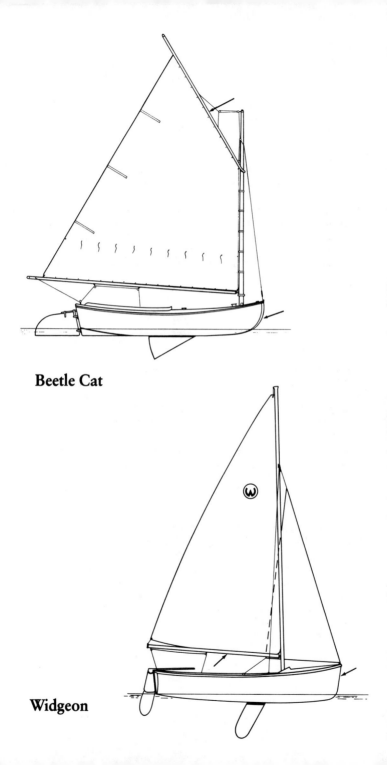

Beetle Cat

Widgeon

Puffer

Length: 12 ft. 6 in.
Beam: 5 ft. 9 in.
Draft: 2 ft. 6 in. (scaled)
Weight: 160 lbs. (hull only)
Sail area: Main, 55 sq. ft.;
jib, 35 sq. ft.
Hull: FRP

Spars: Aluminum
Racing crew: 1-3 (450 lbs.)
Rating: D-PN 110.1
First built: 1972
No. built: Not avail.
Designer: AMF

Open cockpit. Loose-footed main. Spoon bow. Rudder at noticeable angle away from transom. Adjustable jib leads.

Puffer may be sailed or rowed, so she comes with oarlocks. There is also a motor mount. Seats are molded into the double hull, and there is foam under the benches in case both hulls are holed. The rudder kicks up. There are hiking straps, a boom downhaul, and an outhaul. The centerboard and the rudder are mahogany.

Tech Dinghy

Length: 12 ft. 8 in.
Beam: 5 ft. 2 in.
Draft: 6 in. board up
Weight: 250 lbs. (hull only)
Sail area: 72 sq. ft.
Hull: FRP
Designer: Halsey Herreshoff after initial design by Massachusetts Institute of Technology.

Spars: Aluminum
Racing crew: 2
Rating: D-PN 111.2 suspect
First built: 1962
No. built: Not avail.

Cat, loose-footed main, has forestay. Note sheeting. Recessed foredeck, cross seat.

The original design of the Tech Dinghy was by MIT, for use in the Charles River Basin as either a trainer or a collegiate racer. About 20 years ago Halsey Herreshoff and the MIT sailing director, Hatch Brown, redesigned her a little faster, drier, and more forgiving. There is a lever to operate the FRP centerboard. The traveler, outhaul, and boom vang are adjustable, with the latter leading to the maststep casting. MIT has sold the original boats, and if you see a wood model, it may well be one of the originals.

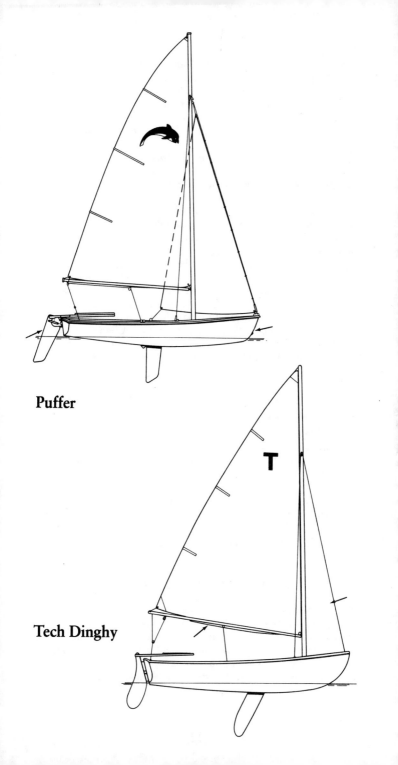

Puffer

Tech Dinghy

Banshee

Length: 13 ft.
Beam: 4 ft. 1 1 in.
Draft: 2 ft. 6 in.
Weight: 120 lbs. (hull only)
Sail area: 88 sq. ft.
Hull: FRP

Spars: Aluminum (two-piece)
Racing crew: 1
Rating: D-PN 94.3
First built: 1969
No. built: 8,000
Designer: Richard L. Reid

Spoon bow. Unstayed mast. Four battens. Loose-footed sail.

A high-performance boat designed for cartopping. Maximum capacity is two, or in a pinch, three. Sail control includes a vang and a Cunningham and an adjustable outhaul. The unstayed, nonrotating mast pivots fore and aft, raking aft when going to weather and forward when running. The loose-footed sail slips over the mast and has a window. The daggerboard is adjustable fore and aft, allowing the boat to be balanced when the sail is reefed around the mast. Rudder kicks up. Banshee is unsinkable, with foam flotation. Racing rules govern the hull, spars, and sail. Modifications are allowed to running rigging, including sail shaping. Originally designed for San Francisco Bay, Banshee now has more than 50 fleets in five countries. A Banshee T modification with a reduced sail area of 73 square feet is available for extra stability and has a Portsmouth Number of 99.9.

Cyclone

Length: 13 ft.
Beam: 4 ft. 11 in.
Draft: 2 ft. 10 in. (scaled)
Weight: 148 lbs.
Sail area: 74 sq. ft.
Hull. FRP

Spars: Aluminum
Racing crew: 1 or 2
Rating: D-PN 96.3
First built: 1972
No. built: 2,350
Designer: Frank Butler

Bendy mast. Short forestay. Loose-footed main. Mid-boom sheeting.

A planing dinghy with a bendy mast. There is an unusually short forestay. For ease of cartopping, the mast may be ordered in two pieces. Both the centerboard and the rudder are fiberglass. A beaching rudder is available as an option. The cockpit is self-bailing, there are hiking straps, and foam flotation is provided. Control includes an outhaul, a Cunningham, and a vang. A sail window is optional. A hatch leads to a forward compartment. Sheets are adjusted with a full-width cockpit traveler.

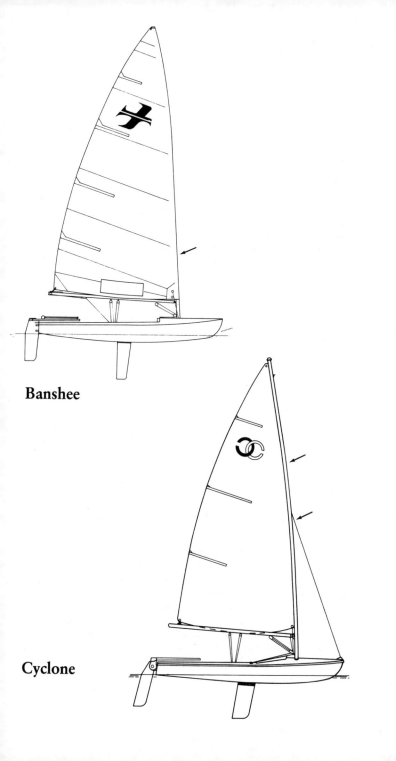

Banshee

Cyclone

Gryphon

Length: 13 ft. 1 in.
Beam: 5 ft.
Draft: 2 ft. 6 in.
Weight: 120 lbs.
Sail area: 82 sq. ft.
Hull: Graphite fiber with PVC
    foam core

Spars: Graphite fiber
Racing crew: 1
Rating: D-PN 94.4
First built: 1980
No. built: 50
Designer: Team. Evolved
    from Banshee.

Lever boom vang. Rudder head perforated. Main loose-footed. Bendy mast. Maximum beam well aft.

A high-technology boat designed to sell against Banshee, Laser, and Finn. The extremely light weight is due to the use of carbon fiber in the mast, hull, and foils. The mast is tapered and unstayed. There are dual controls for the vang, traveler, outhaul, and Cunningham. The foot and leech tension may be adjusted by single controls. There are hiking straps, a daggerboard slot gasket, and a beaching rudder. The traveler is curved. Flotation is provided by the PVC core of the sandwich hull, which is stiff. Because of its light weight, the Gryphon accelerates quickly.

FJ

Length: 13 ft. 3 in.
Beam: 5 ft. 3 in.
Draft: Not given
Weight: 210 lbs.
Sail area: Main, 65 sq. ft.; jib,
    35 sq. ft.; spinnaker, 80 sq. ft.
Hull: FRP

Spars: Anodized aluminum
Racing crew: 2
Rating: D-PN 98.2
First built: 1956
No. built: 4,400 (USA)
Designer: Not known

Compound curve to bow. Roach smoothly curved. Spinnaker pole sets high.

The FJ is recognized by the IYRU for international competition. Many aspects of the boat are strictly controlled. Flotation in three separate bouyancy tanks, plus positive foam flotation is required. Seating is on the gunwales, which are the tops of two of the tanks. Rigging is stainless steel, and the rudder flips up. There is a suction bailer. The jib leads are adjustable, and there is a 4: 1 boom vang. The sail plan is fairly modest, which allows for sailing in most conditions. The main sheets to a traveler on the transom. Light weight allows for cartopping.

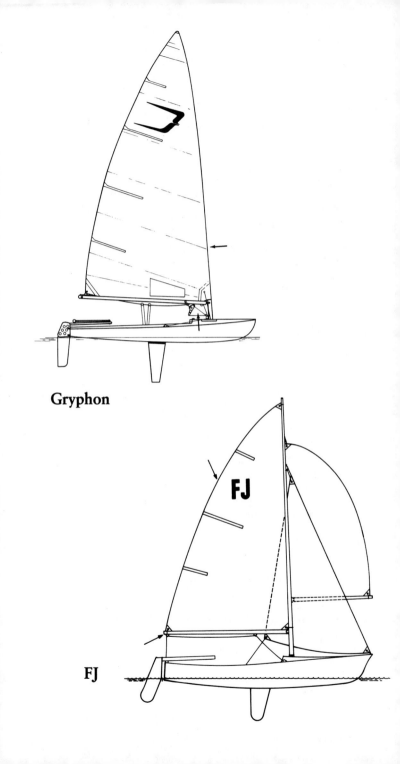

Gryphon

FJ

Spindrift

Length: 13 ft. 4 in.
Beam: 5 ft. 2 in.
Draft: 3 ft.
Weight: 205 lbs.
Sail area: Main, 68 sq. ft.;
jib, 32 sq. ft.
Hull: FRP

Spars: Aluminum
Racing crew: 2
Rating: D-PN 103.6
First built: 1964
No. built. 620
Designer: Hubert Vandestadt

No spreaders. Straight bow. Splash rail. Mid-boom sheeting.

Spindrift is available completed in kit forms and can also be built of wood, from scratch. In fiberglass the deck is a foam sandwich. Crew capacity is four. There is foam flotation in the mast and in buoyancy tanks fore and aft. Both the centerboard and the rudder kick up. There is a boom vang and jiffy reefing. This is a planing dinghy.

Blue Jay

Length: 13 ft. 6 in.
Beam: 5 ft. 2 in.
Draft: 3 ft. 9 in.
Weight: 275 lbs. min.
Sail area: Main, 62 sq. ft.; jib, 28
sq. ft.; spinnaker, 110 sq. ft.
Hull: Plywood

Spars: Aluminum
Racing crew: 2 or 3
Rating: D-PN 108.7
First built: 1949
No. built: 7,200
Designer: Sparkman and
Stephens

Fractional rig. Both jib and main set fairly high. Splash rail. Shrouds slightly aft of mast.

This was originally designed as a junior trainer that would allow for a spinnaker, but many boats are now owned and raced by adults. The rig is relatively short, increasing stability. In line with the original design intent, class rules require anchors, PFDs, bailing equipment, and a paddle to be carried on board while racing. Flotation is optional. Cockpit seats are not permitted, but an adjustable outhaul and hiking straps may be used. The last information available indicated more than 140 fleets, with the majority located on the coasts, including Florida, and also in the Great Lakes. Large numbers are found in San Francisco and on Long Island Sound.

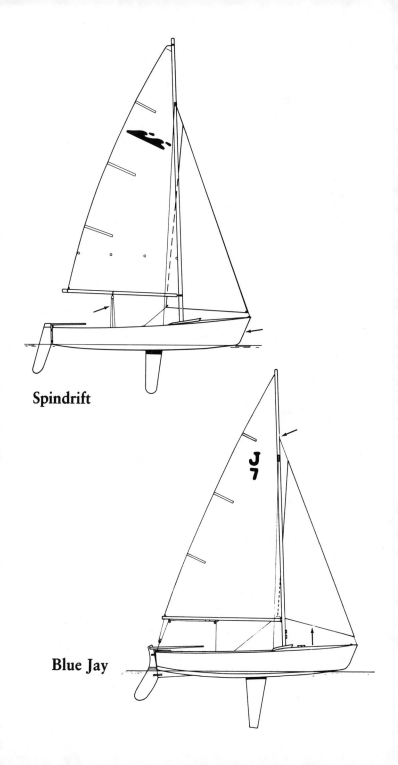

Spindrift

Blue Jay

2.4 Meter

Length: 13 ft. 8 in.
Beam: 30 in.
Draft: 39 in.
Weight: 595 lbs.
Sail area: Main, 50 sq. ft.; jib,
    45 sq. ft.
Hull: FRP or wood
Spars: Aluminum or wood

Racing crew: 1
Rating: None
First built: 1986
No. built: 350 Europe,
    35 USA
Designers: Peter Norlin, Haken
    Sodeergrin, and Lars Bergstrom

Intended to look like a tiny 12 Meter, and does. Crew of one.

The hull weighs 210 pounds, the keel 385 pounds. You sit in the cockpit, facing forward, and with the boom so low hiking is difficult. (The manufacturer points out that disabled sailors can use the boat.) The controls — and there are lots — lead to where you can reach them. The backstay and forestay are adjustable; there is a downhaul for the jib, a ram for the mast, a vang, Cunningham, outhaul, and Barber haulers. And of course, sheets and halyard. The boat has positive flotation. The 2.4 is your personal 12 meter and was designed to the International Meter Rule. It is very popular in Europe, but has only been available in the United States since early 1993.

International 420

Length: 13 ft. 9 in.
Beant: 5 ft. 5 in.
Draft: 3 ft. 2 in.
Weight: 220 lbs.
Sail area: Main and jib, 110 sq.
    ft. total; spinnaker, 95 sq. ft.
Hull: FRP

Spars: Aluminum
Racing crew: 2
Rating: D-PN 98.0
First built: Not avail.
No. built: 45,000
Designer: Christian Maury

Cockpit extends forward of mast and has splash rail. Foredeck quite elevated. Spoon bow, vertical transom.

A light, fast trapeze boat suited for both racing and training, the 420 comes in both options. It is a one-design, governed for international competition by the IYRU. The racing model has a roller traveler, bailers, tapered mast, gasket for the centerboard, and a five-part boom vang. There are hiking straps and hull inspection ports, as well as a downhaul. Windows are allowed in the jib. Flotation lies in the hollow seat tanks. The centerboard is mahogany, and the rudder kicks up. A Cunningham is optional, as are a mast gate and a compass mount. Construction results in a relatively rigid boat.

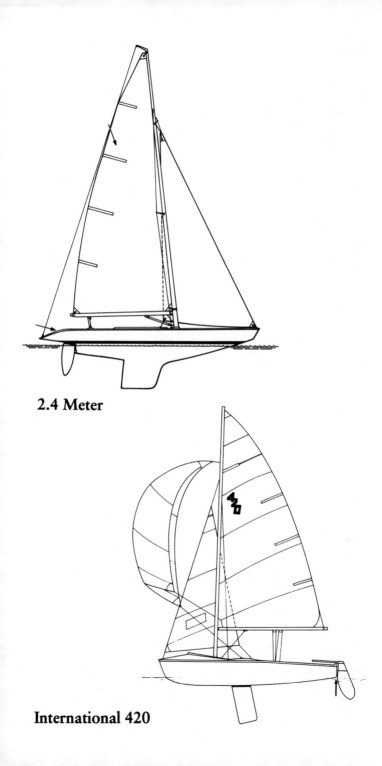

2.4 Meter

International 420

Sunfish

Length: 13 ft. 10 in.
Beam: 4 ft. 1 in.
Draft: 2 ft. 8 in. (scaled)
Weight: 129 lbs. (hull only)
Sail area: 75 sq. ft.
Hull: FRP
Spars: Aluminum

Racing crew: s
Rating: D-PN 103.3
First built: 1955
No. built: Over 248,000
Designers: Alex Bryan and
Cortlandt Heyniger

Most common board boat. Lateen rig. Racing boats have very low boom, others may not. Straight sheer at rail.

Like the Hobie, the Sunfish is found all over the world. The Sunfish was chosen as the "breakthrough board boat" in *Sail* magazine's tenth-anniversary poll. Sunfish has also been honored by *Fortune,* which picked her as one of the 25 best designed products in the U. S. The original model was the Sailfish, made in wood, but without the cockpit. It was lengthened to the Super Sunfish, the same length as the Sunfish, but again without the cockpit. There is a storage compartment, foam flotation, cockpit bailer, and daggerboard retention line. Sail attachment is by sail sets. Class rules prohibit daggerboard gaskets, jibing boards, and Cunninghams. The only option available for use in racing is a mainsheet jam cleat. A window is allowed, and the running end of the halyard may be used as a boom vang.

Barnett 1400

Length: 13 ft. 10 in.
Beam: 4 ft. 7 in.
Draft: 15 in.
Weight: 140 lb
Sail area: 75 sq. ft.
Hull: FRP
Spars: Anodized aluminum

Racing crew: Not applicable
Rating: D-PN 96.0 suspect
First built: 1989
No. built: 600+
Designer: Gerry and Ron Hed
lund

Board boat. Sail loose-footed. Unstayed mast. Kick-up rudder.

The 1400 will carry three adults, but two is better, and the most fun on any board boat is to sail it alone. There is a traditional halyard, and with a loose-footed sail and no stays, preparing the boat for cartopping is simple. The beam is fairly wide, providing higher-than-average board boat stability — but on board boats, expect to get wet. A hiking strap helps you keep the boat upright. For safety, there is positive internal flotation. The main sheet leads to the daggerboard trunk, and there is a 3:1 boom vang.

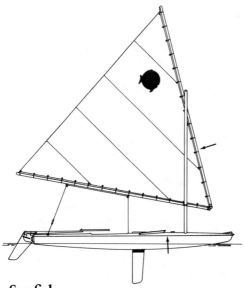

Sunfish

Barnett 1400

Laser (Laser M)

Length: 13 ft. 10¼ in.
Beam: 4 ft. 6 in.
Draft: 2 ft. 8 in. (scaled)
Weight: 130 lbs. (hull only)
Sail area: 76 sq. ft.; M, 60 sq. ft.
Hull: FRP
Spars: Aluminum

Racing crew: 1
Rating: D-PN 91.3;
  93.2 (M)
First built: 1971
No. built: 150,000
Designer: Bruce Kirby

Long, straight spoon bow. Bendy, unstayed mast with sleeved sail. Loose-footed sail. Note angles on rudder.

The Laser M is the same boat as the Laser, but with a modified rig. The Laser has a 20-foot mast and 76 square feet of sail. The Laser M is designed for lighter crews or heavier weather: The top half of the two-piece mast is replaced with a shorter section and the replacement sail has an area of 60 square feet. If the conversion is not made, you can reef the Laser by wrapping the sail around the mast two or three times before attaching it to the boom. (Best done on shore.) Like most boats of this type, the Laser capsizes easily, but floats so high that when it is righted there is no water in the cockpit. (The Laser II, not shown, has a jib; a spinnaker and trapeze are optional.)

Force 5

Length: 13 ft. 10½ in.
Beam: 4 ft. 10 in.
Draft: 6 in. (centerboard up)
Weight: 145 lbs. (hull only)
Sail area: 91 sq. ft.
Hull: FRP

Spars: Aluminum
Racing crew: 1 or 2
Rating: D-PN 96.6
First built: 1972
No. built: 15,000 est.
Designer: Fred Scott

Mono rig. Unstayed mast. Mast slips through main. Four battens. Crew sits well forward.

The Force 5 is a "hot" boat. The normal racing crew is one, but two may be needed to hold her down. The main slips over the three-piece, unstayed mast. Sail control includes an eight-part boom vang, a Cunningham, outhaul, and traveler. All boat controls can be reached from both sides of the boat. She is self-bailing, has positive foam flotation and full-length hiking straps. The rudder kicks up. All fittings are stainless steel, aluminum, or plastic. Only minor modifications are allowed for racing, including a sail window, inspection ports, etc. The use of lever vangs or removal of any foam flotation is specifically disallowed.

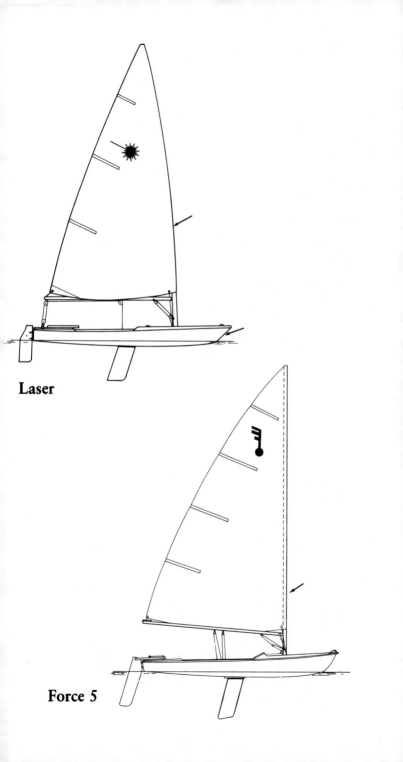

Laser

Force 5

One Design 14

Length: 14 ft.
Beam: 5 ft. 6 in.
Draft: 4 ft
Weight: 200 lbs.
Sail area: Main, 95 or 122 sq. ft.; jib, 38 or 68 sq. ft.; spinnaker, 165 or 280 sq. ft.

Hull: FRP, foam core
Spars: Aluminum
Racing crew: 2
Rating: D-PN 88.2 (Std.)
First built: 1988
No. built: 250
Designer: Jay Cross

Very long bowsprit if spinnaker up. Note curve to roach and windows. Lots of sail.

The One Design 14 is a high performance planing dinghy with trapezes for both members of the crew. Two sail rigs are available and may be used on the same hull. Start sailing on the Standard, and move up to the Grand Prix. The spinnaker is asymmetrical, and both it and its supporting bowsprit are launched from the cockpit. There is no spinnaker pole. Flotation is positive, and because the cockpit is above the waterline and slopes to the transom, water will drain even if the boat is not moving. The boat was picked by *Sailing World* as Boat of the Year. Speeds of 10 knots upwind and 25 knots downwind are claimed. There is roller furling and all shrouds are adjustable, allowing for changes in jib luff tension, mast bend, and mast rake.

Rhodes Bantam

Length: 14 ft.
Beam: 5 ft. 6½ in.
Draft: 4 ft. 2 in.
Weight: 325 lbs.
Sail area: Main, 77.25 sq. ft.; jib, 46.5 sq. ft.
Hull: Wood or FRP (balsa core)

Spars: Wood or aluminum
Racing crew: 2
Rating: D-PN 98.0
First built: 1945
No. built: 1,900
Designer: Philip Rhodes

Vertical bow. Shrouds somewhat aft of mast. Considerable sheer. Fractional rig. Undecked.

This undecked planing one-design was originally intended for home construction in wood. Later construction has used FRP, balsa core with flotation tank, and foam-in-place flotation. Wood boats are competitive with FRP, as the minimum weight is controlled. Note the plumb bow. The hull is an arc-bottomed chine. Capacity is four adults. Spinnakers with an area of 135 square feet are available. There is a strong class association, maintaining strict one-design racing rules. Fleets are in Kansas, Missouri, Ohio, Michigan, Pennsylvania, New York, and Virginia.

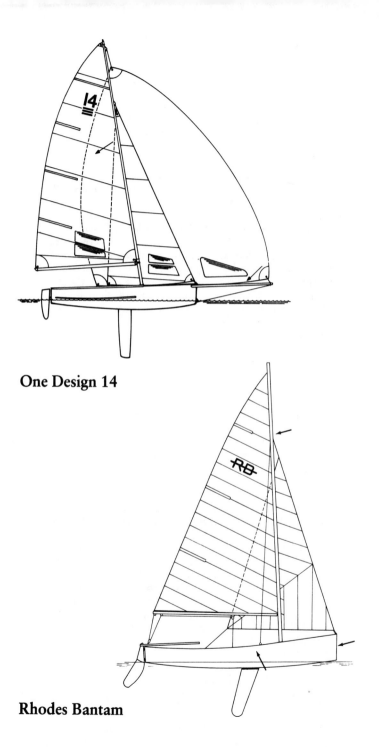

One Design 14

Rhodes Bantam

Cheshire

Length: 14 ft.
Beam: 6 ft. 2 in.
Draft: 2 ft. 1 in.
Weight: 185 lbs.
Sail area: Main, 105 sq. ft.;
  jib, 30 sq. ft.
Hull: FRP

Spars: Anodized aluminum
Racing crew: 1
Rating: D-PN 80.0
First built: 1963
No. built: 500
Designer: Frank Meldau

Two symmetrical hulls with exaggerated elliptical shape. Pivoting centerboards. Three cross members. Six full-length battens. Distinctive rudder head.

The Cheshire catamaran predates the Hobie and has been in production for almost 20 years. The pivoting centerboards are unique to the Cheshire and its sister, the Isotope. The boards are easier to retract than daggerboards. There are three cross members, with the aft supporting the traveler, the middle the mast, and the forward the forestay. Hulls are stiff, as there is an internal tubular frame. The Cheshire is raced single-handed, but can accommodate three adults.

GP-14

Length: 14 ft.
Beam: 5 ft.
Draft: 3 ft.
Weight: 293 lbs. (hull only)
Sail area: Main, 82 sq. ft.; jib,
  30 sq. ft.; genoa, 44 sq. ft.;
  spinnaker, 81 sq. ft.

Hull: FRP, foam, and balsa
Spars: Aluminum
Racing crew: 2
Rating: D-PN 101.1
First built: 1950
No. built: 13,000
Designer: Jack Holt

Hard chine. Note lines of foredeck. Main stops well short of boom end. Wood seats and thwarts. High freeboard.

Relatively dry, with high freeboard, GP-14 is used both as a day sailer and as a highly competitive racer. Used for day sailing, capacity is four adults. Racing, she is light and responsive. In the United States most fleets are found in the mid-Atlantic states; in Canada, on the Great Lakes. There are large fleets overseas in Great Britian, Ireland, South Africa, and Australia.

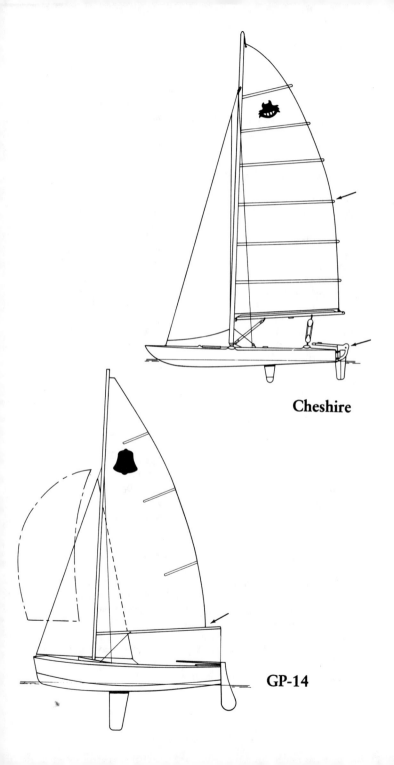

Cheshire

GP-14

Hobie 14

Length: 14 ft.
Beam: 7 ft. 8 in.
Draft: 8 in.
Weight: s
Sail area: Main and jib, 118 sq. ft. total
Hull: FRP and foam

Spars: Aluminum
Racing crew: 1 or 2
Rating: D-PN 86.4
First built: Middle 1960s
No. built: Over 100,000, all lengths
Designer: Hobie Alter

Catamaran. Full-length battens. Asymmetrical hulls.

The Hobie 16 and 18 (not shown) are faster and perhaps more popular, but the Hobie 14 was the first. Hulls are asymmetrical, with no boards. The trampoline or "wing" is elevated above the hulls. This very fast boat has been clocked at over 24 mph. The sail is shaped by full battens, which themselves can be formed. The jib has roller furling as an option on the Turbo TJ model. Hobies are, with Sunfish, found at resorts all over the world. There are racing fleets to match. There are regional area, national, and world championships. The development history is interesting. Hobie Alter's first love was surfboards. He pioneered the substitution of foam for balsa woodcores, and he used the combination again when he first began venturing into catamarans in the mid-1960s.

Javelin

Length: 14 ft.
Beam: 5 ft. 8 in.
Draft: 3 ft. 10 in.
Weight: 524 lbs.
Sail area: Main and jib, 125 sq. ft. total
Hull: FRP

Spars: Hard anodized aluminum
Racing crew: 2
Rating: D-PN 111.8
First built: 1962
No. built: 4,900
Designer: Uffa Fox

Small day sailer. Curved transom. Sharp bow. Big cockpit.

A beamy, stable small day sailer. Javelin has an unusually large (nine-foot) cockpit, a gear locker under the seats, and a lockable storage compartment under the deck. She is self-bailing and self-rescuing. The transom is reinforced to take outboards up to eight horsepower. The fiberglass rudder kicks up. The galvanized steel centerboard is, at 49 pounds, fairly heavy and a definite aid to stability. Freeboard is quite high, and a molded-in splash rail helps keep the boat dry.

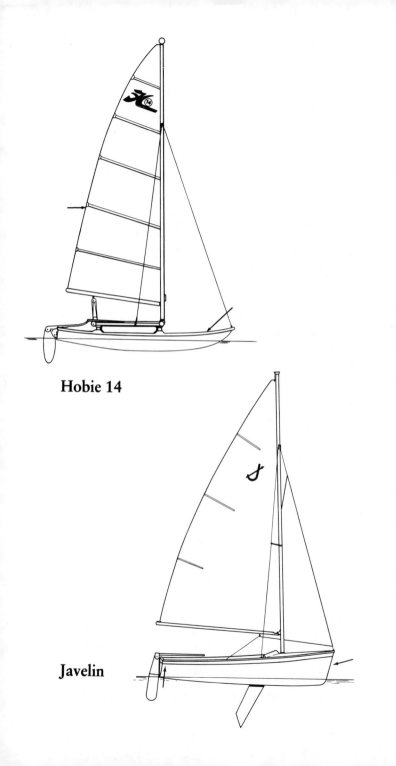

Hobie 14

Javelin

Lido 14

Length: 14 ft.
Beam: 6 ft,
Draft: 4 ft. 3 in.
Weight: 310 lbs.
Sail area: Main, 76 sq. ft.;
  jib, 35 sq. ft.
Hull: FRP

Spars: Anodized aluminum
Racing crew: 2
Rating: D-PN 99.6
First built: 1960
No. built: 4,830
Designer: W. D. Schock

*High freeboard. Deck line. Loose-footed main. Spoon bow.
Gold anodized spars and rudder head.*

Child's boat, racer and sailer. The Lido 14 evolved from the earlier Lehman 14 via a rather complete redesign including sheer, seats, foredeck, and sail plan. The cockpit length allows for six adults on full-length seats. The seats, with a bow compartment, provide flotation. Only limited modifications are allowed for racing, as the intention is to keep Lido a simple, limited boat. Both rudder and centerboard are FRP foam sandwich construction. The latter is not pivoted, but is suspended by two stainless steel straps. There is a two-to-one outhaul and boom vang, and a pad eye for a whisker pole on the mast. Options include the whisker pole and hiking straps. A very strong association exists, particularly in southern California.

Jet 14

Length: 14 ft. 1 in.
Beam: 4 ft. 8 in.
Draft: 4 ft. 2 in.
Weight: 285 lbs. minimum
Sail area: Main, 75 sq. ft.; jib, 38
  sq. ft.; spinnaker, 150 sq. ft.
Hull: FRP or wood

Spars: Wood or aluminum
Racing crew: 2
Rating: D-PN 97.6
First built: 1955
No. built: Over 1,000
Designer: Howard V. Siddons

*Plumb bow. Partially decked. Sharp entry and long waterline.
Rigged like Snipe. Hull same as International 14, but decked.*

The Jet 14 was developed when molds for an International 14, designed by Uffa Fox, became available. She is fast, going well to windward. The long flat run of the hull and the light weight allow her to plane. There may be either a traveler or a head-knocker on the boom. Two cut-outs may be made on the foredeck for spinnaker storage. Usually there is one near the forestay or two outboard of the mast. Size is restricted. A lever vang, not shown, is permitted, as is a jib window. Flotation is required, and with the FRP boats tanks are built in. Spinnakers were allowed in 1971. Fleets are in New York, New Jersey, Maryland, and Ohio. The 14 is often seen with both spinnaker and jib up, except in light air.

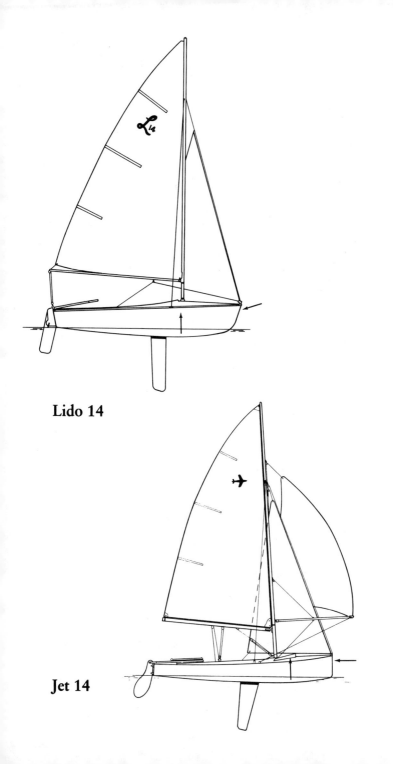

Lido 14

Jet 14

Trac 14

Length: 14 ft 1 in.
Beam: 7 ft. 6 in.
Draft: Unknown
Weight: 195 lbs.
Sail area: Main, 119 sq. ft.;
   jib, 29 sq. ft.
Hull: FRP (Australia)

Spars: Hard-coated aluminum
Racing crew: 2
Rating: D-PN 83.5
First built: 1980
No. built: Not avail.
Designer: Windrush Yachts

Catamaran. Seven battens. Mainsail window. High boom. No trapeze. Trampoline even with top of hulls.

Trac 14 was manufactured by AMF under license from Australia, where it is the most popular catamaran. The jib has roller furling. The outhaul is adjustable, and there is a three-part downhaul. In a novel feature to assist transportation, the hulls fold under the trampoline to reduce the beam to just over six feet. Each hull has a compartment. The single tiller has an extension long enough for hiking. There is no trapeze. Mast rake may be adjusted under way using tweaker lines.

Phantom

Length: 14 ft. 1½ in.
Beam: 4 ft. 5 in.
Draft: 2 ft. 10 in.
Weight: 120 lbs. (hull only)
Sail area: 84.5 sq. ft.
Hull: FRP

Spars: Aluminum
Racing crew: 1
Rating. D-PN 103.7 suspect
First built: 1977
No. built: 15,000
Designer: Jack Howie and
   Jack Evans

Lateen-rigged board boat. Sail luff and foot sleeve over spars.

In order to reduce the common tendency of sailboards to submarine downwind, the designer gave Phantom a sharp forward entry and a high bow design. The coaming is molded in, and the halyard leads through it to the cockpit. There are hiking straps and a storage compartment in the cockpit. Spars and the tiller are hard-coated aluminum. Both the luff and the foot of the sail sleeve over the spars, reducing aerodynamic drag and distributing stress evenly.

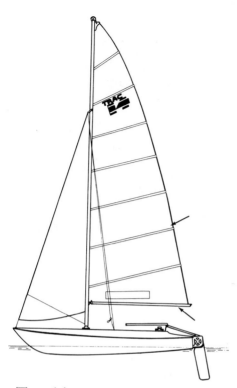

Trac 14

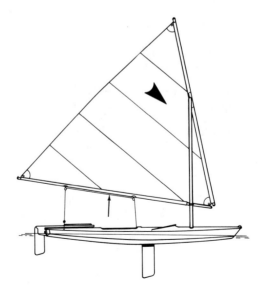

Phantom

Rascal

Length: 14 ft. 5 in.
Beam: 6 ft.
Draft: 3 ft.
Weight: 400 lbs.
Sail area: Main, 72 sq. ft.; jib, 49 sq. ft.; spinnaker, 160 sq. ft.
Hull: FRP and balsa core

Spars: Aluminum
Racing crew: 2
Rating: D-PN 108.9
First built: 1961
No. built: 3,000
Designer: Ray Greene

Sheer. High bow. Recessed foredeck. Jib window.

Sail magazine termed Rascal a "breakthrough boat" as the boat designed for the first-time buyer. Mast, boom, and rudder head are black hard-coated aluminum. The mast is on a tabernacle and is filled with foam for flotation. Jib tracks are adjustable. There is an aft storage locker that can be locked, and there is also a bow locker. The centerboard trunk is enclosed. Trim is teak.

Dolphin Sr.

Length: 14 ft. 6 in.
Beam: 4 ft. 3 in.
Draft: 1 ft. 6 in.
Weight: 170 lbs.
Sail area: 85 sq. ft.
Hull: FRP

Spars: Aluminum
Racing crew: 1
Rating: D-PN 106.2
First built: 1969
No. built: 7,100
Designer: Glen Cororran

Board boat with high freeboard. Lateen rig. Integral, molded splash rail at mast step.

Dolphin is a lateen-rigged cat board boat, slightly longer than most. Capacity for reasonable sailing is two adults. The daggerboard is fiberglass, as is the lower portion of the kick-up rudder. The rudder head is aluminum. There is a small compartment molded into the hull just aft of the mast. The cockpit has hiking bars.

Rascal

Dolphin Sr.

Skipjack

Length: 14 ft. 7 in.	*Spars:* Aluminum
Beam: 5 ft. 3 in.	*Racing crew:* 2
Draft: 3 ft. 6 in.	*Rating:* D-PN 93.1
Weight: 320 lbs.	*First built:* 1966
Sail area: Main, 82 sq. ft.; jib, 43	*No. built:* 800
sq. ft.; spinnaker, 125 sq. ft.	*Designers:* Carter Pyle and
Hull: FRP	Harry Sindle

Full-length battens. Undecked, but wide gunwales. Spreader quite low. Bendy rig. Large roach.

The Skipjack's design combines ideas from the Finn hull, Mobjack (wide side decks, flat cockpit floor), and Flying Dutchman (single spreader, mid-boom sheeting). Upon seeing the design, the U.S. Naval Academy immediately ordered 20. The Skipjack rides high, with the cockpit floor above the water line so transom bailers can be used, and no cockpit cover is necessary at anchor. The full-length fiberglass battens support the full roach. They should also make you stop and think about when and how you use the bar traveler. There is a downhaul and vang, and adjustable jib leads. Simple roller reefing is possible on the boom. The boat may be rigged as a cat by having the mast moved into one of several choices of step. The centerboard must be aluminum, but choice of material for the rudder is optional.

Finn

Length: 14 ft. 9 in.	*Spars:* Aluminum
Beam: 4 ft. 10 in.	*Racing crew:* 1
Draft: 2 ft. 3 in.	*Rating:* Olympic; DN-P91.1
Weight: 319 lbs.	*First built:* 1949
Sail area: 115 sq. ft.	*No. built:* Not avail.
Hull: FRP	*Designer:* Richard Sarby

Mono rig with unstayed, bendy mast. Bow and transom almost vertical. Mid-boom sheeting.

Finn is an Olympic boat, and has been since 1952. The mast is unstayed. The main sheet is a three-part system with a curved traveler. The outhaul has a six-to-one mechanical advantage, and there are dual controls for the inhaul. Other gear that may be controlled from either side of the boat includes the Cunningham, centerboard, and thirty-to-one lever boom vang. The centerboard is aluminum, and its anodized coating is impregnated with Teflon. Flotation tanks, three bailers, and adjustable hiking straps assist in safety, and there are inspection ports for the double hull.

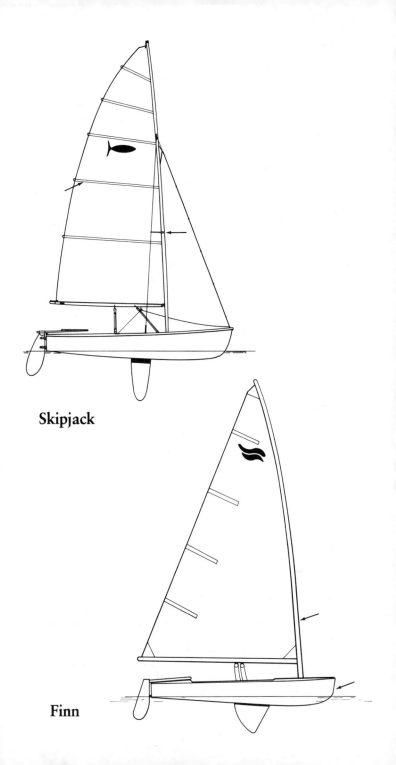

Skipjack

Finn

Scaffie

Length: 14 ft. 9 in.
Beam: 5 ft. 9 in.
Draft: 1 ft. 3 in.
Weight: 460 lbs.
Sail area: 100 sq. ft.
Hull: FRP

Spars: Spruce
Rating: None
First built: 18th century
No. built: Not available
Designer: John Watkinson

Standing lug sail. Mast sharply raked. Bilge fins, no centerboard. Lapstrake hull. Red sails.

The Drascombe Scaffie is a design that has been used in coastal sailing for over 200 years. Scaffies have been built for many years in England, and they are now also built in Maine. The loose-footed lug sail is carried on an unstayed mast. Since there is no centerboard trunk the cockpit has a lot of space, and with a tent, the Scaffie is used for cruising. A three-horsepower outboard may be fitted through the rounded stern. Rowing positions are provided. Other Drascombe types include a Longboat, with mizzen; a Coaster with the same hull but with a cabin; and several other designs. All are lapstrake in appearance, and all have red sails. All have foam flotation.

Designers Choice

Length: 14 ft. 10½ in.
Beam: 5 ft. 1 in.
Draft: 3 ft.
Weight: 315 lbs.
Sail area: Main, 82 sq. ft.;
   jib, 38 sq. ft.
Hull: FRP

Spars: Hard-coated aluminum
Racing crew: 900 lbs. maximum
Rating: D-PN 101.3
First built: 1979
No. built: 1,000
Designer: Sparkman and
   Stephens

Sharp bow, planing hull aft. Rudder head and spars black. Hull seats plus thwart. Loose-footed main. Undecked.

This is a combination boat, meant for training, racing, or general sailing. The Designers Choice has curved sections forward and is relatively dry. With flat surfaces aft, she planes. Spars are anodized with a grooved mast luff and a loose foot. There is an outhaul, vang, and Cunningham. The cockpit sole is above water line, so the scuppers may be left open at anchor or at dock. There is foam flotation. A stowage locker is under the afterdeck. Optional equipment includes a spinnaker and all necessary gear, a motor mount, and hiking straps.

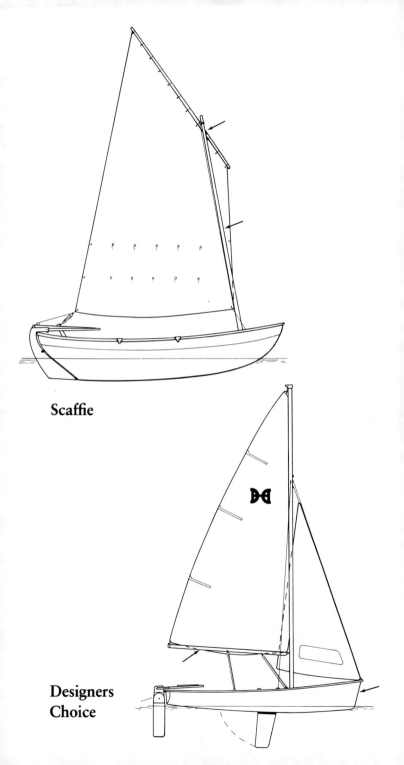

Scaffie

**Designers
Choice**

Albacore

Length: 15 ft.	*Spars:* Aluminum
Beam: 5 ft. 4 in.	*Racing crew:* 2
Draft: 4 ft. 5 in.	*Rating:* D-PN: 90.7
Weight: 240 lbs.	*First built:* Early 1950s
Sail area: Main, 90 sq. ft.;	*No. built:* 7,700
jib, 35 sq. ft.	*Designer:* Uffa Fox
Hull: FRP and wood	

Fractional rig. Four battens. Plumb bow. Foredeck flares up. Unusual jib cut.

The basis for design of this sloop-rigged planing boat was a hot-molded plywood one-design, Swordfish. Construction was originally by the Fairey organization, manufacturers of the World War II Mosquito bomber. Standard features include a four-to-one boom vang, centerboard slot gaskets, and hiking straps. The rudder kicks up. Foam flotation is included. The maximum crew recommended for day sailing is four. Options include Elvstrom bailers, Barber haulers, a ten-to-one vang, Harken package, and simple or remote Cunningham. There are active racing fleets in Connecticut, Pennsylvania, New Jersey, Maryland, Virginia, New York, and Illinois, with a total association membership of about 300.

JY 15

Length: 15 ft.	*Spars:* Aluminum
Beam: 5 ft. 10 in.	*Racing crew:* 2
Draft: 3 ft.	*Rating:* D-PN: 92.6
Weight: 300 lbs.	*First built:* 1989
Sail area: 125 sq. ft.	*No. built:* 800
Hull: ABS with polyurethane	*Designer:* Rodney Johnstone
core	

Flared topsides. Stern cutaway several inches. Fractional rig.

A training boat, designed by Rodney Johnstone, famous for the J/24. Lever adjustments for the stays help set up quickly, and the mast breaks down for transport. The two-to-one mainsheet leads to the centerboard trunk, and there is a four-part vang. The rudder swings up, and there are hiking straps. Storage is under the foredeck. Side decks are rounded, and the edge of the hull and deck is also rounded for comfortable hiking.

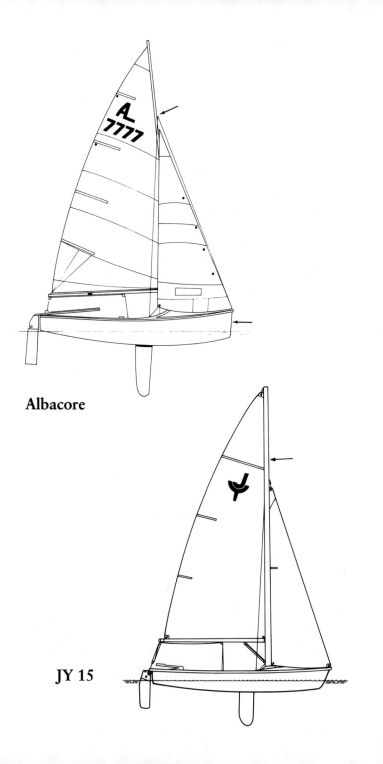

Albacore

JY 15

West Wight Potter

Length: 15 ft.
Beam: 5 ft. 6 in.
Draft: 3 ft.
Weight: 475 lbs.
Sail area: Main, 68 sq. ft.; jib, 23 sq ft.; genoa, 43 sq. ft.; spinnaker, 85 sq. ft.

Hull: FRP
Spars: Aluminum
Racing crew: 1 or 2
Rating: D-PN 135.8
First built: 1966
No. built: 2,000
Designer: Stanley T. Smith

Distinctive. Three battens, with top full-length, give an angular roach.

The Potter was originally built in plywood with a gunter rig. Herb Stewart used one for a fiberglass plug and modified the rig to Marconi. With the top batten full length, appearance is somewhat similar to a gaff rig. The mast and its two shrouds are mounted on the cabin roof. There are three molded-in skegs, which reduce tipping or heeling, with or without sail. There are two 6½-foot bunks in the cabin. The companion-way hatch, which like all trim is mahogany, folds down into the cockpit, making a small table. An outboard bracket is standard and will carry a two-horsepower motor. The Potter has foam flotation and is self-righting and self-bailing. Options include a genoa, a pulpit, railings, and a cockpit tent.

Coronado 15

Length: 15 ft. 4 in.
Beam: 5 ft. 8 in.
Draft: 3 ft. 6 in.
Weight: 385 lbs.
Sail area: Main and jib, 139 sq. ft. total
Hull: FRP

Spars: Aluminum
Racing crew: 2
Rating: D-PN 91.7
First built: 1970
No. built: 3,300
Designer: Frank Butler

Low freeboard. Spoon bow. Considerable sheer. Controllable mast that bends under sail; fractional forestay. Trapeze. High boom.

The planing hull is self-bailing and there is also flotation. There is a forward compartment, with hatch. Spars are black anodized aluminum; rigging, stainless steel. Control assists are an outhaul, boom vang, and mainsheet traveler. An optional barney post (binnacle) with compass may be ordered, as may a trapeze, a beaching rudder, and sail windows in both sails. Hiking straps are standard.

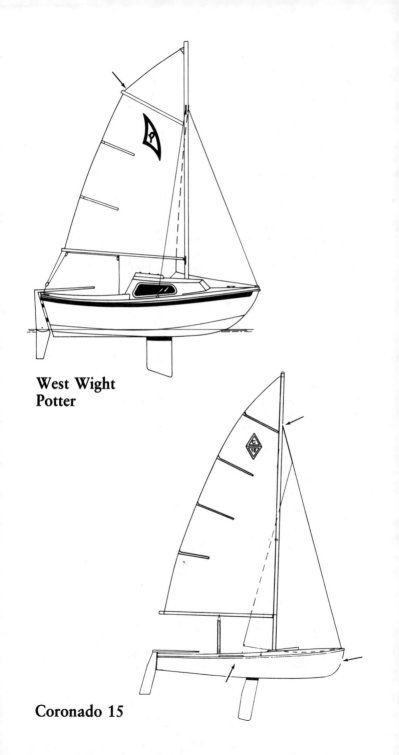

**West Wight
Potter**

Coronado 15

Vanguard 15

Length: 15.3 ft.
Beam: 5.5 ft.
Draft: *3 ft. 2 in.*
Weight: 200 lbs.
Sail area: Main, 77 sq. ft.; jib, 48 sq. ft.
Hull: FRP

Spars: Aluminum
Racing crew: 2
Rating: None
First built: 1991
No. built: 35
Designer: Robert Ames

Low freeboard. Unstayed mast. Perforated black rudder head.

The Vanguard 15 is designed for college/yacht club racing fleets. Rig is simple, and the boat is a strict one-design. The deck is rounded, for easy hiking. There is a vang, and halyards are external. The mast is untapered. The boat will plane upwind with a crew of two. With the daggerboard and light weight, the boat may be easily dry sailed — often helpful for fleet sailing.

470

Length: 15 ft. 5 in.
Beam: 5 ft. 6 in.
Draft: 3 ft. 2 in.
Weight: *260 lbs. minimum*
Sail area: Main, 97 sq. ft.; jib, 40 sq. ft.; spinnaker, 140 sq. ft.
Hull: FRP

Spars: Aluminum
Racing crew: 2
Rating: Olympic; D-PN 86.5
First built: 1963
No. built: 50,000+ world
Designer: André Cornu

Significant mast rake. Top batten full length. Possible windows in main and jib. Tiller passes through opening in transom.

The 470 is an Olympic boat, internationally controlled by the IYRU. The first use in the Olympics was in 1976. Flotation is in the hollow seats and in the mast, which causes the boat to float high when capsized. (Don't sit on the capsized hull or the 470 will turtle.) There are hiking straps and a trapeze. The spinnaker has an uphaul, a downhaul, and guy twings. Various mechanical assists are available for the boom vang. Spars are anodized and tapered. Controls for the Cunningham are dual. There are Barber haulers for the jib and a traveler for the main. Both jib and main have windows. Elvstrom bailers are provided. Although this is not true for most boats, on the 470 the spinnaker pole is best carried at an upward angle, especially in heavy air. There are fleets in more than 45 countries.

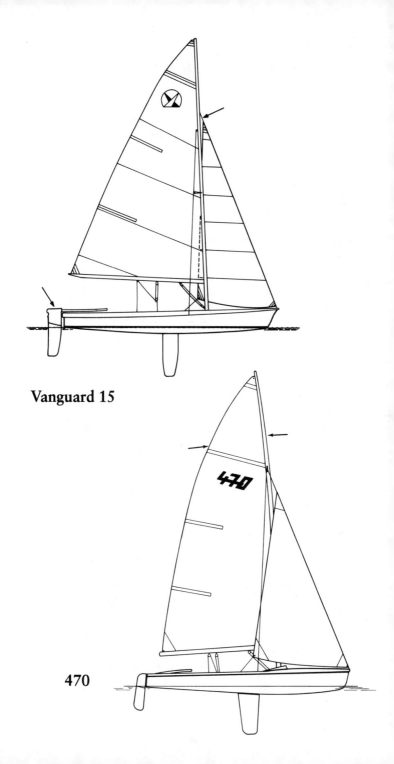

Vanguard 15

470

US 1

Length: 15 ft. 5 in.	*Spars:* Aluminum
Beam: 4 ft. 7 in.	*Racing crew:* 1
Draft: 2 ft. 6 in.	*Rating:* D-PN 91.5
Weight: 190 lbs.	*First built:* 1973
Sail area: 90 sq. ft.	*No. built:* 300
Hull: FRP	*Designer:* Ralph Kupersmith

Cat. High aspect ratio. Sharp bow, rounded deck. Loose-footed main.

US 1 fleets are in Missouri, Ohio, Florida, Pennsylvania, and Texas. Modifications allowed include two bailers, centerboard gaskets, four inspection ports, and redesign and modifications of sheeting, the vang, Cunningham, traveler, outhaul, rudder and tiller controls, and centerboard controls. Crew is limited to one, or two not to exceed 270 pounds. An experiment during which the two-piece mast could be changed to three-piece has been repealed. Both mast and boom are foam-filled. The centerboard and the rudder pivot, which is unusual in a single-hander. Production boats come with dual Cunningham and outhaul control.

Snipe

Length: 15 ft. 6 in.	*Spars:* Wood or aluminum
Beam: 5 ft.	*Racing crew:* 2
Draft: 3 ft. 3 in.	*Rating:* D-PN 93.1
Weight: 381 lbs.	*First built:* 1931
Sail area: Main, 90 sq. ft.;	*No. built:* 28,600
jib, 38 sq. ft.	*Designer:* William F. Crosby
Hull: Wood or FRP	

Significant sheer. Angled transom. Concave curve to rudder.

The International class Snipe has over 800 fleets located on five continents. The class is found throughout the United States and has seven districts, with governors located in Massachusetts, Missouri, Illinois, Florida, Pennsylvania, and northern and southern California. International racing measurements are restrictive. Loose-footed sails and spinnakers are not allowed. Jib windows are permitted. If a chevron appears on the sail, the boat has won a championship. Gold chevron indicates World; Silver, European; Red, National; Blue, Junior National; Black, Fleet.

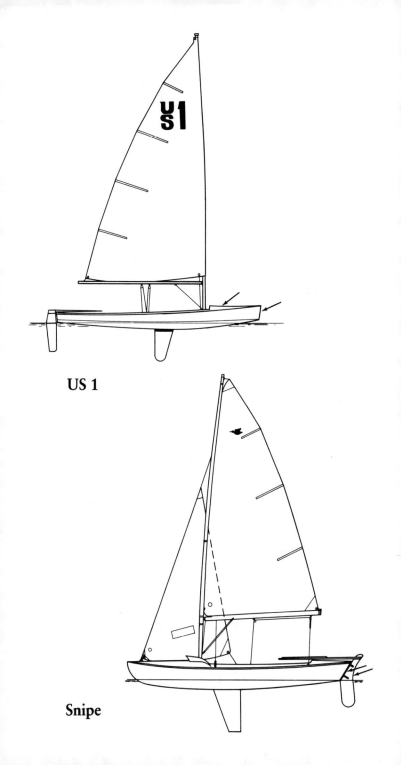

US 1

Snipe

Windmill

Length: 15 ft. 6 in.
Beam: 4 ft. 8 in.
Draft: 4 ft. 2 in.
Weight: 198 lbs.
Sail area: Main, 85 sq. ft.;
  jib, 34 sq. ft.
Hull: FRP and PVC foam

Spars: Aluminum
Racing crew: 2
Rating: D-PN 90.2
First built: 1953
No. built: 5,300
Designer: Clark Mills

Vee bottom, hard chine. Sheer appears cobled. Sail windows.

The Windmill is a high-performance sloop that can be built from plans or from a kit, or purchased complete. She is very light and planes quickly. Class rules are strict, and neither spinnakers nor trapezes are allowed. With a double hull and closed-cell foam, the boat is unsinkable. This type of construction also results in a very rigid boat. The two-to-one outhaul is internal and the four-to-one boom vang leads to the skipper. The Cunningham has a four-to-one purchase. Jib fairleads may be adjusted, as may the traveler. There is an Elvstrom bailer. Almost all sailing equipment is standard, with options for such items as a trailer or compass.

Invitation

Length: 15 ft. 7 in.
Beam: 5 ft.
Draft: 3 ft. (board up)
Weight: 180 lbs. (hull only)
Sail area: 90 sq. ft.
Hull: FRP Center

Spars: Aluminum
Racing crew: 1 or 2
Rating: D-PN 99.3
First built: Not avail.
No. built: Not avail.
Designer: Bombardier Research

Coble sheer for top of deck, with reverse sheer forward, normal sheer aft. Sail wraps around mast and is loose-footed.

A boat designed for ease in cartopping, with two-piece mast and overhanging two-inch gunwale to assist lifting. The loose-footed sail slips over the mast. Control includes adjustable outhaul, vang, and Cunningham. Safety provisions feature foam flotation, hiking straps, and vacuum bailer. The rudder kicks up. Invitation is a one-design with rigid class rules.

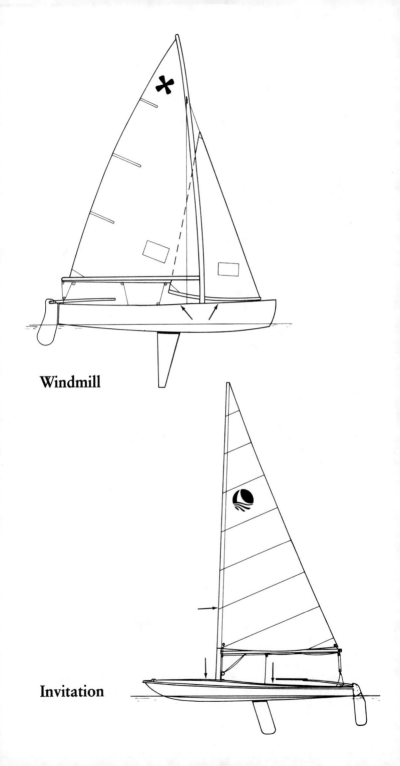

Windmill

Invitation

Bullseye

Length: 15 ft. 8½ in.
Beam: 5 ft. 10 in.
Draft: 2 ft. 5 in.
Weight: 1,350 lbs.
Sail area: Main, 104 sq. ft.; jib, 30 sq. ft.; genoa, 60 sq. ft.; spinnaker, 100 sq. ft.
Hull: Wood before 1950, FRP since

Spars: Aluminum
Racing crew: 2 or 3
Rating: None
First built: 1914
No. built: 2,000 wood, 800 FRP
Designer: N. G. Herreshoff

High bow. Distinctive transom. Wood coamings. Possible jib boom.

A New England classic, designed stiff and heavy for the short, choppy seas of Buzzards Bay. The Bullseye's original wood construction has been updated to FRP, and flotation tanks added under the cockpit floor and in the bow. The jib is self-tending roller-reefing. In addition to the cuddy, there is a lazarette with teak hatch. Teak is also used elsewhere for trim. Rigging and hardware are stainless steel or bronze. The full keel incorporates 750 pounds of lead. Lines are traditional. The Bullseye has active fleets concentrated in Massachusetts, but also in Maine, New Jersey, Florida, and Long Island Sound.

Apollo

Length: 15 ft. 9 in.
Beam: 5 ft. 11 in.
Draft: Unknown
Weight: 300 lbs.
Sail area: Main, 90 sq. ft.; jib, 39 sq. ft.
Hull: FRP

Spars: Aluminum
Racing crew: 2 or 3
Rating: D-PN 92.5
First built: Not avail.
No. built: Not avail.
Designer: Manufacturer

Straight bow, rudder mounting. Jib not on forestay. Overhang at stem.

This one-design has an active racing class. It is designed to carry two to four people comfortably in a large cockpit. Halyards are internal and the mast step is hinged. Sail control includes end-boom sheeting, outhaul, vang, and Cunningham. Both main and jib have leech lines. Rudder and centerboard kick up. Traveler is full width with dual controls. Apollo has a storage bin, hiking straps, and two Elvstrom vacuum bailers. Spinnaker, whisker pole, and jiffy reefing are options. Modifications permitted for racing are minor, with the intention to keep Apollo a true one-design class.

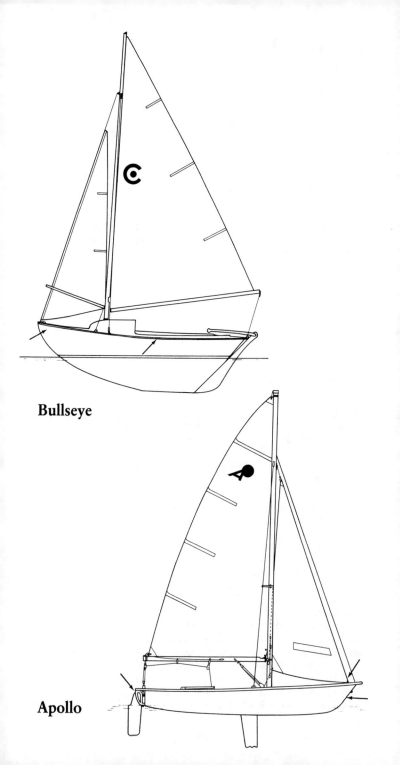

Bullseye

Apollo

Bombardier 4.8

Length: 15 ft.10 in.
Beam: 5 ft.
Draft: 3 ft. 10 in.
Weight: 300 lbs. (hull only)
Sail area: Main, 82 sq. ft.; genoa,
   56 sq. ft.; spinnaker, 140 sq. ft.
Hull: FRP Center

Spars: Aluminum
Racing crew: 2
Rating: D-PN 94.9
First built: Not avail.
No. built: Not avail.
Designer: Bombardier Research

Gunwale wraps around bow. Mast step elevated. Shrouds aft of mast. Mid-boom sheeting.

The 4.8 is a day sailer large enough to seat four. It has polyurethane flotation. Control includes adjustable outhaul, boom vang, Cunningham, and a roller-furling genoa. The genoa leads are adjustable. Both rudder and centerboard flip up. Hiking straps are adjustable, and there is a forward storage compartment. The vacuum bailer operates at low speeds and may be left open when the boat is moored.

Doughdish (Herreshoff 12½)

Length: 15 ft. 10 in.
Beam: 5 ft. 10 in.
Draft: 2 ft. 6 in.
Weight: 1,500 lbs.
Sail area: Main, 109 sq. ft.; jib,
   31 sq. ft.; spinnaker, 125 sq. ft.
Hull: FRP or wood

Spars: Sitka spruce
(Racing?)Crew: 1-4
Rating: D-PN 105.0 suspect
First built: 1914
No. built: 435
Designer: N. G. Herreshoff

Small, gaff-rigged. Jib boom. Coaming. Spoon bow, angled transom. Mast hoops. Strong sheer.

Buzzards Bay, under the hook of Cape Cod, has strong southwest winds and a short, steep chop. This boat was designed to cope with those conditions. It is very similar to the Bullseye, but the Bullseye has a cuddy and less displacement. Since the new version of the original boat is FRP, there are no frames or visible seams. An H Class Association has been formed to preserve activity and interest, and a class championship is conducted each year. Today's hull is sandwich construction, with an Airex core. Trim is teak and is used for seats, the coaming, sheer strake, and elsewhere. To counteract the fixed keel with its 735 pounds of lead, there is positive flotation of foam behind bulkheads. If you see an FRP boat it is the Doughdish. If it's wood, it is a Herreshoff 12½.

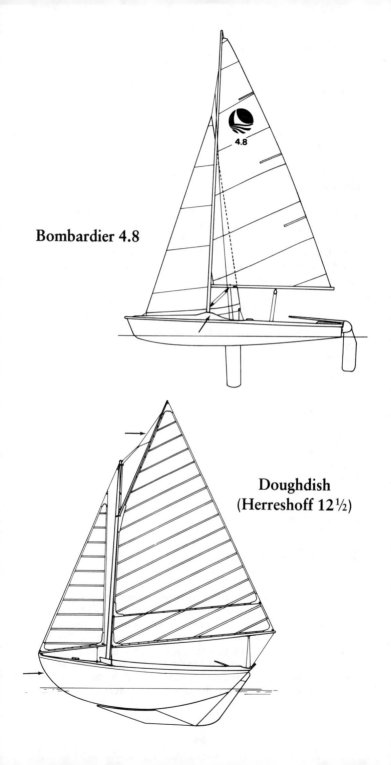

Bombardier 4.8

Doughdish
(Herreshoff 12½)

Wayfarer

Length: 15 ft. 10 in.	*Hull:* Wood or FRP
Beam: 6 ft. 1 in.	*Spars:* Wood or aluminum
Draft: 3 ft. 10 in.	*Racing crew:* 2
Weight: 365 lbs.	*Rating:* D-PN 91.6
Sail area: Main, 95 sq. ft.; jib, 30	*First built:* 1957
sq. ft.; genoa, 46 sq. ft.;	*No. built:* 8,100
spinnaker, 125 sq. ft.	*Designer:* Ian Proctor

Double chine visible when heeled. High-aspect centerboard. High freeboard forward.

There appears to be something about the Wayfarer that makes people want to cruise long distances. It has been sailed across the North Sea, from Scotland to Iceland, and elsewhere. It is particularly popular in Canada and in Britain, where it is a well-known instructional boat. The boat will plane. There are removable floorboards inside the nine-foot-long open cockpit, where six adults can sit. The double chine provides inherent stability, and there are large buoyancy compartments fore and aft that double as watertight storage lockers. The mast pivots and the centerboard and rudder retract. Yearly championships are held for the U. S., Canada, and North America. A world championship is held every two years.

Balboa 16

Length: 16 ft.	*Spars:* Anodized aluminum
Beam: 7 ft. 5 in.	*Racing crew:* 2
Draft: 2 ft. 5 in.	*Rating:* None
Weight: 1,000 lbs.	*First built:* 1980
Sail area: Main, 52 sq. ft.; jib, 65	*No. built:* Not avail.
sq. ft.; genoa, 98 sq. ft. (150%)	*Designer:* W. Shad Turner
Hull: FRP	

Masthead rig. Straight bow. Very slight reverse counter. Straight line from foredeck to coach roof. Backstay.

This day sailer is designed for recreation rather than racing, and it offers overnight accommodation for four in one double and two quarter berths. The mast step is hinged, which adds to the ease of trailering. Standard equipment includes ice chest, Plexiglas sliding hatch, and carpeting. The cockpit is self-bailing. Total ballast is 400 pounds, and the maximum recommended outboard power is six horsepower. Considering the number of berths below, the cockpit is quite large. The manufacturer suggests the Balboa 16 for beginners.

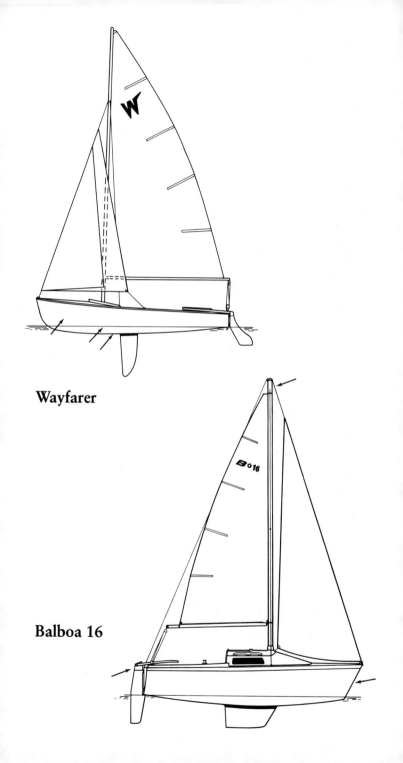

Wayfarer

Balboa 16

Comet

Length: 16 ft.
Beam: 5 ft.
Draft: 3 ft.
Weight: 265 lbs. min. (hull only)
Sail area: Main, 110 sq. ft.;
   jib, 25 sq. ft.
Hull: New boats, FRP

Spars: Aluminum
Racing crew: 2
Rating: D-PN 92.0
First built: 1932
No. built: 4,100
Designer: C. Lowndes Johnson

Jumper stay instead of headstay optional. Spoon bow. Running backstays. Window in main optional.

An older design, the Comet has many modern features. The bottom is flat and the afterbody is broad. She planes. The Comet is a one-design with rigid controls on size, shape, and materials. Minor modifications through the years have kept her up-to-date. These include self-bailers, a full-width traveler, sail windows, and side tanks making the boat self-rescuing. There is a vang, which leads to the cockpit. The backstays have slides and are adjustable. There are two rigging options. The first uses three stays; the second, which has a jumper and backstays, seven. The centerboard, which may be of various metals, has a drum control.

International Contender

Length: 16 ft.
Beam: 4 ft. 8 in.
Draft: 4 ft. 8 in.
Weight: 230 lbs.
Sail area: 120 sq. ft.
Hull: FRP
Spars: Aluminum

Racing crew: 1
Rating: D-PN 91.6
First built: 1969
No. built: 300 U. S., Canada;
   1,500 world
Designer: William Miller

Five battens. Heavily raked mast. Trapeze. Mono rig.

The Contender was designed by Australian Bill Miller to re-place the Finn in Olympic competition. So far it hasn't; but as can be seen by the rating, it is a little faster. Contender is a single-handed trapeze boat, with active fleets throughout the United States and Canada. There is a boom vang for control off the wind.

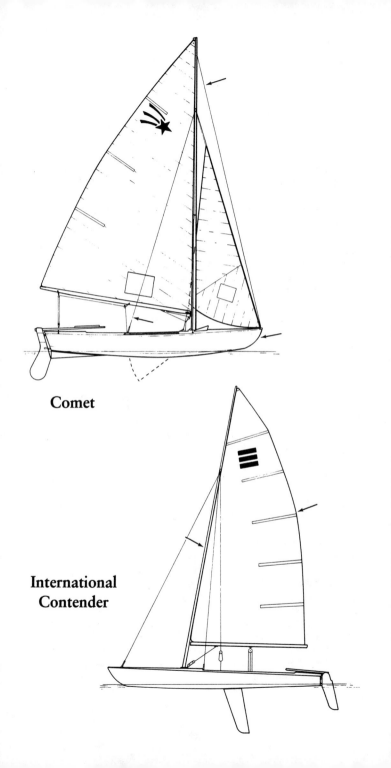

Comet

**International
Contender**

Isotope

Length: 16 ft.
Beam: 7 ft.
Draft: 2 ft. 6 in.
Weight: 275 lbs.
Sail area: Main, 140 sq. ft.;
   jib, 45 sq. ft.
Hull: FRP

Spars: Aluminum
Racing crew: 1
Rating: D-PN 74.0
First built: 1964
No. built: 700
Designer: Frank Meldau

Catamaran. Eight full-length battens. Jib window. Elongated spoon bow. Considerable rocker. Three cross members.

Sister to the Cheshire, the Isotope is two feet longer and five Portsmouth numbers faster. Two sail options are available. When rigged for a total of 200 square feet, Isotope has a D-PN of 77.0. The mast rotates, rudders kick up, and the centerboards are self-tending. There are two storage hatches. A trapeze and mast limiter are optional. Hulls are exaggerated ellipses, and symmetrical. Racing crew is normally one; cruising, three. There is positive flotation and a righting bar.

Leeward 16

Length: 16 ft.
Beam: 6 ft. 3 in.
Draft: 3 ft. 9 in.
Weight: 650 lbs.
Sail area: Main, 95 sq. ft.; jib, 45
   sq. ft.; genoa, 73 sq. ft.
Hull: FRP

Spars: Anodized aluminum
Racing crew: 2
Rating: D-PN 112.3
First built: Not avail.
No. built: Not avail.
Designer: Luger Industries

Bow eye for trailering. High boom. Cuddy angular, with FRP mast tabernacle on top. Curve at back of rudder.

Luger Industries builds kit boats ranging in length from 8 feet to 30 feet. The Leeward 16 is typical. It is delivered without sails and requires 10 to 15 hours to complete. There is a hinged tabernacle fitting for the mast, so that you can lower it for trailering by loosing the forestay. The boom allows for roller reefing of the main. An optional motor mount will carry a two- to seven-horsepower outboard. Sails, trim molding, and running lights are other options. Jib sheets, main sheets, and centerboard control lead to within reach of the tiller. Foam flotation is recommended. All fittings are either stainless steel or anodized aluminum.

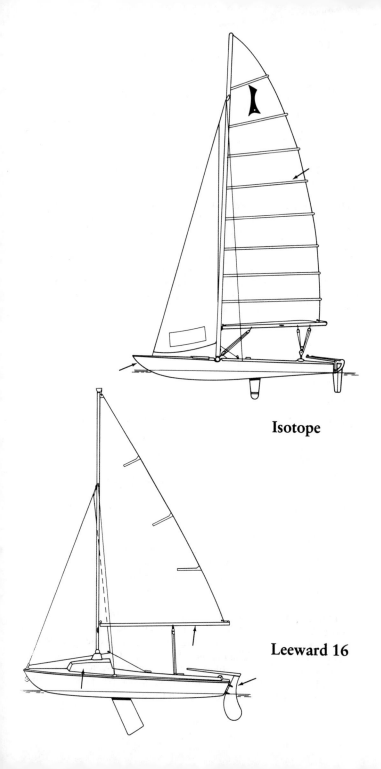

Isotope

Leeward 16

M-16

Length: 16 ft.
Beam: 6 ft.
Draft: 2 ft. 8 in.
Weight: 440 lbs.
Sail area: Main, 107.25 sq. ft.;
  jib, 39 sq. ft.
Hull: FRP or cedar Henry McKee

Spars: Aluminum or wood
Racing crew: 2
Rating: D-PN 89.3
First built: 1957
No. built: Not avail.
Designer: Melges Boat Works,

Scow. End-boom sheeting. Sail windows. Hull sheer almost
straight; deck has reverse sheer.

The M-16 scow is raced on the East Coast, in the Southeast,
and in the Southwest, but most boats are found in the
Midwest. There are bilgeboards and dual rudders and tillers.
As with most scows, the amount of control possible is extensive. There is a boom vang and a Cunningham. There are Barber haulers and a traveler for the jib. The stern-mounted main
traveler is controllable. Spars may not be tapered. Other limit-
ing specifications are issued by the Inland Lake Yachting Association, which holds a championship regatta with 60 to
90 competitors.

MC

Length: 16 ft.
Beam: 5 ft. 8 in.
Draft: 3 ft.
Weight: 420 lbs.
Sail area: 135 sq. ft.
Hull: FRP

Spars: Anodized aluminum
Racing crew: 1-3
Rating: None
First built: 1970
No. built: 750
Designer: Harry C. Melges, Sr.

Scow. Mono rig with no jib. Rake to mast. Reverse sheer.

Single-hander? Catboat? Scow? Well, it has bilgeboards. The
MC can be sailed single-handed, but it is a big boat and will
easily carry more. High aspect ratio. It has a traveler, Cunningham, vang, hiking straps, and adjustable outhaul. Trim is
mahogany. There are many options, most of which involve
hardware or repositioning control leads, such as a boom vang
lead to the skipper. The MC is perhaps not quite as athletic as
most single-handers. There is plenty of mechanical advantage,
with the outhaul three to one, the traveler two to one, and the
vang twelve to one. The mainsheet is four-part. An association
was founded in 1972 and has 21 fleets, some of which are located in Texas, Georgia, Oklahoma, Missouri, Nebraska, North
Carolina, Michigan, Wisconsin, and Iowa.

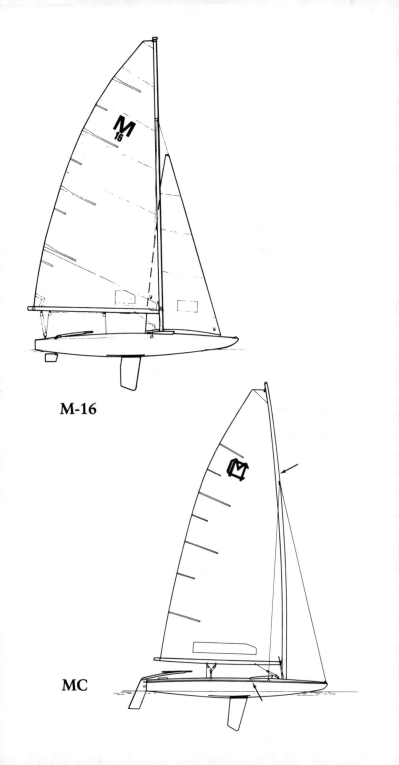

M-16

MC

X Boat

Length: 16 ft.
Beam: 6 ft. 1 in.
Draft: 2 ft. 7 in.
Weight: 500 lbs.
Sail area: Main, 85 sq. ft.;
  jib, 24.75 sq. ft.
Hull: FRP

Spars: Aluminum
Racing crew: 2
Rating: D-PN 97.7
First built: Not avail.
No. built: Not avail.
Designer: Melges Boat Works

Stern bar traveler. Spoon bow. Angled transom.

The X Boat was designed as a low-performance training boat for junior programs. With the exception of the boom vang, sail control is minimal so as to emphasize handling skills. There are two sets of hiking straps. Melges builds this boat and it is common in the Midwest. Since 1984 the Portsmouth Number has dropped dramatically.

Rebel

Length: 16 ft. 1½ in.
Beam: 6 ft. 7½ in.
Draft: 3 ft. 4 in.
Weight: 700 lbs.
Sail area: Main, 120 sq. ft.;
  jib, 46 sq. ft.
Hull: FRP, some balsa and
  foam core

Spars: Hard-coated aluminum
Racing crew: 2 minimum
Rating: D-PN 97.2
First built: 1948 approx.
No. built: 4,000+
Designer: Ray Greene

Straight sheer. Full foredeck. Full-length seats. Black (hard-coated) spars. (Class plans show sheer; manufacturer's drawings do not.)

Rebel was the first production sailboat built in fiberglass. Acceptance was fast, and there have been annual national regattas since 1951. The cockpit will seat eight. There is foam flotation in the bow and under the seats. The mast rotates. Jib tracks are adjustable, and the rudder kicks up. Options include a mast rotation bar, a boom vang, Cunningham, whisker pole, cockpit bailers, and hiking straps. The centerboard is steel and weighs 110 pounds.

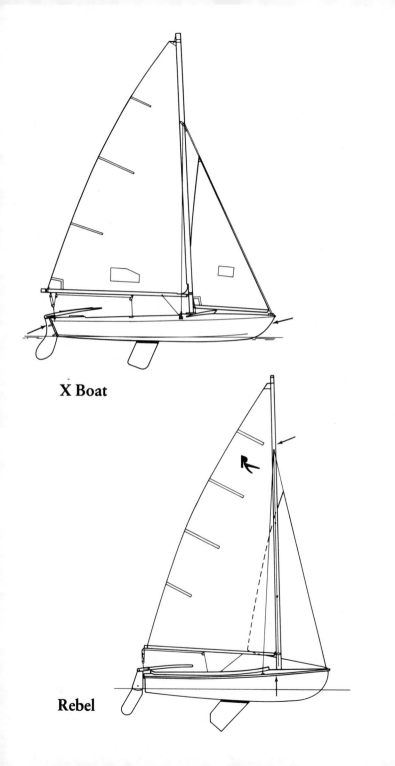

X Boat

Rebel

International Fireball

Length: 16 ft. 2 in.
Beam: 4 ft. 8½ in.
Draft: 4 ft. ½ in.
Weight: 175 lbs.
Sail area: Calculated as triangles: main, 87.5 sq. ft.; jib, 35.5 sq. ft.; spinnaker, 140 sq. ft.
Hull: Wood or FRP

Spars: Aluminum, steel
Racing crew: 2
Rating: D-PN 86.0
First built: 1964
No. built: 125,000 world, 13,000 U. S.
Designer: Peter Milne

Overhanging bow with angled bend. Low freeboard, but not a board boat. Trapeze.

Fireball is a high-performance dinghy, not as fast as an International 505 or Flying Dutchman, but allowing a great deal of latitude in the positioning and adoption of all gear except sails and hull. This scow-shaped boat was originally built in wood, but fiberglass was allowed in 1966. YRU International status was granted in 1970. Major fleets are in Great Britain, South Africa, France, Sweden, Australia, Canada, and the United States, with smaller numbers in many other countries. The (usually) high-cut jibs and the small spinnaker require less strength to control, so that many successful racing crews have had women members. (Adoption of a trapeze in 1965 limits this somewhat.) In addition to jib cut and lead, mast adjustments have seen considerable development. Mast chocks and struts have both been used, but many recent champions have dropped the strut.

Precision 16

Length: 16 ft. 3 in.
Beam: 6 ft. 8 in.
Draft: 3 ft. 8 in.
Weight: 3,901 lbs.
Sail area: Main, 97 sq. ft.; jib, 58 sq. ft.; spinnaker, 162 sq. ft.
Hull: FRP

Spars: Aluminum
Racing crew: 2
Rating: D-PN 100.1
First built: 1981
No. built: 64
Designer: Steve Seaton

Undecked. Long bow, considerable sheer. Aluminum rudder head. Mid-boom sheeting.

The Precision 16 is sold only in Florida. The aspect ratio approximates 2.3 to 1. The boat has a double hull and 10 cubic feet of foam flotation. The cockpit is self-bailing. Precision planes in a breeze. The centerboard and the kick-up rudder are foam-filled FRP. Trim is teak, and there are two storage compartments.

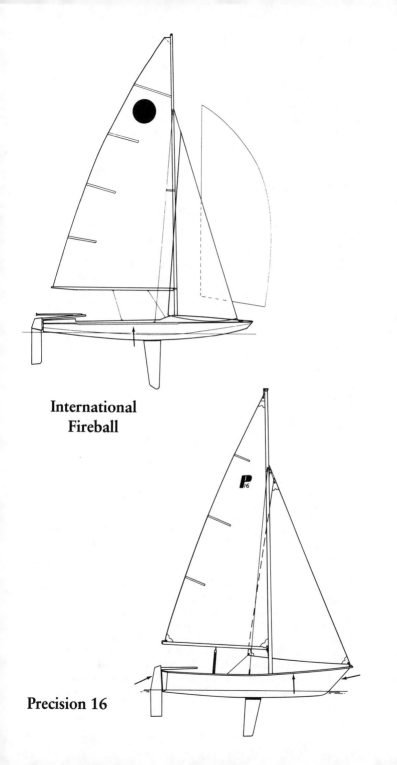

International
Fireball

Precision 16

Tanzer 16

Length: 16 ft. 4 in.
Beam: 6 ft. 2 in.
Draft: 2 ft. 9 in.
Weight: 450 lbs.
Sail area: Main, 100 sq. ft.; jib, 35 sq. ft.; genoa, 45 sq. ft.; spinnaker, 205 sq. ft.

Hull: FRP
Spars: Aluminum
Racing crew: 3
Rating: D-PN 98.3
First built: 1963
No. built: 1,550
Designer: Johann Tanzer

Four battens. Spoon bow. Vertical transom. Possible overnighter configuration with cuddy.

Before a name change the Tanzer 16 was known as the Constellation. She is sold both as a one-design and as an overnighter. The latter has a cuddy with two bunks and an optional boom tent, and the mast is stepped on the cabin roof instead of on the keelson. The boat's wide beam and low center of gravity aid stability. Both the aluminum centerboard and the rudder kick up. There is a roller-reefing boom, with vang. Storage for the day sailer consists of a lazarette compartment, side compartments in the cockpit, and a shelf under the foredeck. Trim is oiled teak. There is foam flotation. The Tanzer will plane.

International 505

Length: 16 ft. 7 in.
Beam: 4 ft. 3 in.
Draft: 4 ft. 10 in.
Weight: 220 lbs. minimum
Sail area: Main, 100 sq. ft.; jib, 50 sq. ft.; spinnaker, 225 sq. ft.
Hull: Plywood or FRP

Spars: Aluminum
Racing crew: 2
Rating: D-PN 80.1
First built: 1953
No. built: Over 8,500
Designer: John Westall

Fast dinghy with end-boom sheeting to traveler. Curved rudder and foredeck. Flat bottom. Transom often open with tiller through.

The length translates to 5.05 meters. She is an International boat and there are extensive (but often liberal) rules for construction and measurement. Centerboard and rudder shapes may vary; but they must have similar profiles on both sides, and the centerboard cannot project below the hull when raised. Rigging may be modified, but the mast cannot be permanently bent. A trapeze is normal. Sail dimensions are rigid. The 505 has buoyancy compartments. Major fleets are in the San Francisco and Chesapeake areas, but there are more than 30 fleets in all.

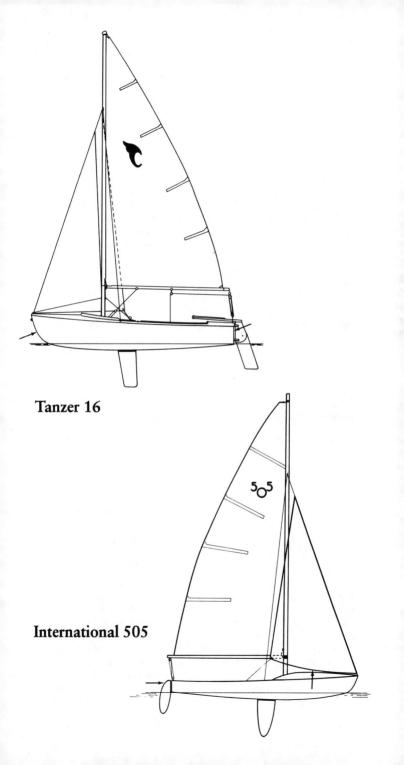

Tanzer 16

International 505

G-Cat

Length: 16 ft. 8 in.
Beam: 8 ft.
Draft: 1 ft. 1 in.
Weight: 340 lbs.
Sail area: Main, 150 sq. ft.;
  jib, 60 sq. ft.
Hull: FRP
Spars: Aluminum
Racing crew: 2
Rating: D-PN 76.0
First built: 1970
No. built: Over 1,000
Designer: Hans Geissier

Catamaran. Symmetrical hulls. No daggerboards. Forestay attached well aft. Full battens.

G-Cat is an unusual catamaran with symmetrical hulls and without daggerboards. Also unusual is the trampoline forward of the mast, upon which an optional tent may be pitched for cruising. (To avoid pitch-poling, remove the forward trampoline in heavy weather.) The hulls are a deep vee section to resist leeway. The boat has substantial rocker that puts lateral resistance well below the center of effort, making the boat pivot easily about the middle. The mast rotates. Shrouds go to chain plates on the hull, while the forestay leads to a bridle. Other control consists of outhaul, downhaul, and main sheeting to a traveler on the aft cross beam. Rudders kick up for beaching. The G-Cat comes in two sizes, 5.0 meters and 5.7 meters. The "number built" figure above reflects production for both types.

Day Sailer

Length: 16 ft. 9 in.
Beam: 6 ft. 3 in.
Draft: 3 ft. 9 in.
Weight: 628 lbs.
Sail area: Main, 102.5 sq. ft.; jib,
  48.75 sq. ft.; spinnaker, 213.5
  sq. ft.
Hull: FRP
Spars: Aluminum
Racing crew: 2
Rating: D-PN 99.9
First built: 1958
No. built: 14,100
Designer: Uffa Fox

Jumper strut is forward of mast. Cuddy. High aspect ratio. Lower jumper strut raked aft of mast.

The original Day Sailer was designed in 1958 for George O'Day, who produced the boat until 1978. Since then, the boat has been produced by both Bangor Punta and Spindrift, and now by Sunfish-Laser. There is also a Day Sailer II. There is no difference in the hull or sails, but there are minor differences in the cuddy. Day Sailer is a relatively dry boat, with high freeboard and a sharp bow entry. The large cockpit seats six adults. Standard and optional equipment vary with the manufacturer but may include storage lockers, a lazarette for the outboard or for storage, and an icebox. Sail control includes adjustable sheet leads, boom vang, and Cunningham. Safety features provided are foam flotation, foam-filled spars, a cockpit drain, and a kick-up rudder. There is a strong class association, with more than 100 fleets.

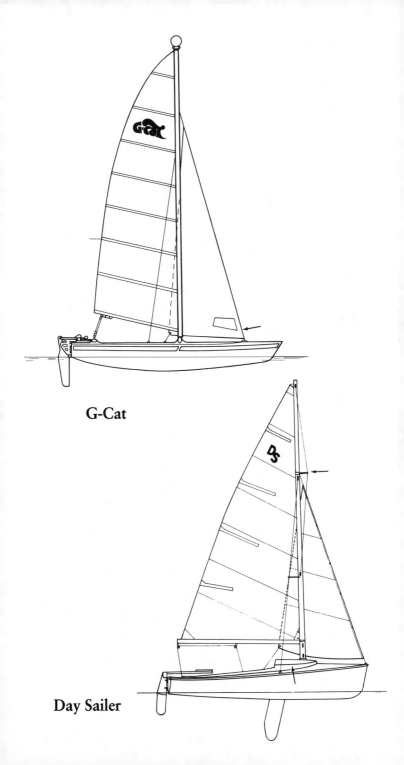

G-Cat

Day Sailer

Dolphin 17

Length: 16 ft. 9 in.
Beam: 6 ft.
Draft: 4 ft. 3 in.
Weight: 725 lbs.
  (800 for Model C)
Sail area: Main and jib, 160 sq.
  ft. total; 130 sq. ft. for
  Model C

Hull: FRP
Spars: Aluminum
Racing crew: 2
Rating: D-PN 97.8
First built: 1973
No. built. 740 (open and cabin)
Designer: Glen Cororran

Jib independent of stay. Two sidestays with one jumper strut. Splash rail molded in. Possible cuddy with one window for Model C.

In addition to the open design, there is a cabin model available. As might be expected, it is slightly heavier and has a reduced sail area. Capacity in either model is six adults; the cabin model sleeps two. The Dolphin 17 has covered storage on both sides of the mast, as well as aft storage. The cockpit is self-bailing. The kick-up rudder and the centerboard are fiberglass. The mast is stayed, and there is both a fore- and a backstay. The traveler is adjustable and there is a boom vang.

Com-Pac 16

Length: 16 ft. 11 in.
Beam: 6 ft.
Draft: 18 ft.
Weight: 1,100 lbs.
Sail area: Main, 65 sq. ft.; .
  Jib, 55 sq ft.;
  Spinnaker, 117 sq. ft.

Hull: FRP
Spars: Aluminum
Racing crew: 2
Rating: PHRF 326
First built: 1974
No. built: Over 2,800
Designer: Clark Mills

Curved bow with short stainless bowsprit. Outboard rudder, with unusual shape. Small cabin with two ports.

A small, trailerable cruiser with a fixed, shoal draft keel. Spars are anodized, and standing rigging is stainless. The rig is a ⅞ fractional and may fly either a working or a genoa jib. There is jiffy reefing. The cockpit is 6 feet 11 inches long, and is self-bailing. There are two 8-foot berths, space for a portable head, and additional storage in the lazaret. Trim inside and outside is teak. A vent hatch is on the foredeck. Halyards lead to the cockpit, and the bow pulpit is stainless steel. Equipment that comes with the boat includes a boarding ladder, navigation lights and cabin lights, and a portable head.

Dolphin 17

Com-Pac 16 XL

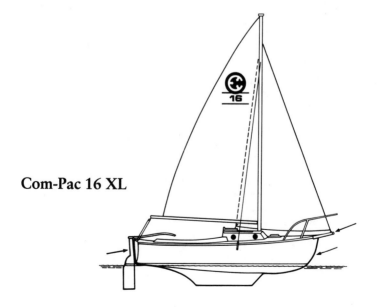

Cape Cod Cat

Length: 17 ft.
Beam: 7 ft. 11 in.
Draft: 4 ft. 10 in. (centerboard); or 1 ft. 11 in. (keel)
Weight: 2,200 lbs.; ballast 500 lbs.
Sail area: 250 sq. ft.
Hull: FRP
Spars: Painted aluminum
Rating: None
First built: Not avail.
No. built: Not avail.
Designer: Charles Wittholz

Traditional lines. Typical (Cape Cod) rudder. Plumb bow. Gaff rig. Mast hoops. High coamings.

A modern version of the classic catboat found near Cape Cod, this cat is produced in fiberglass. Both a keel version and a centerboard version are available, with sales to date giving a two-to-one preference to the keel, undoubtedly because there is then no trunk in either cockpit or cabin. The cockpit is self-draining, with room to seat six adults. There are bunks for two and space for a sink, shelves, lockers, head, and stove. A diesel or gasoline inboard engine may be installed, or an outboard may be mounted. While indigenous to the Cape, the boat may also be found in the Great Lakes and Florida, and on the West Coast.

Marsh Hen

Length: 17 ft.
Beam: 6 ft.
Draft: 3 ft.
Weight: 650 lbs.
Sail area: 150 sq. ft.
Hull: FRP
Spars: Aluminum
Rating: None
First built: 1980
No. built: 40
Designer: Reuben Trane

Spritsail rig. With canvas dodger up she is distinctive. Unusual rudder. Mast unstayed. Double-ended.

Hull shape has evolved from working boats of the Chesapeake, and the rudder and spritsail rig are also traditional. The Marsh Hen was designed as a pocket cruiser. The dodger, which unlike a boom tent allows sailing when it is raised, is standard. There is provision for rowing, but that is not the prime intention. There are six lockers for stowage, a portable toilet, and a built-in ice chest. The tiller is teak, there is flotation, and the fully open cockpit is self-bailing.

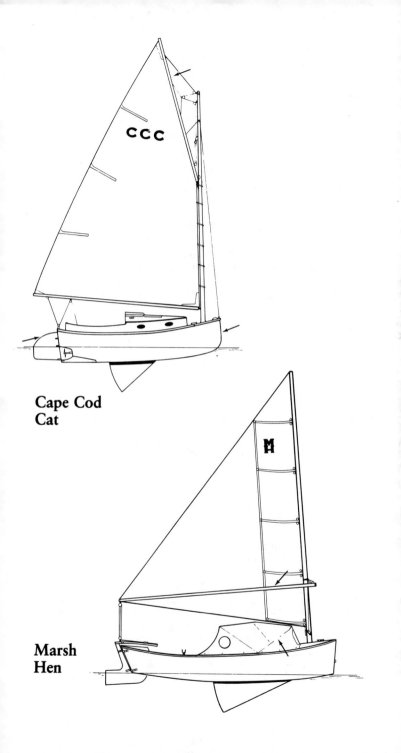

Cape Cod
Cat

Marsh
Hen

Nacra 5.2

Length: 17 ft.
Beam: 8 ft.
Draft: 2 ft. 6 in.
Weight: 375 lbs.
Sail area: Main, 170 sq. ft.;
  jib, 50 sq. ft.
Hull: FRP

Spars: Anodized aluminum
Racing crew: 2
Rating: D-PN 72.0
First built: 1975
No. built: 2,500
Designer: Tom Roland

Catamaran. Nine full-length battens. Plumb bow. Jib bridle well aft. Daggerboards. Symmetrical hulls.

The 5.2 has evolved from Tom Roland's designs for the Alpha 18, Roland 36, and Nacra 5.5. Sister ships are the 5.5 and 5.8. The hulls are wide at the bottom and narrow at the top to create extra buoyancy. Adjustments include mast rotation, trapeze wires, shroud tension, outhaul, and jib luff and main downhaul. The daggerboards and rudders are fiberglass. There are fleets in Australia, Europe, Japan, and the United States. In spite of the high aspect ratio, the center of effort is low.

Thistle

Length: 17 ft.
Beam: 6 ft.
Draft: 4 ft. 6 in.
Weight: 515 lbs. (hull only)
Sail area: Main, 136 sq. ft.; jib,
  55 sq. ft.; spinnaker, 220 sq. ft.
Hull: FRP

Spars: Aluminum
Racing crew: 3
Rating: D-PN 83.0
First built: 1945
No. built: Over 3,875
Designer: Gordon K. Douglass

Sharp vertical bow. Undecked. Wood cross members forward of mast. Round bilges. Three spreaders.

The Thistle was influenced by English dinghy design and is similar to the International 14, another racing dinghy with a plumb bow and flat run. Originally, boats were of molded wood. Racing crew is three, but the Thistle will carry six. She will fit into a garage. The Thistle has a lot of sail and a lot of speed. Class rules are strict. Gear that may be technically legal but provides an advantage is not allowed. There is built-in flotation. The centerboard operates off a drum. Decks and seats are sandwich construction. The tall rig is supported by three diamonds and sidestays. There are more than 150 local fleets of this planing boat. The Thistle is the boat used as the primary yardstick for Portsmouth Numbers.

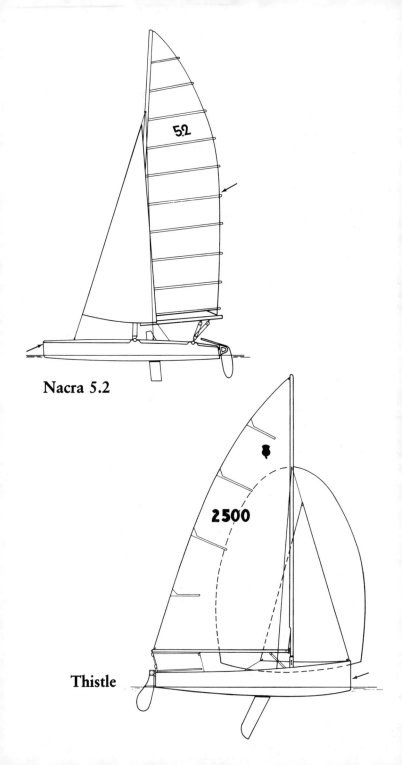

5.2

Nacra 5.2

2500

Thistle

Vagabond 17

Length: 17 ft.
Beam: 7 ft. 3 in.
Draft: 4 ft. 2 in.
Weight: 950 lbs.
Sail area: Main, 82 sq. ft.; jib, 65 sq. ft.; genoa, 87 sq. ft.; spinnaker, 210 sq. ft.

Hull: FRP
Spars: Anodized aluminum
Racing crew: 2
Rating: None
First built: Not avail.
No. built: Not avail.
Designer: Ron Holder

Wide beam. Pulpit. Backstay. Two windows. Rudder and keel have high aspect ratio.

A little overnighter, the Vagabond 17 will sleep four in two quarter berths and a split vee berth. There is a galley sink and water storage. A bulkhead runs halfway across the cabin, giving some privacy to a head. There is a bridled backstay. Handrails are of teak. When the 150 percent genoa is used, optional winches are available. The keel swings down and locks into place, with a lifting wire going through a hole in the cabin sole. The bow pulpit is stainless steel, and there is foam flotation.

Siren

Length: 17 ft. 2 in.
Beam: 6 ft. 8 in.
Draft: 4 ft. 3 in.
Weight: 750 lbs.
Sail area: Main and jib, 145 sq. ft. total
Hull: FRP

Spars: Aluminum
Racing crew: 2 or 3
Rating: D-PN 112.8
First built: Not avail.
No. built: Not avail.
Designer: Hubert Vandestadt

High boom with end sheeting. Large cabin windows.

Day sailer and weekender. There are berths for two, but an optional tent will provide shelter for two more in the cockpit. The icebox is molded in, as is a tank that may be converted to a head. An alcohol stove is optional. There is a well for outboards up to seven horsepower. The cockpit is seven feet long and self-bailing. Trim is mahogany. The mast step is hinged, and there is a boom vang and jiffy reefing. Siren has foam flotation.

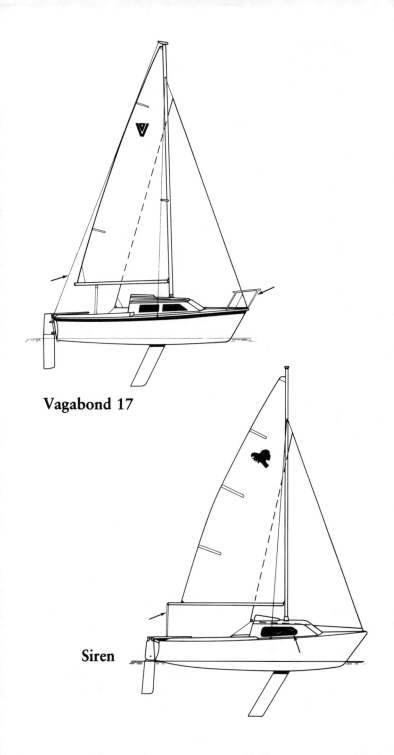

Vagabond 17

Siren

Buzzards Bay 14 Footer

Length: 17ft. 9 in.
Beam: 5ft. 10 in.
Draft: 2 ft. 6 in.
Weight: 2,000 lbs.
Sail area: Main, 103 sq. ft.; jib,
   35 sq. ft.; spinnaker, 140 sq. ft.
Hull: FRP

Spars: Aluminum standard
Racing crew: Not applicable.
Rating: None
First built: 1945
No. built: 17 in FRP
Designer: L. Francis Herreshoff

Curved bow, sloped transom — a bigger H-12. The forefoot has a slight cutaway.

The boat was originally designed for Llewellyn Howland as a larger version of the H-12. Concordia was to manufacture it. Concordia chose, however, to build the Beetle Cat, and plans for the Buzzards Bay were shelved until the mid-eighties. Still, there is a wood "feel" to the boat, as all seats, seat backs and other trim are teak, and fittings are either wood or bronze. Wood spars are an option to the standard painted aluminum. Sails include the main, with one set of reef points. The jib is club-footed, and optional sails are available. There are two locking compartments, and storage under hinged seats is available as an option. The lead ballast is encapsulated. There is a garboard drain, and six copper seat scuppers.

Ideal 18

Length: 17 ft 10 in.
Beam: 6 ft. 2 in.
Draft: 3 ft. 11 in.
Weight: 1,240 lbs.
Sail area: Main, 109 sq. ft., Jib,
   60 sq. ft.; Spinnaker, 240 sq. ft.
Hull: FRP

Spars: Aluminum
Racing crew: 2
Rating: D-PN 99.6
First built: 1991
No. built: 60
Designer: Bruce Kirby

Fractional rig. Straight bow. Notched transom. Spreaders raked aft.

A strong little keelboat designed for club racing, with rigid rules, such as only one set of sails a year, and no hiking. The jib barely overlaps, is a decksweeper, is self-tacking, and has roller furling. (The roller furling gear is set below deck level.) The lead keel is glass-encased. Bench seating in the large cockpit is built in and will take four adults, although the normal racing crew is two. The mast is hinged for easy rigging and has a mast holder, as the boat is designed for trailering. Winches are not needed. The main rigs to a bridle on the transom, aft of the tiller, which fits to the inboard rudder. The Ideal does not plane. Flotation is built in.

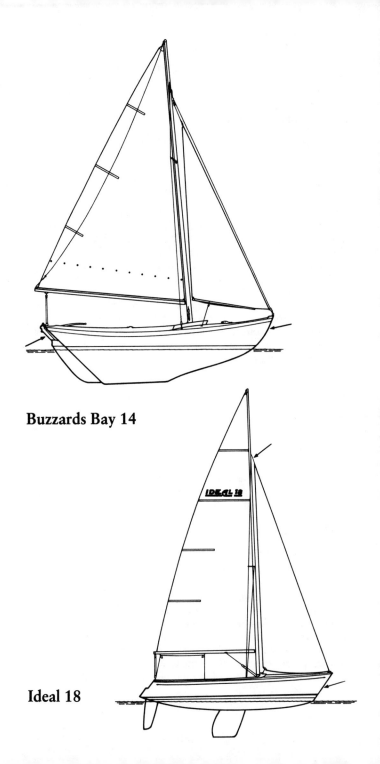

Buzzards Bay 14

Ideal 18

Buccaneer

Length: 18 ft.	*Spars:* Aluminum
Beam: 6 ft.	*Racing crew:* 2 minimum
Draft: 3 ft. 10 in.	*Rating:* D-PN 87.9
Weight: 500 lbs.	*First built:* 1968
Sail area: Main, 114 sq. ft.; jib,	*No. built:* 4,000
61 sq. ft.; spinnaker, 178 sq. ft.	*Designer:* J. R. Macalpine-
Hull: FRP	Downie

Four battens. Medium spoon bow, continuous curve from rudder through head to tiller. Straight sheer.

Buccaneer, originally built by Chrysler, is a big boat with a 7-foot 3-inch cockpit, seating six. The boat was designed to be easy to sail and maintain. The hull is planing, with the wide beam well aft and a lean bow. Standard controls include adjustable jib fairleads and roller furling for the jib. Optional controls are a vang, jib hauler, and spinnaker launching tube. All controls lead to the cockpit. There is an enclosed lazarette as well as an under-deck storage compartment. Trim is wood. The anodized aluminum spars are foam filled, and there are two suction bailers. Mooring eyes may be used for lifting. Both rudder and centerboard kick up and both are fully adjustable. Safety equipment is required.

Geary 18

Length: 18 ft.	*Spars:* Aluminum or wood
Beam: 5 ft. 5 in.	*Racing crew:* 2
Draft: 1 ft. 4 in. (centerboard up)	*Rating:* D-PN 92.2
Weight: 525 lbs.	*First built:* 1929
Sail area: Main and jib, 200 sq.	*No. built:* 1,450
ft. total	*Designer:* Ted Geary
Hull: FRP or wood	

Full roach. Hard chine, flat bottom. Decked. Looks flat. Trapeze. Inboard rudder.

The Geary was designed in 1928 as a club racer; it was originally built of cross-planked cedar, then plywood, and now of FRP. A trapeze has been allowed but not a spinnaker. The Geary's stability comes from her beam, as the centerboard is quite light. A whisker pole is used downwind, and she will plane. Vangs are used. When the Geary is FRP, a balsa core is common. The centerboard is aluminum and the rudder FRP.

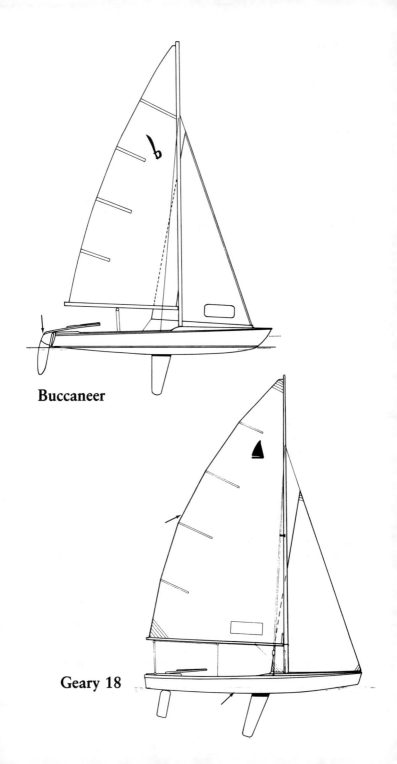

Buccaneer

Geary 18

Hampton One-Design

Length: 18 ft.
Beam: 5 ft. 9½ in.
Draft: 3 ft. 6 in.
Weight: 500 lbs.
Sail area: 195 sq. ft.
Hull: FRP or cedar

Spars: Aluminum or wood
Racing crew: 1 or 2
Rating: D-PN 92.0
First built: 1934
No. built: 710
Designer: Vincent Serio

Hard chine. Probably windows in both jib and main. Notice shape of rudder.

Look for Hamptons in the Chesapeake Bay. A very strict, one-design class association was established in 1938, when 70 boats were racing. The original wood design was converted to fiberglass in 1961 and 1962, at which time spars were changed to aluminum, and trapezes were allowed. Hamptons have a lot of sail area, but no spinnaker and no genoa. They have always been quick in light airs, but with the trapeze, they may also be sailed in heavier conditions. A fleet of about 40 boats is based in St. Marys.

Interlake

Length: 18 ft.
Beam: 6 ft. 3 in.
Draft: 4 ft. 7 in.
Weight: 650 lbs.
Sail area: Main, 125 sq. ft.; jib, 50 sq. ft.; spinnaker, 200 sq. ft.
Hull: FRP, balsa core

Spars: Aluminum
Racing crew: 2 or 3
Rating: D-PN 89.9
First built: 1932
No. built: 1,250
Designer: Francis Swiesguth

Hard chine. Sharp bow. Forward flare. Considerable rocker. Medium aspect ratio.

Interlake was designed for Sandusky Bay, Ohio, known for its short chop. She will plane fairly readily. The bow and sheer are classic, and the forward flare throws spray down, keeping her dry. She was originally built in wood, but fiberglass was allowed in 1955. Interlake is one of the older one-design classes in the United States. Sandwich construction with a balsa core is used for the hull and deck, and there is foam flotation. The boom is roller reefing, has a vang, and uses a bridle for a traveler. The centerboard winch has a ten-to-one mechanical advantage. While there are fore- and sidestays, there are no jumpers or backstays. Storage is in pan lockers under the foredeck. There are hiking straps. Rudder and centerboard are of fiberglass.

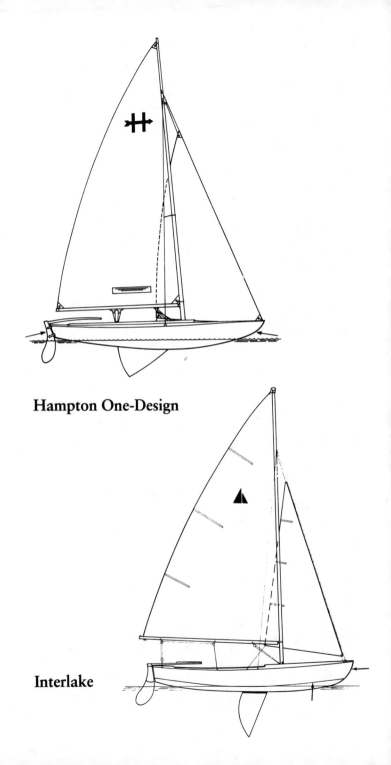

Hampton One-Design

Interlake

Mercury

Length: 18 ft.
Beam: 5 ft. 4 in.
Draft: 3 ft. 1 in.
Weight: 1,175 lbs.
Sail area: Main, 121 sq. ft.;
 jib, 56 sq. ft.
Hull: Wood or FRP

Spars: Wood or aluminum
Racing crew: 2
Rating: None
First built: 1938
No. built: 1,060
Designer: Ernest Nunes

Backstay. Note counter and transom. Rudder not visible. Long spoon bow. Hard chine. Two jumpers, with topmost raked forward.

This classic-design, full-keel sloop is usually found in the Northeast or on the West Coast. There is no ballast, and the keel must weigh at least 675 but not more than 700 pounds. Until 1952 hulls were of wood; since then, of fiberglass. Plans are available for home construction, as are FRP hulls. For the West Coast boat there is an active association. Flotation is not required; but preservers, bilge pump, and other safety equipment are necessary. Cape Cod Shipbuilding makes a Mercury with the same winged insignia on the sail, but with the letters CC instead of M. This very different Mercury was designed by Sparkman and Stephens, is 15 feet long, has a single sail with an area of 119 square feet, and is available with either keel or centerboard.

Prindle 18

Length: 18 ft.
Beam: 7 ft. 11 in.
Draft: 7 in.
Weight: 335 lbs.
Sail area: Main, 170 sq. ft.;
 jib, 48 sq. ft.
Hull: FRP

Spars: Aluminum
Racing crew: 2
Rating: D-PN 74.5
First built: 1978
No. built: 2,000
Designer: Geoff Prindle

Two asymmetrical hulls. Nine battens. No centerboards or daggerboards. Mesh trampoline. Single or double trapeze. Lots of rocker.

The Prindle fleet consists of the 15, 16, 18, and 19. The 16 was the first. The beaching rudders have an adjustable tiller crossbar. The mast step is hinged. The Prindle has a four-to-one downhaul system, an outhaul, and mast rotation controls. The jib luff is zippered. Battens are foam and FRP, and halyards are internal. There are two trapezes. Rake of the spreaders is adjustable. All of the Prindles are actively raced.

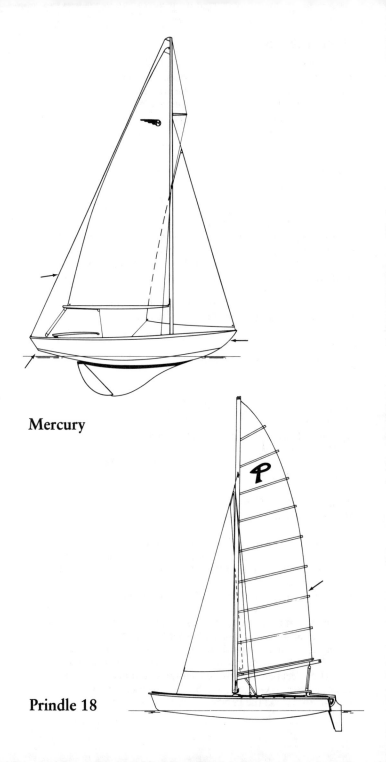

Mercury

Prindle 18

Windrose 5.5

Length: 18 ft.
Beam: 8 ft.
Draft: 2 ft. 3 in.
Weight: 1,500 lbs.
Sail area: Main, 82.5 sq. ft.; jib, 69 sq. ft.; genoa, 94 sq. ft.

Hull: FRP
Spars: Aluminum
Racing crew: 2-4
Rating: None
First built: 1980
No. built: Unknown
Designer: W. Shad Turner

Wide beam, wide transom. Straight bow. High boom. Comes close to a masthead rig.

Windrose is designed as a little cruiser and has bunks for four, with a double berth forward and two quarter berths. Space remains for cabin seating, shelf storage, and a head. This shoal-draft boat has 500 pounds of ballast in the keel. The manufacturer claims that the special shape of the keel makes Windrose track unusually well. An outboard with six horsepower may be used. There is under-deck storage in the cockpit. The mast is stepped on the keelson and therefore comes down through the cabin just aft of the foredeck hatch.

Y Flyer

Length: 18 ft. 2 in.
Beam: 5 ft. 8 in.
Draft: 4 ft.
Weight: 500 lbs. minimum
Sail area: Main, 110 sq. ft.; jib, 51 sq. ft.
Hull: Wood or FRP

Spars: Wood or aluminum
Racing crew: 2
Rating: D-PN 88.1
First built: 1952
No. built: 2,600
Designer: Alvin Youngquist

Scow. Long bow. Counter. Bridle traveler. Centerboard rather than bilgeboards.

The Y Flyer has a hard chine and flat bottom and is unusually stable. A slight heel reduces wetted surface dramatically, however, as may be seen from the rating. Sheer is reverse, but this is difficult to see in a boat with such low freeboard. Although there are two builders, the boat may also be built from plans using spruce and plywood. The centerboard is steel or aluminum. The mast can rotate, and the rig is flexible. The traveler may be moved amidships and bailers, barber haulers, transom flaps, and hiking assists may be used. Spinnakers are used in Canada, where there are fleets in Alberta, Manitoba, Ontario, and Quebec. U. S. fleets are heavily concentrated in Indiana, Illinois, Ohio, Missouri, Georgia, and South Carolina, but are also in the Northeast, on the Pacific coast, and elsewhere.

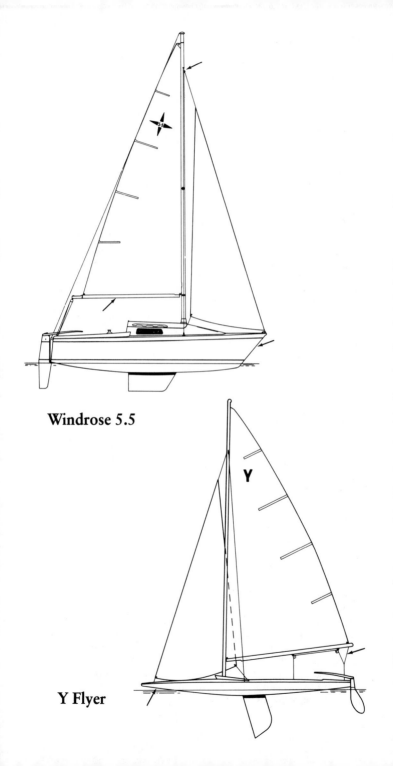

Windrose 5.5

Y Flyer

Victoria

Length: 18 ft. 5 in.
Beam: 5 ft. 6 in.
Draft: 2 ft.
Weight: 1,200 lbs.
Sail area: Main, 83 sq. ft.; jib, 51 sq. ft.; genoa, 81 sq. ft.; spinnaker, 120 sq. ft.
Hull: FRP
Spars: Tapered, anodized aluminum
Racing crew: 1-3
Rating: None
First built: 1977
No. built: 1,000
Designer: G. William McVay

Long counter. Pulpit. Keel. Traditional lines above water. Duplicate ports.

Victoria has two versions, with one for families and one for racing. The first has standard rigging and allows only main, jib, and genoa. The racing class permits adjustable backstay, boom vang, Barber haulers, and a spinnaker. The cockpit is six feet long and an optional boom tent is available. There are genoa tracks and winches. Below, there are two berths and a cooler. Roller reefing is standard, as are opening ports, a lazarette, and a boom crutch. An optional outboard bracket will carry a 4.5-horsepower motor. With her shallow-draft keel, Victoria is designed for trailering.

Typhoon

Length: 18 ft. 6 in.
Beam: 6 ft. 3½ in.
Draft: 2 ft. 7½ in.
Weight: 2,000 lbs.
Sail area: Main and jib, 160 sq. ft. total
Hull: FRP
Spars: Anodized aluminum
First built: Not avail.
No. built: Not avail.
Designer: Carl Alberg

Heeled, look for full keel. Cuddy. Wood coamings. Diagonal end-boom sheeting. Cruiser bow.

There is a weekender version of this day sailer. The significant visual differences are an extension of the cabin aft and the addition of a round porthole and a top hatch for entry. The jib may be working or genoa. The weekender has a vee berth and two quarter berths, with room for an optional head. The boat has a 900-pound keel and is very steady. On the day sailer, seats are teak, as are the rub strakes and toe-rails. Both boats have balsa-cored decks and teak coamings and taffrails. Storage in the day sailer is in a forepeak locker, while in the weekender there are two cockpit lockers and cabin shelves. Both have a genoa track, winches, and cleats.

Victoria

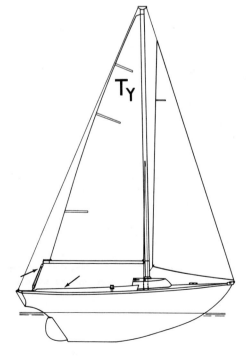

Typhoon

Appledore

Length: 19 ft.
Beam: 3 ft. 3 in.
Draft: 4 in. (board up)
Weight: 1,000 lbs.
Sail area: Main and mizzen, 40 sq. ft. each

Hull: FRP
Spars: Aluminum
Racing crew: 1 or 2
Rating: None
Designer: Arthur E. Martin

Unmistakable two-masted sliding gunter rig. Double-ended hull. Full-length battens.

A very unusual design based upon sailing canoes, and intended for both sailing and rowing. The center of effort is quite low. Sails roll on booms for reefing. There is an anodized aluminum kick-up rudder and a daggerboard. Deck and bulkheads are mahogany, with the latter providing flotation in conjunction with foam. Note the teak belaying pins. There are no halyards or stays, and the boat may be converted for rowing with sliding seats for two oarsmen.

Flying Scot

Length: 19 ft.
Beam: 6 ft. 9 in.
Draft: 4 ft.
Weight: 850 lbs.
Sail area: Main, 138 sq. ft.; jib, 53 sq. ft.; spinnaker, 200 sq. ft.
Hull: FRP, balsa core

Spars: Aluminum
Racing crew: 3
Rating: D-PN 90.3
First built: 1957
No. built: 4,900
Designer: Gordon K. Douglass

Normal sheer at rail, but reverse sheer at deck. Very large cockpit. Big boat.

A big, fast centerboard boat, the Flying Scot has an unusual reverse sheer. Capacity is eight adults. With hard bilges and a slightly tunneled hull, stability is good. Rigging is relatively simple, and the class rules discourage complexity. Required or allowed are vangs and roller furling for the main. Specifically not allowed are hiking straps and trapezes, leech cords, Barber haulers, twings, and self-bailers. No mast adjustment is allowed while racing. The centerboard is heavy — 105 pounds — so control usually includes a 6:1 assist. Foam flotation is provided under the seats, which have a drain to the transom. The boat is a one-design and all hulls are made from the same mold.

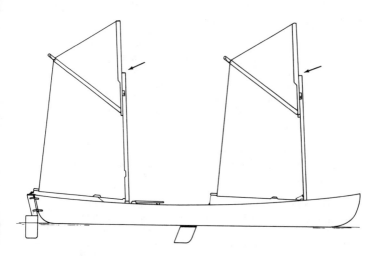

Appledore

Flying Scot

Lightning

Length: 19 ft.
Beam: 6 ft. 6 in.
Draft: 4 ft. 11 in.
Weight: 700 lbs.
Sail area: Main and jib, 177 sq. ft. total; spinnaker, 300 sq. ft.
Hull: Wood or fiberglass

Spars: Wood or aluminum
Racing crew: 4
Rating: D-PN 88.4
First built: 1938
No. built: Over 14,600
Designer: Olin Stephens

Raked mast. Permanent backstay. May have windows. If wood mast, there is a jumper stay from the head to the spreader. Long vee coaming.

Lightning may be bought complete, built from hull kits, or built from scratch. Most of the older boats are wood, but replacements are mostly FRP. If the boat is to be raced, rigid one-design specifications intended to keep costs within bounds must be met. Lightning is an International class, supervised by the IYRU. There are over 460 fleets in the U. S., Europe, Canada, and South America. The large cockpit holds five adults. There is a clear area forward of the centerboard and aft of the mast from which crew may handle sails. The backstay is permanent and lands at the chain plate off center, so as to clear the tiller. There is good freeboard and stability.

Mariner

Length: 19 ft. 2 in.
Beam: 7 ft.
Draft: 4 ft. 11 in.
Weight: 1,250 lbs.
Sail area: Main and jib, 185 sq. ft. total
Hull: FRP; deck balsa core

Spars: Hard-coated aluminum
Racing crew: 2
Rating: D-PN 104.0
First built: 1966
No. built: 4,100
Designer: George O'Day

Backstay. Same hull as Rhodes 19. Cuddy. Two windows. Black headboard, mast, boom. Possible sail window in jib.

The Mariner, a very typical day sailer, was originally built by the O'Day Corporation. There is sharp bow entry and high freeboard; like the Rhodes 19, the Mariner can handle heavy weather. This capability is enhanced by the 210-pound centerboard. There is seating for six adults. The mast is deck mounted. In the cuddy are two forward berths, two quarter berths, under-berth storage, opening windows, space for a portable head, and teak trim. The cockpit is self-draining and has a storage compartment. A vang, 105-square-foot genoa, and spinnaker package are optional.

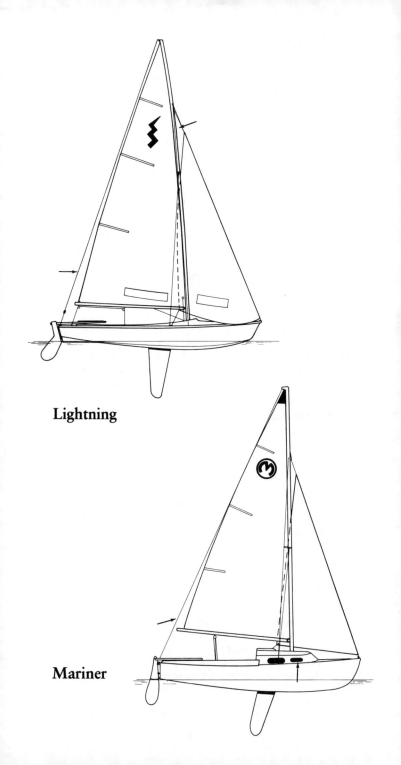

Lightning

Mariner

Rhodes 19

Length: 19 ft. 2 in.
Beam: 7 ft.
Draft: 4 ft. 11 in. (centerboard);
  or 3 ft. 3 in. (keel)
Weight: 1,000 lbs. (centerboard);
  or 1,240 lbs. (keel)
Sail area: Main, 112.5 sq. ft.;
  jib, 60.5 sq. ft.
  spinnaker, 326 sq. ft.

Hull: FRP
Spars: Aluminum
Racing crew: 2
Rating: D-PN 97.4 (centerboard)
  or D-PN 99.0 (keel)
First built: 1959
No. built: 4,000
Designer: Philip Rhodes

Triangular spreaders forward of mast, second set below. Backstay. Cuddy.

A *Sail* magazine "breakthrough boat" with tremendous influence upon sailing, the Rhodes 19 is the first popular day sailer. Centerboard and keel versions are available, with the former found mostly on lakes and the latter in coastal waters. The large cockpit will hold six to eight, while the cuddy can sleep two. There is a built-in icebox. The traveler is mounted on the stern. Jib leads are adjustable. In the centerboard model the rudder kicks up. In both, there is foam flotation. Optional features are a boom tent, boom vang, Cunningham, cockpit bailers, a tapered mast, a whisker pole, and a spinnaker package. Portsmouth Numbers shown date from the early 1980s. For some reason, the latest edition of the numbers does not show the 19, but only the Rhodes Bantam. The 19 is actively raced.

Flying Dutchman

Length: 19 ft. 10 in.
Beam: 5 ft. 11 in.
Draft: 3 ft. 8 in.
Weight: 347 lbs. minimum
Sail area: Main, 116 sq. ft.;
  genoa, 84 sq. ft.; spinnaker,
  190 sq. ft.
Hull: Wood, FRP, composite

Spars: Optional, usually
  aluminum
Racing crew: 2
Rating: Olympic; D-PN 79.9
First built: 1951
No. built: 10,500
Designer: Uus van Essen

Sharp spoon bow. Hull extends far aft of boom. Straight sheer. Trapeze.

The Flying Dutchman (FD) is the first trapeze boat selected for the Olympics. It is an International class boat, controlled by the IYRU. FD is a compromise between a "rule" boat and a strict one-design. Hull shape, centerboard and rudder, and sail plan are controlled. There are guidelines for standing and running rigging, layout, and cockpit size. There is a sharp, hollow bow which reduces pounding. Initial stability is high because of the hard bilges. She is fast, but not nervous. The boat is frequently built from hull kits, sometimes from plans. Fleets are scattered over the East Coast, Florida, Michigan, Texas, Washington, and California; there is also one in Green River, Wyoming.

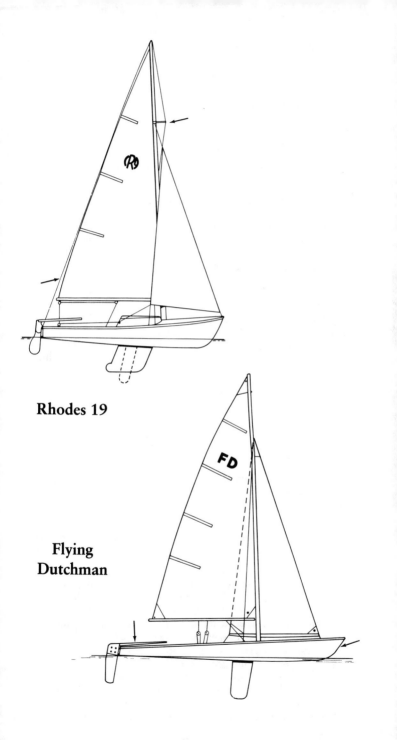

Rhodes 19

**Flying
Dutchman**

C-Scow

Length: 20 ft.
Beam: 6 ft. 10 in.
Draft: 3 ft. 3 in.
Weight: 650 lbs. minimum
Sail area: 216 sq. ft.
Hull: FRP
Spars: Aluminum or wood

Racing crew: 2 or 3 (475 lbs. max.)
Rating: D-PN 79.7
First built: Early 20th century
No. built: 2,000
Designer: Inland Yacht Association

Scow. No jib. Running backstays. Mast raked aft. Boom close to deck.

The C-Scow was first built early in the century. Sources differ, with one claiming 1906 and the other, 1923. As may be seen from the rating, this cat-rigged scow is fast. Scows were developed in the Midwest, but the C-Scow can also be found in Texas and California. There is extensive control. Forestays may be adjusted while the boat is sailing; a lever aft of the vang track is used, and of course the backstays must be released. Sidestay adjustment is by turnbuckle, but the mast may not be pulled to windward while sailing. There is an adjustable ballbearing traveler. The boom vang leads to a radial recessed track. (The boom is low, which makes installation of a conventional vang difficult.) The double-ended 6:1 outhaul and Cunningham also control shape. These boats are one-design, with strict control of hull shape. They have polystyrene foam flotation.

Flying Fifteen

Length: 20 ft.
Beam: 5 ft.
Draft: 2 ft. 6 in.
Weight: 697.4 lbs. minimum
Sail area: Main, 100 sq. ft.; genoa, 50 sq. ft.; spinnaker, 150 sq. ft.

Hull: FRP or wood
Spars: Aluminum
Racing crew: 2
Rating: D-PN 91.0
First built: 1948
No. built: 2,900
Designer: Uffa Fox

Long spoon bow. Unusual counter. Rudder post well forward of stern.

The Flying Fifteen is an ultra-light-displacement keel boat that has been clocked at 16 knots. The cockpit is self-bailing, and there is airbag flotation. She became an International class in 1981. The majority of boats are in Great Britain, Australia, New Zealand, South Africa, and Hong Kong. In the U. S., fleets are in San Francisco, Maine, and Connecticut. Class rules require positive buoyancy, hiking straps, and other safety equipment. Instrumentation and mast adjustment under way are not allowed. Championships must be sailed on tidal waters. All controls lead to the cockpit just forward of the traveler. Included are sheets, Cunningham, vang, down- and outhaul, and spinnaker sheet and guy. Roller furling for the jib is available.

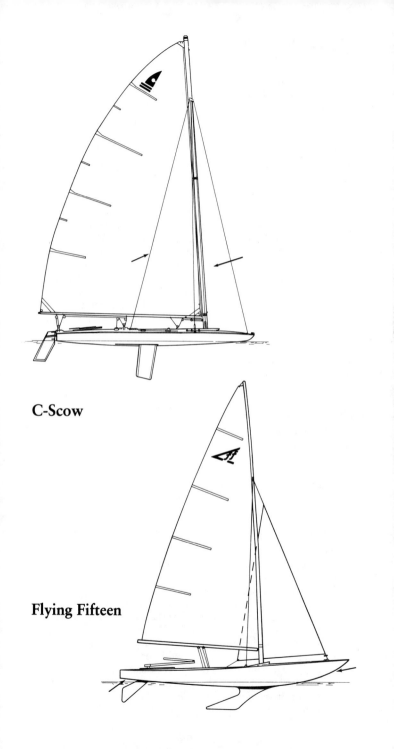

C-Scow

Flying Fifteen

Highlander

Length: 20 ft.
Beam: 6 ft. 8 in.
Draft: 8 in. (centerboard up)
Weight: 830 lbs.
Sail area: Main and jib, 225 sq. ft. total; spinnaker available, used for racing.

Hull: FRP
Spars: Aluminum
Racing crew: 3
Rating: D-PN 84.6
First built: 1951
No. built: 1,000
Designer: Gordon K. Douglass

Three jumper struts. Reverse sheer similar to Flying Scot. Jib window possible. Curved rudder.

The Highlander evolved from the same designer's dinghies and from the Thistle. It predates the Flying Scot (also by Gordon Douglass) and was originally built of molded plywood. The bow is similar to the Thistle, while the reverse sheer foretells the Scot. The mast has a triple diamond-shroud system. While apparently heavy, the Highlander has a low length-to-displacement ratio of 69.8, and she planes. The cockpit is 11 feet long and 5 feet wide and will hold ten people. Wood is used for seats, foredeck rail, and elsewhere. Standing rigging is adjustable. Running rigging is simple and includes a vang, Cunningham, and centerboard adjustment with a high mechanical advantage. Fleets are mostly in Ohio, with others in Tennessee, Maryland, Massachusetts, Kentucky, North Carolina, and New York.

Yngling

Length: 20 ft. 4 in.
Beam: 5 ft. 6 in.
Draft: 3 ft. 6 in.
Weight: 1,320 lbs.
Sail area: Main 95 sq. ft.; jib, 55 sq. ft.; spinnaker, 180 sq. ft.
Hull: FRP

Spars: Aluminum
Racing crew: 3
Rating: None
First built: 1968
No. built: 3,500-4,000
Designer: Jan Linge

Small cuddy. Similar to Soling. Fractional rig. Spoon bow.

Yngling was designed and is built in Norway. Jan Linge also designed the larger Soling, and the lines are very similar. The boat is designed for racing and has had International status since 1979. There are also National associations in Austria, Belgium, Germany, Norway, Switzerland, Denmark, the Netherlands, Sweden, the United States, and Australia. All are very active, as is the International Association. The Yngling is highly stable, with a beam-to-waterline ratio of .37 and with 50 percent of the weight in ballast. It is unsinkable, with foam-filled tanks. Sail area is not large, so that the boat may be sailed by younger sailors. While one-design rules are strict, every effort has been made to keep the cost of allowable modifications down. Sails have windows. Main sheeting is end-boom.

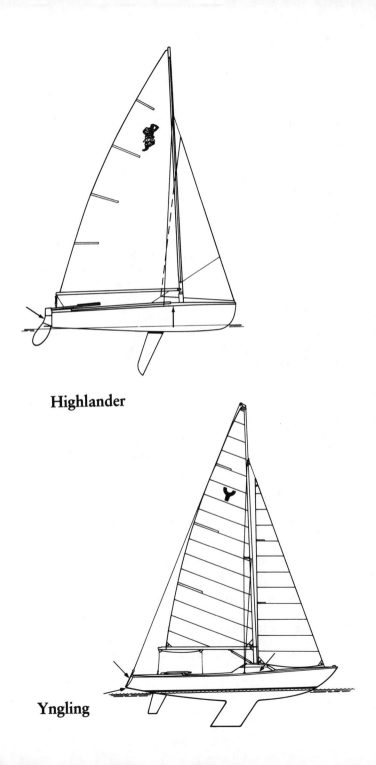

Highlander

Yngling

Impulse 21

Length: 21 ft.	*Spars:* Aluminum
Beam: 8 ft.	*Racing crew:* 2
Draft: 3 ft. 4 in.	*Rating:* D-PN 183
Weight: 1,300 lbs.	*First built:* 1986
Sail area: Main, 126 sq. ft.; jib,	*No. built:* 120
82 sq. ft.; spinnaker, 340 sq. ft.	*Designer:* William E. Cook
Hull: Klegecell core and FRP	

Raised base for mast. Strongly raked transom, shows cut out area from behind.

A day sailer with room for lots of crew, the Impulse's most unusual feature is a center console housing the control lines for the jib sheet, jib traveler, jib Cunningham, main Cunningham, boom vang, spinnaker halyard, spinnaker retriever, and backstay adjustments. The cockpit is 9 feet long, with seating on the wide decks. The cuddy is small enough to store sails and a cooler, but isn't for sleeping. The spinnaker is "launched" from a tube located below the foredeck. The jib is self-tacking. The cutout in the transom makes for easy boarding for swimmers. Keel depth is moderate, so that Impulse may be trailered. However, the keel, taken with the wide beam and deck, provides good stability, and foam-filled compartments provide flotation.

Tornado

Length: 20 ft.	*Spars:* Aluminum
Beam: 10 ft.	*Racing crew:* 2
Draft: 2 ft. 7 in.	*Rating:* Olympic; D-PN 64.0
Weight: 279 lbs.	*First built:* 1967
Sail area: Main and jib, 235 sq.	*No. built:* 3,600
ft. total	*Designer:* Rodney Marsh
Hull: Wood	

Two symmetrical hulls. Trapeze. Very high aspect ratio. Very high jib. Ten battens in loose-footed main.

In use since 1976, the Tornado is the only Olympic catamaran. There are very few boats with lower Portsmouth numbers than this daggerboarder. No spinnaker is used. This International boat is self-rescuing. Hiking assists allowed are straps, usually used by the skipper, and a trapeze ridden by the crew.

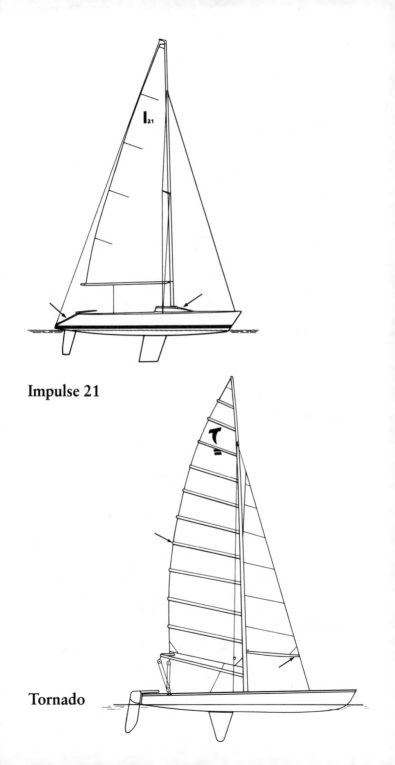

Impulse 21

Tornado

Sirius

Length: 21 ft. 2 in.
Beam: 7 ft. 11 in.
Draft: 5 ft.
Weight: 2,000 lbs.
Sail area: Main, 93 sq. ft.; jib,
   110 sq. ft.; genoa, 156 sq. ft.;
   spinnaker, 385 sq. ft.

Hull: FRP
Spars: Aluminum
Racing crew: 2 or 3
Rating: D-PN 95.5 suspect
First built: 1976
No. built: 565
Designer: Hubert Vandestadt

Very high boom. Foremost cabin windows slightly smaller. Possible bow and stern pulpit. Note straight lines of rudder. Masthead rig.

The Sirius is built in Ontario and is mostly found on the Great Lakes. There are berths for five, a dinette, and a galley. Sink, five-gallon water tank, and pump are extra. The interior is finished, with hull and deck liners and teak trim. Sirius has a wide beam; and this, combined with the hard bilge and a retractable cast-iron keel, gives good stability. She is unsinkable and, if the keel is locked down, self-righting. There is a well for the anchor. In the cockpit is a compartment for a gas tank. A pop-top is standard. Rudder kicks up, and she has a boom vang, jiffy reefing, and topping lift.

Santana 20

Length: 20 ft. 2½ in.
Beam: 8 ft.
Draft: 4 ft.
Weight: 1,350 lbs.
Sail area: Main, 36 sq. ft.; jib,
   109 sq. ft.; genoa, 149 sq. ft.;
   spinnaker, 359 sq. ft.

Hull: FRP
Spars: Aluminum
Racing crew: 3 or 4
Rating: D-PN 91.3
First built: 1976
No. built: 630
Designer: W. Shad Turner

Straight bow, counter, reverse transom. High aspect ratio. Stern support for lifeline. Distinctive deckhouse.

This large day sailer has a cabin with two opening windows that will sleep four. There is storage under the vee berth, and under the cockpit seats. The cabin has a liner and teak trim. Cockpit layout is split. Forward, controls for halyards and the vang lead to the top of the cuddy. There is a traveler, and aft is the helmsman's station. Note the size of the main in relation to the jib or genoa. Most fleets are on the West Coast, but some are also in Oklahoma, Indiana, Florida, and Texas. Sail the Santana 20 heeled about seven degrees, and roll tack.

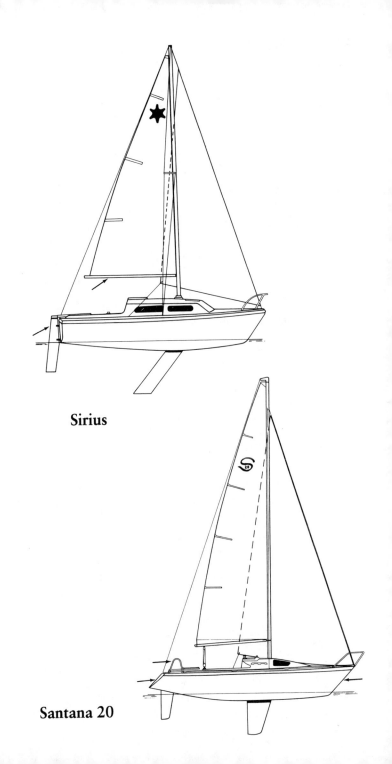

Sirius

Santana 20

Atlantic City

Length: 21 ft. 3 in.	*Spars:* Wood
Beam: 9 ft. 6 in.	*Rating:* None
Draft: *5 ft.*	*First built:* 1982
Weight: 5,300 lbs.	*No. built:* Not avail.
Sail area: 350 sq. ft.	*Designer:* Mark-O-Boats
Hull: FRP	

Catboat, mast hoops, gaff rigged. Ports unusual shape. Typical plumb bow.

The basic design of this catboat is classic. Note the high coaming and the rudder design, typical of boats built for this part of the Atlantic coast. (For contrast, see Marshall 22 for a Cape Cod-style rudder.) Below, there is an area for the galley and for a chart table and locker (all optional). The opposing settees can be used for berths, and each has a pilot berth above. A door isolates the head, forward, and a rope locker in the forepeak. Typically, the cockpit is large. With available options including a 12-horsepower diesel engine, cockpit table, marine head, and even a fireplace, the Atlantic City is ready for short cruises. Tiller steering, a bilge pump, and bronze hardware are standard.

Dovekie

Length: 21 ft. 5 in.	*Spars:* Aluminum
Draft: 4 in. leeboards up	*Racing crew:* —
Beam: 6 ft. 8 in.	*Rating:* NA
Weight: 600 lbs.	*First built:* 1979
Sail area: 143 sq. ft.	*No. built:* 152
Hull: Airex foam and FRP	*Designer:* Phillip Bolger

Raked mast. Leeboards. Rounded transom.

A cruising sailboat for two, with power available, but not necessary. Spirit used in place of a boom. Meant for short cruises, and with the exceptional draft, gunkholing. (For minimum draft the leeboards are raised, and the small centerboard forward and the rudder reduce leeway.) The leeboards provide more space in the cabin. Since Dovekie is very light, oars, which are provided, may be used for auxillary power. There are two sets of reef points, and an unusual method of furling: the sail is rolled forward on itself, but not on the mast.

Dovekie tacks through 84 degrees and has a speed of about four knots. Under cover forward are two large, canvas-covered storage bins. The cockpit has seating for three or four under way, and the seven-foot open bottom provides a sleeping area. While Dovekie has a location for a Porta Potti, sleeping and eating require camping equipment such as sleeping bags , air mattresses, and portable stoves. The boat will float if swamped. Sails, an anchor, anchor warp, life jackets, and a signaling kit come with the boat.

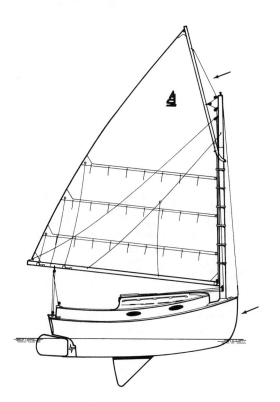

Atlantic City

Dovekie

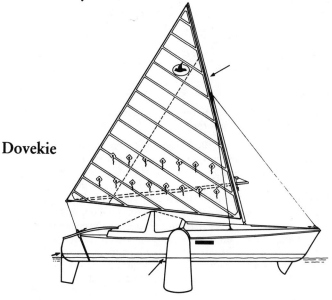

Tempest

Length: 21 ft. 11¼ in.
Beam: 6 ft. 5½ in.
Draft: 3 ft. 7 in.
Weight: 977 lbs.
Sail area: Main, 164 sq. ft.;
  jib, 82.78 sq. ft.; spinnaker,
  225 sq. ft.

Hull: FRP
Spars: Aluminum
Racing crew: 2
Rating: None
First built: 1965
No. built: 850
Designer: Ian Proctor

Keel boat, rudder submerged. Aft deck. Note foredeck line down to hull at mast.

The International Class Tempest was an Olympic boat in 1972 and 1976. She is fast. Tempest is a one-design, and class rules are strict. Trapezes are allowed. The mast's design and material are optional, but the mast may not rotate. Older boats have thicker, stiffer masts and, in addition to the diamond shrouds and spreaders found today, additional swept-back spreaders. Good racing boats are light at the ends and rigid, although this is not necessary in the deck. Windows are allowed in the jib and main, with size controlled. Tempests are often dry sailed. There are three transverse bulkheads for flotation. Items prohibited include mast jacks, trim tabs, and more than two spinnakers. Only one person may use the trapeze, and safety equipment is required.

Ensign

Length: 22 ft. 6 in.
Beam: 7 ft.
Draft: 3 ft.
Weight: 3,000 lbs.
Sail area: Main, 140 sq. ft.; jib,
  61 sq. ft.; genoa, 150 and 111
  sq. ft.; spinnaker dimensions
  restricted by class: leech and
  luff, 25 ft; foot from clew to
  clew, 15 ft.

Hull: FRP; deck balsa core
Spars: Anodized aluminum
Racing crew: 2 or more
Rating: D-PN 95.8
First built: 1962
No. built: 1,775
Designer: Carl Alberg

Long spoon bow, counter, reverse transom. High coamings. Mast splits two shrouds fore and aft. End-boom sheeting.

There are more than 1,700 Ensigns sailing in 47 fleets in 20 states. Fleets are concentrated in Long Island Sound, Massachusetts, Maine, the Great Lakes, and Texas. Ensign is the largest full-keel one-design class in the country. The cuddy has two berths, optional head, and 3-foot 10-inch headroom. In the 8-foot 8-inch cockpit are teak sole, seats, and coamings. Mast adjustments during racing are not permitted, except to the backstay, which is controlled with a turnbuckle. Roller reefing on the boom is allowed. There is a boom vang, and mid-boom sheeting is an allowed modification. Barber haulers, geared sheet winches, and internal halyards are not permitted.

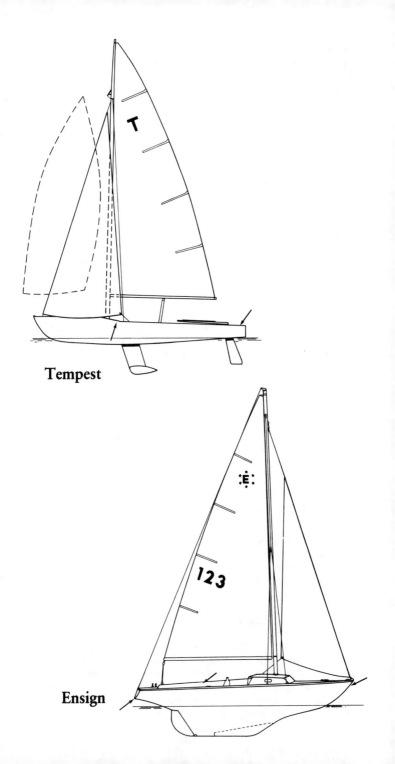

Tempest

Ensign

J/22

Length: 22 ft. 6 in.
Beam: 8 ft.
Draft: 3.7 ft.
Weight: 1,790 lbs.
Sail area: Main, 120 sq. ft.;
   jib, 103 sq. ft.;
   Spinnaker, 361 sq. ft.
Hull: Baltex core and FRP

Spars: Aluminum
Racing crew: 3 (605 lbs. max.)
Rating: PHRF 180-183, D-PN
   82.4
First built: 1983
No. built: 1,200 est.
Designer: Rod Johnstone

Straight bow, single porthole, shaped rudder.

Ready to race when delivered, but the J/22 can still be tuned to fit conditions. Sailors adjust upper and lower shrouds, the backstay, and the outhaul depending upon wind strength. There seems to be general agreement that sail trim is very sensitive. The jib car, for example, should be located very precisely for best boat speed. There is a cabin into which four or five people might fit, but the J/22 is meant to be raced, not cruised. (However, in light air, it is suggested that one or more of the crew go below to reduce windage and to keep weight forward and low.) Hatches are designed for offshore, and the 700-pound keel is lead. The main sheets to a traveler across the cockpit, and there are winches on the coach roof. J/22s are in 61 fleets in eight continents, qualifying for International status.

Star

Length: 22 ft. 8½ in.
Beam: 5 ft. 8¼ in.
Draft: 3 ft. 6 in.
Weight: 1,480 lbs. minimum
Sail area: Main, 240 sq. ft.;
   jib, 78 sq. ft.
Hull: Wood or FRP
Spars: Wood or aluminum

Racing crew: 2
Rating: Olympic
First built: 1911 (present length)
No. built: 7,700
Designer: William Gardner in
   1906, Francis Swiesguth in
   1910

Inboard rudder. Small cockpit. Relatively low boom. Running backstays.

Roller reefing in the twenties and thirties. Vang very early, and circular vang in the fifties. Flexible rig in the thirties. Mast benders in the twenties. Now, almost everything is adjustable, and the Star rig must be fine-tuned very carefully. Adjustments include the traveler, backstays, low backstays, jib leads, and mast partners. There is a lever-operated mast bender. Most of these lead to amidships in the cockpit. The Star originally had a gaff or gunter rig which changed to Marconi in 1921. The original wood hull changed to FRP in 1967; the spars to aluminum in 1971. Hull shape has changed very little, with the major change a lengthening from 18 feet to the present length in 1911. Measurement rules are extensive. There are about 160 fleets on five continents, with about 3,000 boats actively racing. Buoyancy has been required since 1979.

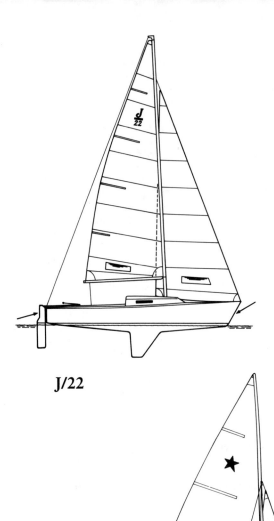

J/22

Star

Ranger 23

Length: 23 ft.	*Spars:* Aluminum
Beam: 7 ft. 11 in.	*Racing crew:* 2-3
Draft: 3 ft. 9 in.	*Rating:* PHRF 232
Weight: 3,394 lbs.	*First built:* 1970
Sail area: 263.56 sq. ft.	*No. built:* 825
Hull: FRP	*Designer:* Gary Mull

Bow and stern almost parallel. Masthead rig. Cabin quite large.

This Ranger was originally designed to the MORC racing rules, and it became very well known in MORC and PHRF racing. There are both tall and short rigs. In the cabin are four berths, lockers, a sink, icebox and a 12-gallon water tank. There is also an enclosed head. Rigging is stainless steel. The main sheet has a four-to-one purchase and the outhaul, two to one. There are two winches in the cockpit, and a halyard winch on the mast. The main sheet traveler has a car, and there is an internal boom topping lift. D-PN for the tall mast version is 91.0.

Sonar

Length: 23 ft.	*Hull:* FRP
Beam: 7 ft. 10 in.	*Spars:* Aluminum
Draft: 4 ft.	*Racing crew:* 3 or 4
Weight: 2,160 lbs.	*Rating:* D-PN 82.5
Sail area: Main, 153.55 sq. ft.;	*First built:* 1980
jib, 99 sq. ft.; spinnaker, 360	*No. built:* 510
sq. ft.	*Designer:* Bruce Kirby

Large, keel day sailer. Sharp bow. Reverse transom. Backstay. Very large cockpit.

The Sonar was designed for the same market as the Etchells 22, Soling, Tempest, and Ensign. The basic concept was generated by a committee of the Noroton Yacht Club (Connecticut), then designed by Bruce Kirby. The cockpit is huge. Seven adults can sit in its 11-foot length. The boat is very stable, with a 935-pound keel. Notice that the rudder is inboard. Only three sails are allowed — main, jib, and spinnaker. There are three cockpit lockers and a locking cabin that is sometimes rigged for two berths. The tapered boom has internal slab reefing. Adjustment is with a four-to-one sheet, and there is a vang. Class rules prohibit hiking. Production figures for this fairly new boat may be misleading, as 60 were sold the first month it was approved.

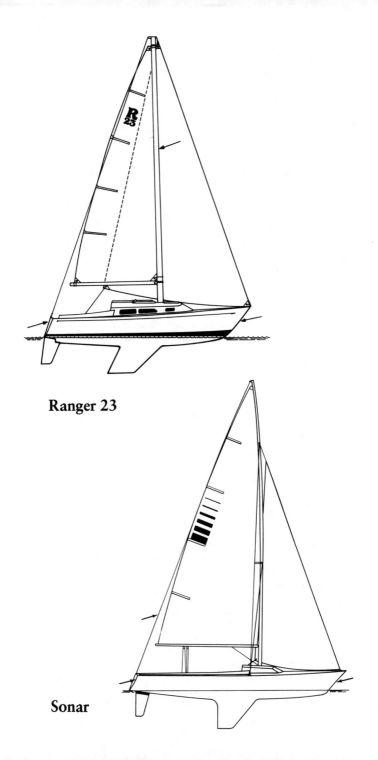

Ranger 23

Sonar

Balboa 24

Length: 23 ft. 7 in.
Beam: 8 ft. 4 in.
Draft: 2 ft. 11 in.
Weight: 2,666 lbs. or 2,800 lbs.
Sail area: Main, 115 (124.5) sq. ft.; jib, 105 (127) sq. ft.; genoa, 158 (190) sq. ft.; spinnaker, 360 (462) sq. ft.

Hull: FRP
Spars: Anodized aluminum
Racing crew: 2
Rating: D-PN 99.0
First built: 1980
Designer: W. Shad Turner

Masthead rig. Bow pulpit, stern pulpit. Three windows. Straight bow, almost vertical transom.

Two rigs are available for this sloop. The first has a 26½-foot mast; the taller rig has a 28-foot mast and 200 additional pounds of ballast. The latter is the better rig for racing.
Both are equipped for cruising, with five berths, a galley with fixed ice chest and sink, separate head area with sink, and a recessed area for an alcohol stove. The boat opens up with a Plexiglas foredeck hatch and pop-top allowing six feet of headroom. Storage includes an anchor locker, two cockpit lockers and a cockpit lazarette for gas can, under-berth storage, galley storage, shelves, and a hanging locker. Interior trim is teak. Safety items include a pulpit, lifelines, integral toe-rails, and a stern pulpit.

110

Length: 24 ft.
Beam: 4 ft. 3 in.
Draft: 2 ft. 9 in.
Weight: 910 lbs.
Sail area: Main and genoa, 167 sq. ft. total; spinnaker, 200 sq. ft.

Hull: Plywood
Spars: Wood or aluminum
Racing crew: 2 or 3
Rating: D-PN 89.6
First built: 1939
No. built: 700
Designer: C. Raymond Hunt

Untraditional double-ender. Low freeboard, narrow hull. Vertical sides.

This fin-keeler was a breakthrough design of the late thirties. Rule changes, allowing a trapeze, enabled the 110 to win the Keel Division of the One-of-a-Kind Regatta in 1969. She points extremely well, planes on the flat bottom, and goes well downwind, but unless weight is kept well aft the bow tends to bury. Because of the very simple lines, the 110 is easy to build. In spite of her weight, which includes the 300-pound keel, she is unsinkable. The most frequent racing crew is two. A third crew member has to fight the boom vang for space. Many boats have been made of fiberglass. There is a roller-furling jib, a trapeze, and a spinnaker tube. The cockpit is small and, with the narrow beam, it is difficult to work off the foredeck. Most boats are in New England, the West Coast, and the upper Midwest.

Balboa 24

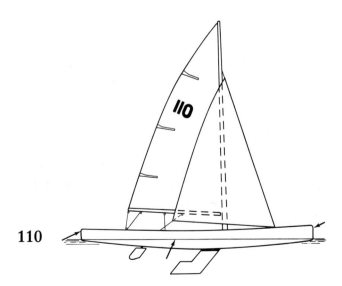

110

J/24

Length: 24 ft.
Beam: 8.9 ft.
Draft: 4 ft.
Weight: 3,100 lbs.
Sail area: I, 26.25 ft.; J, 9.50 ft.;
P, 28.0 ft.; E, 9.75 ft.
Hull: FRP, balsa core

Spars: Tapered aluminum
Racing crew: 5
Rating: D-PN 81.1; PHRF
174 average.
First built: 1977
No. built: 5,024
Designer: Rodney S. Johnstone

Fractional rig. Straight bow, vertical stern. Cutaway rudder.

While the J/24 is primarily raced, the cabin makes it suitable for weekend cruising. In the cabin are two settee berths, a vee berth, and a sink. There is a foredeck hatch serving for both ventilation and sail handling. The boat is very popular, with a number of fleets. It is an International class. The cockpit is self-bailing, and there are two water-tight compartments for flotation. There are two two-speed primary winches. The backstay is adjustable, and the boom vang has an eight-to-one purchase. There is a Cunningham. The traveler has a car, and there is an internal outhaul with a five-to-one advantage. The bow pulpit is stainless steel, and the spars are anodized.

Raven

Length: 24 ft. 3 in.
Beam: 7 ft.
Draft: 5 ft. 4 in.
Weight: 1,170 lbs.
Sail area: Main and jib, 300 sq.
ft. total
Hull: FRP

Spars: Anodized aluminum
Racing crew: 3
Rating: D-PN 82.6
First built: 1949
No. built: Over 300
Designer: Roger McAleer

No visible tiller or rudder. Continuous curve to bow. Two spreaders. Adjustable jib leads.

Raven, originally in molded plywood, was a forerunner of today's planing boats. Construction was switched to FRP in 1951, and the Coast Guard Academy took the first eight. Coamings and centerboard trim remain in wood. The boom is fitted with roller reefing and a six-part outhaul. There are two self-bailers. Rule changes, most in 1970, allow for a one-piece aluminum centerboard, trapeze, full-width traveler on the large aft deck, and hiking straps.

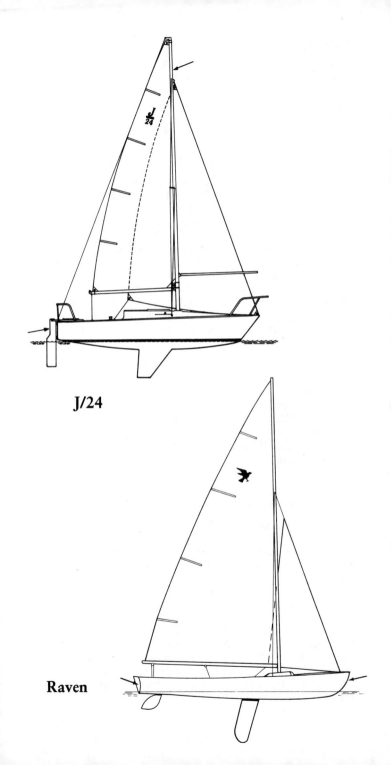

J/24

Raven

Folkboat

Length: 25 ft. 1 in.
Beam: 7 ft. 2½ in.
Draft: 3 ft. 11 in.
Weight: 5,000 lbs.
Sail area: 235 sq. ft.
Hull: Lapstrake, wood
Spars: Wood

Racing crew: 2-4
Rating: D-PN 103.2
First built: 1942
No. built: Unknown, over 110 U.S.
Designer: Tord Sunden

Lapstrake construction. Fractional rig. Jumper stays above jib.

The Noridska Folkbaten, or people's boat, was originated by Tord Sunden of Sweden in 1942. It incorporated ideas by Jac N. Iversen, also of Sweden. By 1942 there were 20, but the total to date is not known. Since then, at least two other similar boats — the International 25 and the Olsen 26 — have followed. There are fleets in Germany, Denmark, Sweden, Finland, Latvia, Estonia, and in San Francisco Bay in the United States. The boat is noted for its seaworthy character. With an iron keel, it has raced in winds of 40 knots and often carries full sail in 20-25. Most boats have two bunks, and perhaps a vee-berth forward, with camping gear used for cooking. There are lockers. The interiors are apt to vary widely, with some minimized for racing, and others adapted for cruising.

Soling

Length: 26 ft. 11 in.
Beam: 6 ft. 3 in.
Draft: 4 ft. 3 in.
Weight: 2,277 lbs.
Sail area: Main, 146 sq. ft.; jib, 87 sq. ft.; spinnaker, 340 sq. ft.
Hull: FRP

Spars: Aluminum
Racing crew: 3
Rating: Olympic
First built: 1965
No. built: 3,000
Designer: Jan Herman Linge

Backstay. Big sloop with no cabin. Long spoon bow. Long counter, reverse transom. Rudder not visible.

An Olympic class since 1972. The Soling is heavy, but she planes. There are active class associations in 35 countries, and about 750 Solings in the United States. There are strict class rules covering more than 150 items. All boats are built from an official mold. The Soling is self-bailing, but it has been known to sink despite flotation compartments fore, aft, and below the floor. There is a cabin of sorts, which may contain a galley and other types of storage. There are also storage lockers in the cockpit. While the Soling can be found almost anywhere in the U. S., because it is a keel boat it is most often found on the coasts or on large bodies of water. The areas listed for the U. S. include the Atlantic, West, Midwest, South, Northwest, and Mideast. The International one-design class is administered by the IYRU. About 950 Solings are members of the International Soling Association.

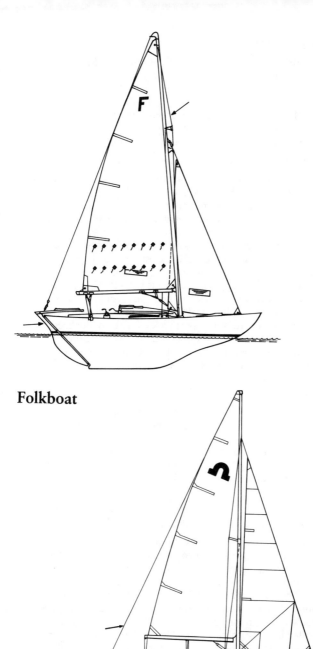

Folkboat

Soling

Stuart Knockabout

Length: 28 ft.
Beam: 6 ft. 11 in.
Draft: 2 ft. 9 in. to 5 ft. 6 in
Weight: 4,000 lbs.
Sail area: Main; 185 sq. ft.; jib 80 sq. ft.; genoa, 160 sq. ft.; spinnaker; 330 sq. ft.

Hull: Airex cored FRP
Spars: Aluminum
Racing crew: 2-4
Rating: PHRF 185
First built: 1932
No. built: 16
Designer: L. Francis Herreshoff

Overhanging transom, classic bow, inboard rudder.

While there are not too many Knockabouts, the design warrants inclusion. The original boats were wood, and while now in fiberglass, the classic wood lines are retained. The first boat was built in 1933, and construction began again in 1989. The first boat was used in Maine, but the present manufacturer is in Marion, Massachusetts. The cockpit is over 9 feet long, has bench seats, and the coaming is a backrest. Forward, shelves and a decked-over space provide storage for sails. In addition, there is a stern locker. The centerboard is solid PVC, is not ballasted, and has a two-part tackle to assist in raising. A detachable bracket allows for the installation of a three-to-four-horsepower outboard. There is four-part tackle for the mainsheet, leading to the aft corners of the cockpit. Headsail options include a club-footed self-tending jib, a genoa, and a spinnaker. As with many Herreshoff designs, the Knockabout is shallow draft.

E Scow

Length: 28 ft.
Beam: 6 ft. 9 in.
Draft: 4 ft.
Weight: 965 lbs. (hull only)
Sail area: Main, 228 sq. ft.; jib, 95 sq. ft.; spinnaker, 550 sq. ft.
Hull: Wood or FRP

Spars: Aluminum, wood permitted
Racing crew: 2 or 3
Rating: D-PN 73.2
Designer: Evolved through many designs

Large scow. Rudder concealed. Bilgeboards. Windows in jib and main. Running backstays. Forestay attached well aft of bow.

This is a very fast and sophisticated boat with a long history of development. Scows probably evolved from sharpies, and the first scows were in evidence around 1895. E Scows were born at a meeting of the Inland Lake Yachting Association in 1923. Wood has been used for many years, but since 1976 FRP has predominated. Manufacturers now use sandwich construction. The E Scow has twin bilgeboards and rudders. Transom bailers are provided by both Johnson and Melges. Sail control is sophisticated. Main shape devices can include outhaul, downhaul, Cunningham, vang, and leech cord. Luff wire and downhauls are allowed for the jib. Other control includes radiused traveler and jib tracks. Artificial hiking assists other than hiking straps are not allowed. Fleets are found in Texas, Colorado, Wisconsin, Minnesota, Michigan, New York, and New Jersey.

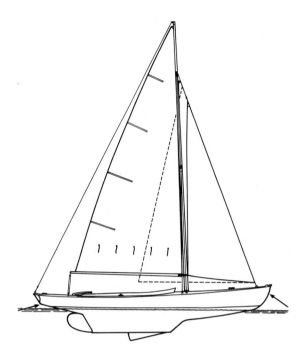

Stuart Knockabout

E Scow

Dragon

Length: 29 ft. 2 in.	*Hull:* Wood or FRP
Beam: 6 ft. 5 in.	*Spars:* Wood or aluminum
Draft: 3 ft. 11 in.	*Racing crew:* 3
Weight: 3,740 lbs.	*Rating:* D-PN 89.5
Sail area: Main, 135 sq. ft.;	*First built:* 1928
genoa 150 sq. ft.; spinnaker,	*No. built:* 4,500
155 sq. ft.	*Designer.* Johan Anker

Long overhangs at bow and stern. Classic lines. Very high aspect ratio. Two jumper struts. Very small cabin. Narrow beam.

This fractional sloop-rigged keel boat has celebrated more than 50 years of international popularity. Originally built of pine and subsequently of mahogany, it is now built of both FRP and laminated wood. A major change was made in 1945, when spinnakers and genoas were allowed. Dragon then served as an Olympic boat from 1952 through 1972. It is maintained as a one-design class by the IYRU. Although there is a cuddy that was designed to sleep two, the elegant lines of the Dragon proclaim its use in international and national racing. There are over 288 Dragons registered in the United States and 130 in Canada. Fleets are at Rochester, Toledo, Cleveland, Chicago, Long Beach, Santa Barbara, San Francisco, and Seattle.

International 210

Length: 29 ft. 10 in.	*Spars:* Aluminum
Beam: 5 ft. 10 in.	*Racing crew:* 3-4
Draft: 3 ft. 10 in.	*Rating:* One design
Sail area: Main, 210 sq. ft.; jib,	*First built:* 1945
75 sq. ft.; genoa, 130 sq. ft.	*No. built:* 450
spinnaker, 320 sq. ft.	*Designer:* C. Raymond Hunt
Hull: Foam cored FRP	

Double ended. Bow curve similar to stern. Fractional rig.

This is the big brother of the 110, by the same designer. The 110, however, has no curve to the bow or stern. The 210 is a fast boat and frequently beats Shields, Stars, and J/24s. It is light, but with the keel, stable. Originally built of plywood, the 210 is now glass-reinforced plastic. There have been continual updates over the 48-year history of the 210, but when the older boats have been maintained, they continue to compete with newer boats. Styrofoam blocks provide flotation. Woodwork on boats being produced now is of teak. Halyards and the outhaul are internal. The majority of fleets are in Massachusetts Bay, but there are also fleets in Michigan, Wisconsin, Maine, and on the Chesapeake Bay.

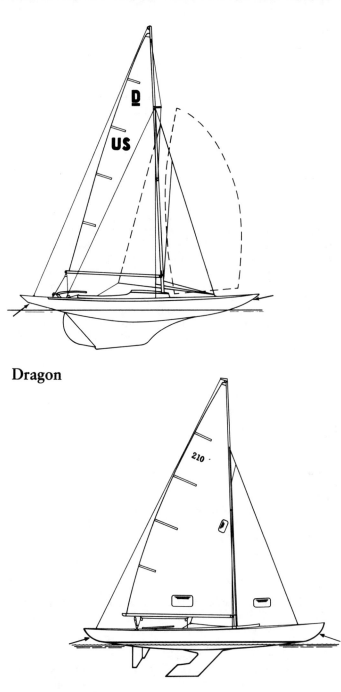

Dragon

International 210

Shields

Length: 30 ft. 2½ in.
Beam: 6 ft. 5¼ in.
Draft: 4 ft. 9 in.
Weight: 4,600 lbs.
Sail area: Main, 222 sq. ft.;
   jib, 138 sq. ft.; spinnaker,
   490 sq. ft.

Hull: FRP
Spars: Aluminum
Racing crew: 5
Rating: D-PN 83.8 suspect
First built: 1963
No. built: 248
Designer: Olin Stephens

Big, classic sloop. Note bow and especially the very long counter. Sheeting just aft of large cockpit. (In new boats, to the center of the boom.) No cabin. No genoa.

This beautiful boat is used for day sailing and, particularly, for racing. Class rules are rigid. For example, only one set of sails is allowed per year. Cape Cod Shipbuilding first built the Shields; then Chris Craft and Hinkley; and now, again, Cape Cod. This design was the concept of Cornelius Shields. As currently built, the Shields has teak coamings, toerails, handrails, floor grating, and cockpit seats. There is a console for halyard winches with cleats mounted vertically. There are flotation compartments under the seats, and in addition, there are watertight bulkheads fore and aft. The lead keel weighs 3,080 pounds. The backstay, the vang, and the mainsheet have a mechanical advantage not to exceed eight to one.

Knarr

Length: 30 ft. 4 in.
Beam: 7 ft.
Draft: 4 ft. 3 in.
Weight: 4,630 lbs.
Sail area: Main, 202 sq. ft.; jib
   107 sq. ft.
Hull: Mahogany or fir, then FRP

Spars: Spruce
Racing crew: 3-4
Rating: D-PN 91.0
First built: 1942
No. built: Over 360
Designer: Erling Kristofersen/
   Jan Linge

Long overhang, long smooth curve to spoon bow. Forestay set aft of bow.

During WW II there was a severe shortage of metals, and several designs, including the Knarr and the Folkboat, were designed in wood, with wood blocks and tackle, few or no winches, and simple construction. They have worn well. The Folkboat is still of wood, but since hull 129 the Knarr has been converted to fiberglass. It is manufactured in Denmark. There are 41 boats in the active San Francisco fleet. The International Championship was held in Oslo in 1993.

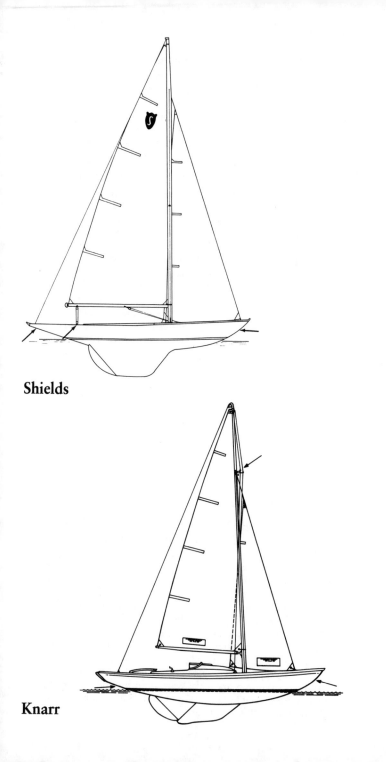

Shields

Knarr

E 22 (Etchells 22)

Length: 30 ft. 6 in.
Beam: 6 ft. 11½ in.
Draft: 4 ft. 6 in.
Weight: 3,400 lbs.
Sail area: Main, 188 sq. ft.; jib, 102 sq. ft.; spinnaker, 400 sq. ft.

Hull: FRP
Spars: Anodized aluminum
Racing crew: 3
Rating: None
First built: 1968
No. built: 500
Designer: E. W. Etchells

Large boat, classic lines, long overhangs at bow and stern. High aspect ratio. Forestay fractional, well back from bow. Keel.

Big, fast, and stiff, and with an association that tends to resist complex mast and sail control mechanisms, the E 22 is designated for International competition by the IYRU. There are builders and classes around the world. The cuddy is for storage and there are no bunks. The Etchells 22 is for day sailing or for racing. An unusual feature of the cockpit is a control console, and the jib halyard (8:1), foreguy, topping lift, Cunningham (4:1), and mainsheet (4: 1) lead to it. On the aft bulkhead of the cuddy are the coarse jib sheet (2:1), jib fine tune (6:1), Barber hauler (2:1), and spinnaker halyard. The backstay (6:1) is adjustable, as is the traveler. United States fleets are in Long Island Sound, Seattle, Maine, Massachusetts, Detroit, Chicago, Minneapolis, San Francisco, and San Diego. In Canada, there are fleets in Toronto and Halifax.

Atlantic One-Design

Length: 30 ft. 7 in.
Beam: 6 ft. 6 in.
Draft: 4 ft. 9 in.
Weight: 4,559 lbs.
Sail area: Main, 276 sq. ft.; jib, 100 sq. ft.; spinnaker, 210 sq. ft.
Hull: Originally wood, now FRP

Spars: Aluminum
Racing crew: 4
Rating: D-PN 81.0
First built: late twenties
No. built: 140
Designer: W. Starling Burgess

Overhanging transom and bow. Forestay set back. Tall rig.

The original boats were built of wood during the twenties, and the boat was popular on Long Island Sound, where many famous names in sailing — Cunningham, Mosbacher, Romagna, Bavier, Shields, etc. — raced the boat. Later, the wooden hulls were replaced with FRP, with the original keels, spars, rudder and rigging transferred to the new hulls. Beginning in 1962, the boat was built totally new. A few boats have been modified for cruising and have a small deckhouse, with a Vee berth, a sink, and a head. There are halyard and jib sheet winches, the vang is four-part, and all running rigging leads to the large cockpit. The jib is a deck sweeper, and genoas are not used. Toe-rails, coamings, and floor gratings are teak. Watertight bulkheads fore and aft assist in providing flotation. The Class Association has found 7 of the original 100 wood boats.

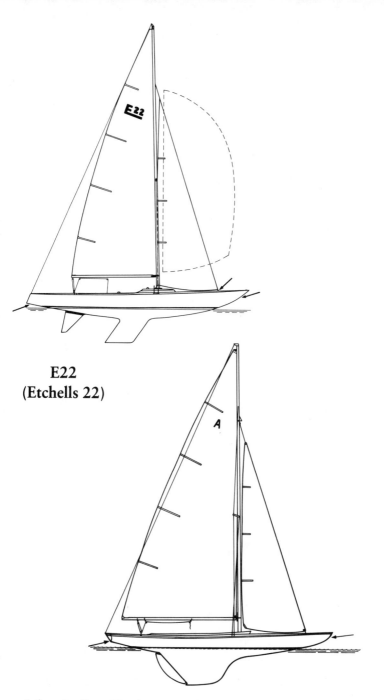

E22
(Etchells 22)

Atlantic One-Design

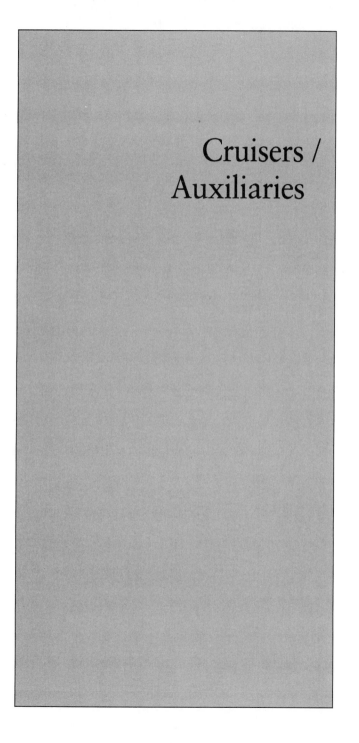

Cruisers /
Auxiliaries

Com-Pac 19

Length: 19 ft. LOA;
  16 ft. 4 in. LWL
Beam: 7 ft.
Draft: 2 ft.
Displacement: 2,000 lbs.
Sail area: Main and lapper,
  188 sq. ft.
Hull: FRP

Spars: Anodized aluminum
Berths: 4
Engine: None
Head: Optional
Galley: Optional
Water: With galley
Rating: None
Designer: Bob Johnson

Cruiser bow. Deep sheer. Round ports. Long, diagonal end-boom sheeting. Short rig.

This little cruiser has berths for four, and with the optional head and galley it is self-contained. Com-Pac was first built in 1981; unlike its sister, the 23, it has not yet been rated.
When fitted, the galley is placed in the notch between the vee berths, and the head goes at the bottom of the companionway.

The cockpit has two scuppers and two seat lockers as well as a gas-tank storage locker for the outboard if it is fitted. There is a large chain locker in the forepeak. Four bronze ports open, and additional ventilation is through a cowl vent on the foredeck. The boom is fitted for an outhaul. Options include sheet and halyard winches, a genoa track, and pulpits.

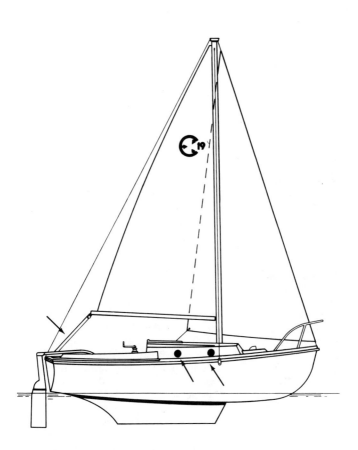

Com-Pac 19

Falmouth Cutter

Length: 20 ft. 10 in. LOA;
  20 ft. 10 in. LWL
Beam: 8 ft.
Draft: 3 ft. 6 in.
Displacement: 7,400 lbs.
Sail area: Main, 170 sq. ft.; jib,
  102 sq. ft.; staysail, 85 sq. ft.
Hull: FRP
Spars: Painted aluminum

Berths: 3
Engine: Yanmar 7 HP
Fuel: 23 gals.
Head: Portable
Galley: 2-burner, kerosene
Water: 30 gals.
Rating: None
Designer: Lyle Hess

Wide beam, wide transom. Bowsprit and boomkin. Boxy deck house. Plumb bow.

This cutter is designed and built for cruising. The first cutter was the "Renegade," somewhat larger and with a gaff rig. Larry Pardey asked for a similar but Marconi-rigged boat and made the result, "Seraffyn," famous. The Bristol Cutter, larger at 28 feet, followed; and the latest design is the Falmouth. Beam is wide and displacement heavy. The keel is full and bilges are firm. Because of the wide beam there is a remarkable amount of space below.

The two quarter berths double as seats for the dinette. When it is not in use, the table slides aft under the cockpit. The gimbaled kerosene stove is to port with a chart table and icebox opposite. The starboard quarter berth is the seat for the navigation station. A hanging locker is forward. In the bow is a double bunk and the head. There is stowage below for sails and the ground tackle. A large hatch is above the forward cabin and is obvious in the profile view. There are also six bronze opening ports.

Bulwarks, taffrail, boomkin, and trim are mahogany. The fir bowsprit is the reefing type. It may be retracted to the deck (or "housed"), which shortens the boat by four feet. There are two winches on the mast for halyards and four at the cockpit for sheets. All deck fittings are bronze. A skylight is just aft of the mast, over the main cabin.

Falmouth Cutter

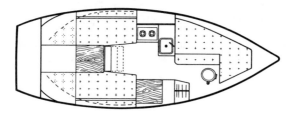

Catalina 22

Length: 21 ft. 6 in. LOA;
19 ft. 4 in. LWL
Beam: 7 ft. 8 in.
Draft: 3 ft. 6 in. (fixed keel) or
5 ft. (swing keel)
Displacement: 2,490 lbs. (fixed)
or 2,250 lbs. (swing)
Sail area: Main, 105 sq. ft.; 100%
foretriangle, 107 sq. ft.
Hull: FRP

Spars: Aluminum
Berths: 4 or 5
Engine: Outboard
Head: Optional, marine
Galley: Optional
Water: 7.5 gals.
Rating: DPN 99.0 (fixed keel);
99.2 (swing keel); PHRF 270
Designer: Frank Butler

Unlike other Catalinas, top of sail logo diamond is not shaded. Continuous taper to ports. End-boom sheeting angles back.

This boat was voted the best small cruiser for trailering in *Sail* magazine's tenth-anniversary issue. There are over 11,000 Catalinas, with 70 racing fleets in 10 regions across the United States. Racing was originally restricted to main and genoa, but recent changes allow spinnakers. Racing rules now include working jib, 150 percent genoa, and spinnaker.

There are vee berths forward that may be isolated with a privacy curtain. Under the port berth is space for a head. In the main cabin there is a dinette to port and a seat and galley to starboard. A fiberglass pop-top lifts to provide standing headroom. The galley is of molded fiberglass. It slides aft under the cockpit for stowage. A hatch on the foredeck provides light and air in the forecabin.

The cockpit is self-bailing. Trim is teak. Under the seats are two lockers. Winches are provided for the genoa sheets.

Catalina 22

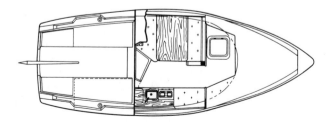

Edel 665

Length: 21 ft. 10 in. LOA;
  18 ft. 2½ in. LWL
Beam: 8 ft. 2½ in.
Draft: 3 ft. 3 in.
Displacement: 2,403 lbs.
Sail area: Main and jib,
  203 sq. ft.
Hull: FRP

Spars: Anodized aluminum
Berths: 4
Engine: Outboard
Head: Optional, recirculating
Galley: 1-burner propane
Water: Manual
Rating: None
Designer: Not known

Very wide beam. Single, long portlight. Straight bow. Two blocks on boom. In port, may have pop-top.

The Edel was designed in Europe, where it was awarded "Boat of the Year" at the Paris Boat Show. While it is certainly capable of cruising, many appointments suggest this boat for day sailing and racing. There is a lifting eye built into the keel for dry sailing, and she may be trailered.

A berth in the peak, a convertible settee, and a quarter berth sleep four. The portlights are fixed, but there is a hatch in the foredeck. A hydraulic pop-top is available for additional head room. Woodwork is mahogany.

Rigging includes jiffy reefing, a vang, a downhaul, a genoa tracks and winches, and a traveler for the main. The cockpit has seat and coaming stowage. Some of the options are spinnaker gear, recirculating toilet, lift-up top, and winches.

Edel 665

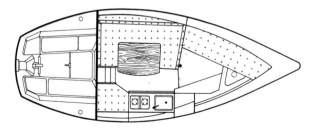

Alberg 22

Length: 22 ft. LOA: 16 ft. LWL
Beam: 7 ft.
Draft: 3 ft. 1 in.
Displacement: 3,200 lbs.
Sail area: Main, 114 sq. ft.; jib
  85 sq. ft.; genoa, 182 sq. ft.
Hull: FRP
Spars: Aluminum

Berths: 4
Engine: Outboard
Head: Standard
Galley: Butane
Water: 5 gals.
Rating: None
Designer: Carl Alberg

Masthead rig. Coamings. Two equal-size ports. Counter.

The 22 is a small boat that, because of its weight and full keel, feels and handles like a much larger boat. The masthead rig has a large sail plan.

There is a double berth forward and two quarter berths. The galley has a sink and a pump; the icebox is removable. Cabin trim is teak.

On deck are genoa tracks and fairleads, and genoa turning blocks leading to winches. Halyards are internal and lead to two winches mounted on the cabin roof. There is jiffy reefing and a Cunningham. Taffrail and handrails are teak. There is an outboard well suitable for a five- or six-horsepower motor and lazarette storage for a five-gallon gasoline tank.

Alberg 22

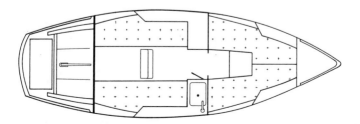

Marshall 22

Length: 22 ft. 2 in. LOA;
   21 ft. 4 in. LWL
Beam: 10 ft. 2 in.
Draft: 3 ft.
Displacement: 5,660 lbs.
Sail area: Cat main, 388 sq. ft.;
   sloop main, 338 sq. ft.;
   sloop jib, 100 sq. ft.
Hull: FRP

Spars: Aluminum
Berths: 4
Engine: Yanmar 21 HP
Fuel: Diesel, 19 gals.
Head: Marine
Galley: Optional, has sink
Water: 20 gals.
Rating. None
Desitner: Breckenridge Marshall

Gaff-rigged cat. Distinctive rudder shape. Mast hoops. May be a sloop, with long bowsprit and bobstay. Round bottom.

A cruising size of the traditional Cape Cod catboat, the 22 is also available as a sloop.

The port settee extends into the forepeak and has storage below and behind. The head is to starboard, and there is an opening hatch above. In the main cabin the galley is to port and the dropleaf table rests on the centerboard trunk. A second locker is in front of the starboard berth, which has the water tank below. (Photographs show a hanging locker forward of the galley and a counter extension that slides out from below the galley to rest on the centerboard trunk.) There are two ports in the forecabin and four in the main.

Rigging for this cat is simple, with only a forestay for the mast and a mainsheet. The boom and gaff are grooved for bolt ropes while the mast has hoops. A portion of the cockpit sole is raised to accommodate the engine. There is wheel steering. Standard equipment supplied includes a boat hook, foghorn, fire extinguisher, and life preservers.

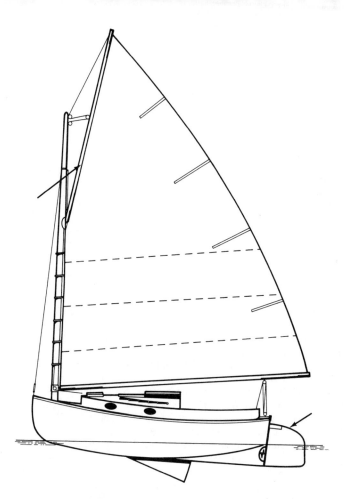

Marshall 22

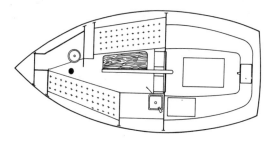

Cape Dory 22

Length: 22 ft. 4 in. LOA;
  16 ft. 3 in. LWL
Beam: 7 ft. 4 in.
Draft: 3 ft.
Displacement: 3,200 lbs.
Sail area: Main, 114 sq. ft.; jib,
  102.25 sq. ft.; genoa, 183 sq.
  ft.
Hull: FRP

Spars: Aluminum
Berths: 4
Engine: Yanmar 7½ HP
Fuel: Diesel, 13 gals.
Head: Optional, marine
Galley: 2-burner alcohol
Water: 24 gals.
Rating: PHRF 265 average
Designer: Carl Alberg

Mastbead rig. End-boom sheeting. Long bow, short counter.

The Cape Dory Company and Carl Alberg believe in full-keel design, strongly built. The rudder is attached directly to the keel, and the propeller is protected. The hull is beamy and the rig high-aspect. Lines are traditional.

There are berths for four, with a curtain giving some privacy between the main cabin and the vee berths. A marine toilet can be installed forward, under the vee-berth filler. The galley is split, with the sink and portable ice chest to port and the stove starboard. Counter tops are hinged. A hatch opens over the vee berth and there are four opening bronze ports. Joinery is teak, and the sole is teak and holly. An inboard diesel comes with the D model and is located behind the companionway ladder.

On the balsa-core deck rub strakes, taffrails, coamings, drop boards, and companionway framing are teak. There are fuel tank, sail, and lazarette lockers. The anchor rode has a roller and there are genoa tracks. The main is roller reefing and there is a topping lift and an adjustable outhaul.

Cape Dory 22

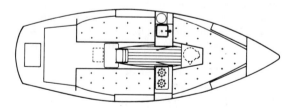

Stone Horse

Length: 23 ft. 4 in. LOA; 18 ft. 4 in. LWL
Draft: 3 ft. 4 in.
Beam: 7 ft. 1 in.
Head: Portable
Sail area: 339 sq. ft.
Hull: FRP with Airex foam
Spars: Spruce
Berths: 3

Engine: Optional, inboard or outboard
Fuel: Not stated
Displacement: 4,490 lbs.
Water: 11 gals. Kerosene
Rating: None
Galley: 2-burner kerosen
Designer: Samuel S. Crocker

Railed deck. Twin jibs. Possible wishbones on main and staysail. Bowsprit.

The Stone Horse was designed in 1931 and saw life again when revived in 1968. Thirty-eight were built before World War II, and some still sail. The boat was originally designed as a small, fast cruiser for use near Cape Cod and Buzzards Bay, and it is meant to be easily handled by a crew of two. Beam is relatively wide, and with the keel, stability is good.

The cabin benefits from the raised deck and has good headroom for a boat this size. Since there are only three bunks, the layout is somewhat unusual, with the Porta Potti, just behind the mast, also used for "normal" seating. The galley is on both sides and has fiddles. An optional cabin heater fits on the port side, with the sink and icebox. The sink does not have a drain; instead, an insert is picked up and emptied over the side. (Even from inside the cabin.) The sole is carpeted. Quarter berths and storage space are aft, although the quarter berths are admittedly small. Forward, there is a lot of additional storage. A 7 horsepower BMW or 10 horsepower Westerbeke are optional, as is outboard power.

The rig is unusual, as either the main or the staysail may have a boom or an optional wishbone. The staysail is self-tending, and the jib is roller furling. With two reef points on the main, lots of sail reductions are available. The manufacturer calls Stone Horse a sloop, not a cutter, as the headsails are small, with more than 50 percent of the area in the main. All running rigging leads to the cockpit. Many options are available, including safety, deck, and navigational equipment.

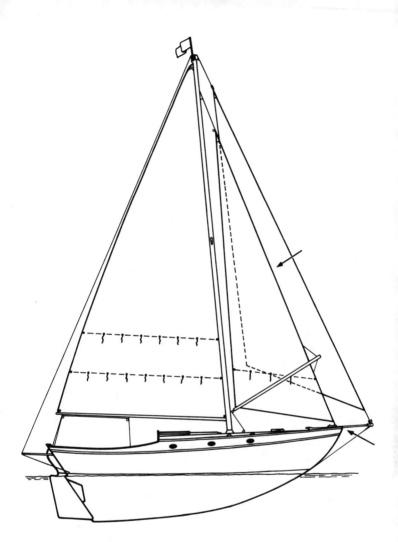

Stone Horse

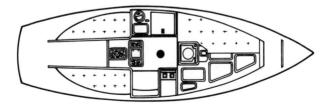

Achilles 24

Length: 23 ft. 9 in. LOA;
  20 ft. LWL
Beam: 7 ft. 1½ in.
Draft: 3 ft. 9 in. (fin keel)
Displacement: 2,600 lbs.
Sail area: Main and 100%
  foretriangle, 210 sq. ft.
Hull: FRP

Spars: Aluminum
Berths: 4
Engine: Outboard
Head: Chemical
Galley: 2-burner alcohol
Water: 20 gals.
Rating: None
Designer: C. J. Butler

Single, very long window. Moderate beam and wetted-surface area. May have triple keel.

The Achilles was designed in England, where tides are extreme. The English like triple keels, so that when the tide goes out the boat will sit high and dry; Achilles has an optional triple keel. The manufacturer claims the triple keel causes only a 3 percent drop in performance as opposed to the bulb-fin keel. Sail area is moderate.

There are two quarter berths and a vee berth. The chemical head is under the aft cushion of the vee berth. Ahead of the saloon the galley is split, with the double sink to port and the two-burner stove to starboard. Trim is teak.

The mast is stepped on the coach roof and does not penetrate the cabin. Jib/genoa tracks, two halyards, and two sheet winches are shown on the deck plan. In the forepeak there is a self-draining anchor well. All exterior timber is oiled teak. There are two seat lockers in the cockpit, and two lazarette storage compartments. An outboard is standard, but an inboard can be fitted beneath the cockpit sole.

Achilles 24

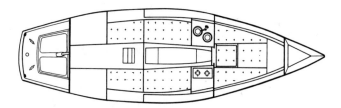

Flicka

Length: 24 ft. LOA;
  18 ft. 2 in. LWL
Beam: 8 ft.
Draft: 3 ft. 3 in.
Displacement: 5,500 lbs.
Sail area: 250 sq. ft.
Hull: FRP
Spars: Painted aluminum

Berths: 4.
Engine: Yanmar 1GM10, 10 hp
Fuel: 12 gal. diesel
Head: Standard, holding tank
Galley: 2-burner alcohol
Water: 20 gal.
Designer: Bruce Bingham

Gaff rigged, with single or twin headsails. Bowsprit. Outboard rudder. Exposed chainplates.

The design follows that of Newport boats used lobstering on Block Island Sound early in the twentieth century. The boat is intended as a small cruiser, and the designer lived and cruised on Flica for more than two years. Notice the marine head, and the amount of water and fuel contained aboard, as well as the substantial engine. The cabin roof is high, providing the maximum headroom, while the cockpit is kept fairly small. In addition, the mast is mounted on the cabin roof, so that the cabin below is unobstructed.

Vee berths are forward and have a filler. It is difficult to tell from either drawings or photographs, but the head is stated to be enclosed, with storage and a hanging locker. The galley is amidships, across from seating, which could double as a berth. A hinged table swings up from the front of the icebox. There is a hatch forward, and four opening ports, as well as two fixed windows in the deckhouse. There is standing headroom. Storage is below all berths. Trim is teak and the sole is holly. Two batteries are provided, with three dome lights and an antenna lead.

The companionway is large. There are storage lockers under both the port and starboard seats, as well as in the aft end of the cockpit. The boat may be single-handed, and the bilge pump may be operated from the helm. The backstay is split, as the rudder is outboard. Aluminum toe rails serve as tracks for the sheets. The rig shown is a gaff cutter, but a masthead sloop is also available. Two sheet winches are included, as is a bow roller for the anchor, which has a bow locker. Deck hardware is bronze. There are teak caprails on the bulwarks, and the handrails are also teak. Stainless bow and stern pulpits are standard. Sails provided are the main and a working jib. The cutter rig is an option, as is an option for single-handing, including hardware to lead lines aft, and coach roof-mounted winches for the halyards. Also available is a navigation and communication package, and many optional jibs, genoas, yankees, drifters, and a spinnaker.

Flicka 20

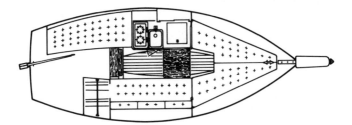

Seidelmann 245

Length: 24 ft. 2 in. LOA;
20 ft. 6 in. LWL
Beam: 8 ft.
Draft: 4 ft. 5 in.
Displacement: 3,000 lbs.
Sail area: Main and jib, 276 sq.
ft. total
Hull: FRP
Spars: Aluminum

Berths: 4
Engine: Outboard
Head: Portable chemical
Galley: 1-burner alcohol
Water: 10 gals.
Rating: D-PN none. (Seidelmann
25 is 92.0)
Designer: Bob Seidelmann

Rudder on transom. Straight bow. ⅞ rig. Sheer virtually straight.

This is a tall rig. The mainsail luff is 27 feet; the foot, 9.75 feet.
The foretriangle base is 10.75 feet and the height 27 feet. The
Seidelmann, however, is meant to be trailered, so the mast is
stepped in a tabernacle and there is a bow eye. With centerboard
up, the draft is 1 foot 11 inches.

The galley has the stove to starboard, the sink to port, and
the icebox under the ladder. Water tank loads from on deck.
Both main-cabin berths have stowage under. The trim is teak;
the sole, holly and teak. The table folds away against the bulkhead. Two of the four ports open. The chemical head is private,
with a door. Forward are two vee berths with a hatch overhead.

Pulpits and liferails are standard. On-deck storage includes a
cockpit locker and an anchor locker. The jib has track-mounted
blocks and two winches. The halyard winch is mounted on
deck. Outhaul and reef lines are internal, as are the halyards.

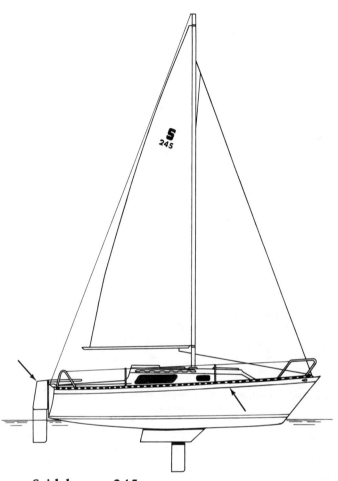

Seidelmann 245

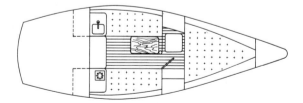

Capri 25

Length: 24 ft. 7 in. LOA;
   19 ft. 2 in. LWL
Beam: 9 ft. 2 in.
Draft: 4 ft. 2 in.
Displacement: 2,785 lbs.
Sail area: Main and 100%
   foretriangle, 276 sq. ft.
Hull: FRP

Spars: Aluminum
Berths: 4
Head: Chemical
Galley: Sink, icebox
Water: Not stated
Rating: D-PN 83.6;
   PHRF 169
Designer: Frank Butler

Masthead rig. Spoon bow. Vertical transom. Sheer almost straight.

This is a tall rig, with an aspect ratio of about 3 to 1. She is medium stiff, reducing heel, and has a ballast/displacement ratio of 32 percent. The Capri is intended as a one-design racer.

The main cabin has two berths, the sink, and an icebox under the ladder. There is no table shown. Forward, the port berth extends over the chemical head and a storage locker. While the bulkhead is not full height, it can be extended for privacy. There is storage under the port and starboard settees in the main cabin.

The cockpit is split level, and the traveler extends across just in front of the tiller steering. There are lockers under both seats. Two winches are provided here, and two on the cabin roof for the halyards. Spinnakers are used, as is a boom vang.

Capri 25

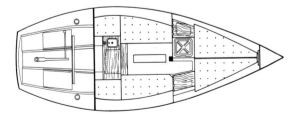

Bayfield 25

Length: 25 ft. LOA;
  19 ft. 8 in. LWL
Beam: 8 ft.
Draft: 2 ft. 11 in.
Displacement: 3,500 lbs.
Sail area: Total, 240 sq. ft.
Hull: FRP, balsa core
Spars: Aluminum
Berths: 4

Engine: 7.5 HP
Fuel: Diesel, 11.1 gals.
Head: Standard
Galley: 2-burner alcohol
Water. 20 gals.
Rating: D-PN 97.0 suspect;
  PHRF 270
Designer: H. Ted Gozzard

Cutter. Clipper bow. Slight counter. Hull, except cabin, similar to larger Bayfield 32. Masthead rig.

Bayfield calls this a pocket cruiser. Lines are traditional. Bayfield ornamentation is used.

All berths have storage under. Forward, there is a vee berth with optional filler. The starboard berth runs forward from the main cabin under a vanity and locker. The head is to port and has a 20-gallon holding tank. In the main cabin there are two settee berths, with lockers over and under. The alcohol stove stores under the starboard berth. Fresh water has a manual pump. Aft of the port berth is a hanging locker.

Above there are three lockers in the cockpit, and an anchor locker forward. Halyards are internal; the four-part mainsheet leads to a traveler; and there is slab reefing and a topping lift. Two single-speed cockpit winches are standard, and a halyard winch is optional. There is tiller steering, with a wheel optional. The genoa track is aluminum and all deck trim is teak.

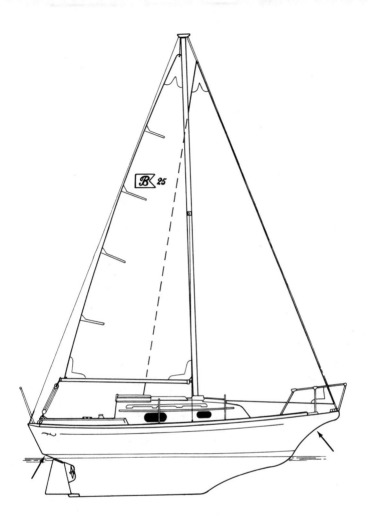

Bayfield 25

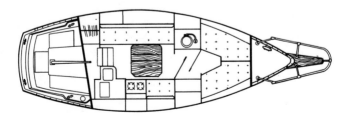

Merit 25

Length: 25 ft. LOA;
  20 ft. 6 in. LWL
Beam: 8 ft.
Draft: 4 ft.
Displacement: 3,000 lbs.
Sail area: Main and jib,
  285 sq. ft.
Hull: FRP
Spars: Aluminum

Berths: 4
Engine: Outboard
Head: Portable
Galley: Stove optional
Water: 5 gals.
Rating: PHRF 170 average;
  D-PN 84.0 suspect
Designer: Paul Yates

Fifteen-sixteenths rig. Smoked acrylic over the windows. Straight bow. Split backstay. Long slope from cabin roof to foredeck.

The accent is on racing rather than cruising. Wetted surface is low, lines aft are flat, the keel and rudder are high aspect. She planes.

To save space, the main-cabin berths extend slightly under the cockpit. Both have stowage under. The icebox serves as the companionway ladder. Forward of the berths a curtain gives privacy to the portable head. A sink and the storage for the galley are opposite. There is a steel mast support splitting the foot of the vee berth, which has storage beneath. A hatch is above. Trim is teak.

There are lots of controls above. Two halyards, the spinnaker pole lift, and the outhaul are internal. There is an internal reefing system. The mainsheet is four to one, with a mid-cockpit traveler, a Cunningham , and a vang standard. The split backstay has a four-to-one adjuster. Jib tracks lead to two cockpit winches, and two winches on the cabin roof serve the halyards. In the cockpit are two lockers. Steering is tiller.

Merit 25

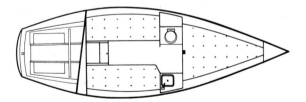

Dufour 1800

Length: 25.09 ft. LOA;
  22 ft. LWL
Beam: 8.9 ft.
Draft: 4.27 ft.
Displacement: 3,968 lbs.
Sail area: Main, 152.9 sq. ft.;
  jib, 100.1 sq. ft.;
  storm jib, 35.5 sq. ft.
Hull: FRP
Spars: Aluminum

Berths: 4
Engine: Outboard in well, or
  Volvo MD-5A
Fuel: Diesel, 6 gals.
Head: Chemical; marine optional
Galley: 2-burner
Water: 25.1 gal.
Rating: None
Designer: Laurent Cordelle-
  Dufour

*⅞ rig. Very high aspect ratio — over 3 to 1. One port well aft.
Backstay adjustment tackle.*

Dufour built France 3 and builds the Dufour 24, 27-1, and 31.
The boats are fairly heavily built and are moderate displacement. Over 1,000 boats have been built in four years. The wetted surface is low, but the waterline length is 88 percent of LOA.

Below, there are four berths. In the main cabin the port berth
extends back under a navigation table. The starboard berth extends forward under the basin of the head. The dinette table can
be stored under the starboard berth or may be moved into the
cockpit. There is storage behind both berths and above and below the galley. The cross-boat head is private and has a hanging
locker behind it. The fo'c'sle is lit and ventilated by a hatch. The
bunk is full width.

There are tracks for both the main sheet and the jib. One
winch serves the main and jib halyards and there are two more
for jib sheets. The tiller has an extension. There are two locking
seat lockers in the cockpit. A boom vang and four-part tackle on
the backstay are standard.

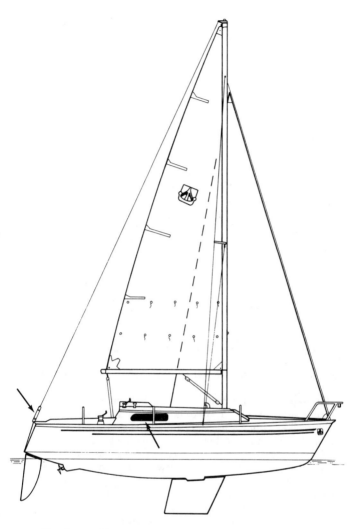

Dufour 1800

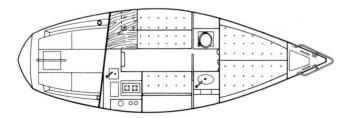

Cal 25

Length: 25 ft. 3 in. LOA;
  22 ft. LWL
Beam: 9 ft.
Draft: 4 ft. 6 in.
Sail area: Main, 133 sq. ft.;
  100% foretriangle,
  181.5 sq. ft.
Hull: FRP
Spars: Painted aluminum
Berths: 5

Engine: Optional Universal
  11 HP
Fuel: Diesel, 12.5 gals.
Displacement: 4,500 lbs.
Head: Chemical, marine optional
Galley: 2-burner alcohol optional
Water: 22 gal.
Rating: D-PN 90.0; PHRF 222
  average
Designer: William Lapworth

If boat is heeled, look for rudder mounting. Long slope to coach roof.

Bill Lapworth designs boats with long waterlines, spade rudders, and moderate to light displacement. The result is a compromise between a cruiser and a racer. There is a short keel option.

The galley spans the hull. To port is the stainless sink and the 4.5-cubic-foot icebox. The two-burner stove stores under the cockpit, sliding out for use. A counter extension also stores. The quarter berth could possibly be used as a double. Amidships the large dinette between two settee berths folds against the bulkhead when not in use. The head, forward of a sliding teak door, has a chemical toilet with a marine head as an option. There is a hanging locker and a vanity. The vee berth has a filler inset. Teak trim is used throughout. Ventilation is through a flush forward hatch and two opening ports in the head. Main cabin ports are fixed.

Halyards are internal, as are the double reef and outhaul. She has a topping lift and a boom vang, a traveler for the main, tracks for the jib and genoa, a winch for the halyard, and two genoa winches. A locker in the peak holds the anchor. The tiller, handrails, and slides for the hatch are teak.

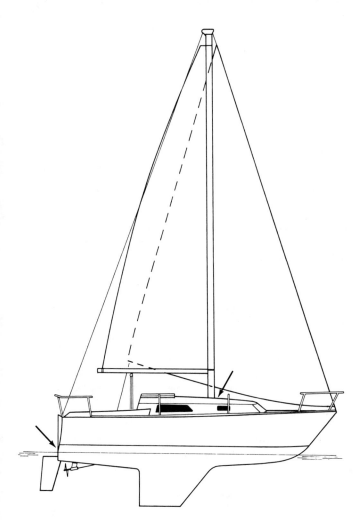

Cal 25

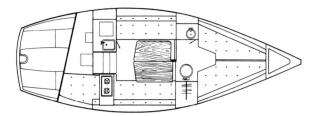

Beachcomber 25

Length: 25 ft. 4 in. LOA;
25 ft. 3 in. LWL
Beam: 8 ft.
Draft: 1 ft. 3 in. (board up)
Displacement: 5,300 lbs.
Sail area: Main, 182 sq. ft.;
mizzen, 93 sq. ft.
Hull: FRP
Spars: Aluminum

Berths: 4
Engine: Optional, inboard or
outboard
Fuel: Diesel, 19 gals. (inboard)
Head: Portable
Galley: 2-burner alcohol
Water: 20 gal.
Rating: None
Designer: Walter Scort

*Cat-ketch or sloop. Plumb bow. High freeboard. Cat-ketch has
wishbone booms, roller-furling masts.*

The Beachcomber may be purchased either as a cat-ketch or as a
sloop. Designed in Florida and with 1,400 pounds of ballast in
the grounding shoe, it is intended to have extremely shallow
draft. Still, you'll have to put the board down for windward
work. Sails are controlled by sheet, clew outhaul, and topping
lifts only; there is no traveler or vang.

Below, to port there is a quarter berth. Starboard is an L-
shaped settee that converts to a berth. No masts below-they
both mount on the coach roof. The galley and a hanging locker
are to starboard. The head has a teak door, storage space, and
ventilation. Another hanging locker is to port. In the bow are
vee berths and a chain locker which may be reached from inside.

Both masts rotate, with sail-furling lines leading to the cockpit. The centerboard has four-part tackle, and it and the two-
part sheets lead to the cockpit. Masts are unstayed. There are
cockpit lockers, and a bimini top is optional.

Beachcomber 25

Parker Dawson 26

Length: 25 ft. 7 in. LOA;
22 ft. 2 in. LWL
Beam: 8 ft.
Draft: 5 ft. 4 in.
Displacement: 5,700 lbs.
Sail area: Total, 271 sq. ft.
Hull: FRP
Spars: Aluminum
Berths: 5

Engine: Outboard; inboard
Yanmar 7.5 HP optional
Fuel: Diesel, 15 gals. (inboard)
Head: Portable standard;
additional marine optional
Galley: 2-burner alcohol
Water: 25 gals.
Rating: None
Designer: Bob Finch

Aft cabin and rudder distinctive.

Parker Dawsons have crossed the Atlantic single-handed. The two cabins are unusual on a boat of this size, and since there is an optional cockpit tent, a third cabin is possible. The iron swing keel has a 50:1 worm gear control, and draft can be reduced to 1 foot 8 inches. The rudder is also adjustable and raises and lowers inside an aluminum frame to one of three draft settings.

The aft cabin has two bunks, its own sink, and space for either the portable head or a marine installation. It is reached from the cockpit. In the main cabin the galley is to port. The forward cabin has two berths, and since there are no bulkheads, it is part of the main cabin. To starboard, the head is under the settee, and when the table is removed, this settee makes into a berth. The four ports in the forward cabin are fixed. In the aft cabin, two are fixed and one opens.

The hinged mast step is on the cabin trunk. Jiffy reefing is provided on the boom. Two winches are provided for sheets; one, for the jib halyard. There is storage for the anchor rode and a port-side cockpit seat locker.

**Parker
Dawson 26**

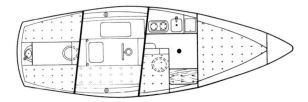

Freedom 25

Length: 25 ft. 8 in. LOA;
   20 ft. LWL
Beam: 8 ft. 6 in.
Draft: 4 ft. 6 in.
Displacement: 2,900 lbs.
Sail area: 300 sq. ft.
Hull: FRP
Spars: Carbon fiber

Berths: 4
Engine; Optional diesel
Head: Standard
Galley: 2-burner
Water: Not stated
Rating: PHRF 182 average
Designer: Garry Hoyt

Catboat. Mast appears heavy. Full battens. Spinnaker pole fixed to bow pulpit, not mast.

This cat has distinctly modern lines, with a fin keel, flat sections aft, and a transom-mounted spade rudder. The mast is not stayed and the main is fully battened. This Freedom is designed to be sailed from the cockpit, single-handed.

Below deck, colors are light, with ash and white predominating. The sole is teak and holly. There are two main-cabin berths, which extend under the cockpit; a private head; and a small galley. Forward are vee berths. A portable cooler is used for the ice chest.

The mast is designed as an airfoil, and it rotates. You furl the main by dropping it into a cradle formed by lazy jacks, at which time the full battens fold somewhat like a venetian blind. The spinnaker pole rides through a sleeve mounted on the pulpit. When not in use it slides to one side and rotates back with one end on deck. In use, the spinnaker is raised from the cockpit. Since most of the load is taken by the "gun mount" fixing it to the pulpit, control of the sheet and guy does not require a winch.

Freedom 25

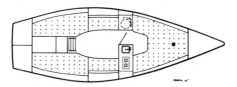

Pearson 26

Length: 26 ft. ½ in. LOA;
   21 ft. 8 in. LWL
Beam: 8 ft. 8¼ in.
Draft: 4 ft.
Displacement: 5,400 lbs.
Sail area: Main, 138 sq. ft.;
   100% foretriangle, 183 sq. ft.
Hull: FRP
Spars: Aluminum

Berths: 5
Engine: Outboard
Head: Optional, portable
Galley: Stove optional
Water: 22 gals.
Rating: PHRF 210 average;
   D-PN 89.1
Designer: William Shaw

Straight bow, vertical transom. Aft port is large. Vertical cabin roof aft leads to cockpit. No coaming.

This Pearson was designed in 1970 and has sold very well. Note the cut-away rudder and the aft-slanting keel. Ballast/displacement ratio is 40 percent. Waterline is 83 percent of overall length.

A double folding door gives the forepeak privacy. There is a double berth and under-berth storage. A translucent hatch overhead gives light and air. Aft, the optional, portable WC is to port with a hanging locker opposite. A solid door isolates this area from the main cabin. There is a dinette with seats facing fore and aft which converts to a double berth. The settee opposite becomes a single. The galley lies across the hull with the sink to port, the optional stove to starboard, and the ice chest under the ladder.

In the cockpit there are two under-seat lockers and a well in the transom for the outboard. A separate locker holds the gas tank. There is also storage for the anchor in the forepeak. The main cabin has four fixed ports. The backstay is adjustable and there are two winches for sheeting and a topping lift. Genoa tracks are on the rail.

Pearson 26

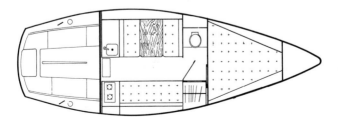

Yamaha 26

Length: 26 ft. 2 in. LOA;
    21 ft. LWL
Beam: 9 ft. 2 in.
Draft: 5 ft. 1 in.
Displacement: 4,349 lbs.
Sail area: Main and 100%
    foretriangle, 330.6 sq. ft.
Hull: FRP
Spars: Aluminum
Berths: 3-5

Engine: Yanmar 7.5 HP
Fuel: Diesel, 6.6 gals.
Head: Standard
Galley: 1-burner
Water: 18.5 gals.
Rating: IOR 19.2 approximate;
    PHRF for Yamaha 25 about
    217
Designer: Yamaha

Stern distinctive, with reverse curve to counter and unusual transom curve. Beam is midships. Bow is straight. Long slope to cabin roof. Small foretriangle.

Many aspects of the Yamaha 26 are unusual, and it almost appears that the designers decided to throw out all traditional ideas and design for function only.

The vee berth forward is full width over the water tank and must be considered standard. The head, to starboard, is also normal. In the main cabin, the stove stores in the port quarter berth and slides out for use. Seat backs can be used to convert the entire cabin into one big berth that is level with the quarter berths, so it is difficult to say just how many can sleep aboard. There is a hanging locker and fresh- and salt-water footpumps. A small table over the starboard seat can be used as a chart table and stowed when not in use.

The cockpit is large, although the traveler crosses it. There is a notch in the transom that accepts a permanently mounted swimming ladder. Two primary and two secondary winches are outboard of the coaming, and there are two multipurpose winches on the coach roof. The genoa tracks are inboard and recessed. Spinnaker gear is standard.

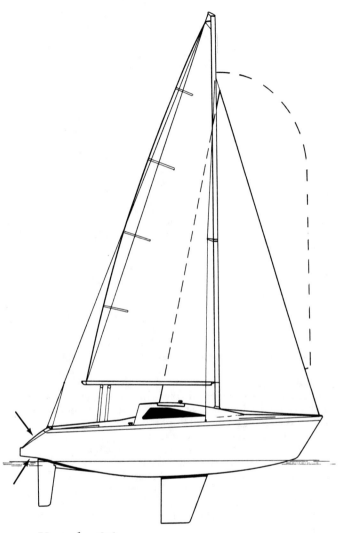

Yamaha 26

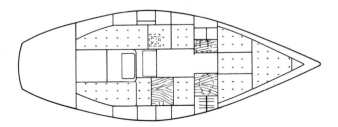

H-26

Length: 26 ft. 4 in. LOA;
    22 ft. 3 in. LWL
Beam: 9 ft.
Draft : 3 ft. 11 in.
Displacement: 6,500 lbs.
Sail area: 360 sq. ft.
Hull: FRP
Spars: Aluminum

Berths: 4
Engine: 12 hp Diesel
Fuel: 12 gals.
Head: Standard
Galley: Alcohol
Water: 47 gals.
Designer: Nathaniel Herreshoff

Transom overhangs. Raised cabin with four portholes. Masthead rig.

Nathaniel Herreshoff converted his earlier design for the H12½ to a keel day sailer, the Goldeneye, in 1930. Subsequent requests for a cruising model resulted in the H26, enlarged from the 14-foot Goldeneye by Sidney and Halsey Herreshoff, and Gorden Goodwin.

Layout below is fairly standard, with vee bunks forward, the head to port, bunk-seating and the galley amidships. There is a hatch just forward of the mast, and with the large windows, lighting is good. A folding table is optional.

Above decks, the cockpit is large, and there is a locker in the lazarette, as well as two sail lockers. While the boat was originally designed for tiller steering, there is presently a wheel pedestal. Two halyard winches, two sheet winches, and jiffy reefing operate from the cockpit. The companionway is large. Optional equipment consists of roller furling for the jib, self-tailing winches for the halyards, a stern ladder, and a connection for shore power.

H-26

Tanzer 26

Length: 26 ft. 4 in. LOA;
 22 ft. 6 in. LWL
Beam: 8 ft. 8 in.
Draft: 3 ft. 10 in.
Displacement: 4,350 lbs.
Sail area: Main, 143 sq.
 117 sq. ft.;
 165% genoa, 265 sq. ft.;
 spinnaker, 500 sq. ft.
Hull: FRP
Spars: Aluminum

Berths: 5
Engine: Outboard, inboard
 optional
Fuel: 12 gals. (inboard)
Head: Portable or marine
Galley: 2-burner alcohol
Water: 15 gals.
Rating: PHRF 216 average for
 inboard model
Designer: Johann Tanzer

Transom-mounted rudder. Split backstay. Self-tacking jib. Single long port.

This is a combination boat, for racing or cruising. The cockpit is large, so she is also a day sailer, with capacity for six or more. With a fairly high ballast/displacement ratio, she can be expected to be stiff.

The forward cabin has a double berth and a hatch above. It is separated from the head by a folding door. The head is to port, with a hanging locker; it, in turn, is separated from the main cabin by a door. The large settee converts to a double, and there is a quarter berth in the main cabin. The table folds against the bulkhead for stowage. The galley is to starboard.

The cockpit is self-bailing and has a sail locker and a locker for the outboard gas tank. There is also an anchor locker. The mast is mounted on the cabin roof and the step is hinged. Tracks for the jib sheets are mounted on the toe-rail, and the traveler for the main is on the bridge deck. There is also a translucent hatch over the main cabin, and a forward-facing opening port lights and ventilates the head.

Tanzer 26

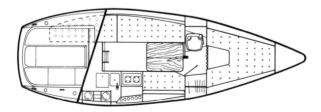

Stiletto

Length: 26 ft. 10 in. LOA;
　24 ft. LWL
Beam: 13 ft. 10 in.
Draft: 4 ft.
Displacement: 1,100 lbs.
Sail area. Main, 230 sq. ft.; jib
　106 sq. ft.; genoa, 159 sq. ft.;
　spinnaker, 7SO sq. ft.
Hull: FRP and honeycomb

Spars: Coated aluminum
Berths: 4
Engine: Outboard
Head: Portable
Galley: Space and storage
　allocated
Water: 25 gals.
Designer: Bill Higgins

*Cruising catamaran. Full-length battens and very full roach.
Cabin windows unusual.*

Stiletto is available in either a cruising or a racing configuration.
The racing version is heavier and has additional sails, sheet
winches, and a six-to-one downhaul. A spinnaker package and
pivoting centerboards are available for either model.

　The starboard hull contains a double berth, the galley, and
storage. Both hulls have a Lexan skylight and a forward hatch
for light and ventilation. The port hull also has a double berth,
and to give more space a tent is available for complete enclosure
of the bridge deck. Access to either hull is through the skylights,
which slide forward. The head is in the port hull.

　The headsails may be roller furling. Jiffy reefing, a halyard
winch, sheet winches, and a small cruising mainsail are also optional. Stiletto breaks down for trailering. The bridge deck and
mast can be removed and the hulls telescope to a beam of 7 feet
11½ inches.

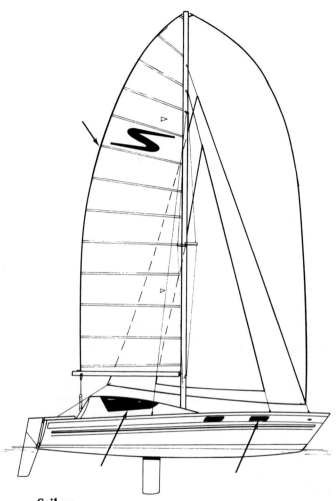

Stiletto

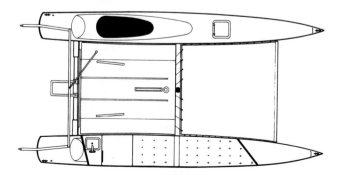

Hotfoot 27

Length: 27 ft. LOA; 22 ft. LWL
Beam: 9 ft. 4 in.
Draft: 5 ft. 6 in.
Displacement: 3,600 lbs.
Sail area: Main and jib, 346 sq. ft. total
Hull. FRP, foam core
Spars: Aluminum

Berths: 4
Engine: Outboard
Head: Chemical
Galley: 1-burner alcohol
Water: 12 gals.
Rating: None
Designer: Douglas Hemphill

Single trapezoidal port. Note shape of rudder. Bent mast. Running backstays.

The Hotfoot is a new design that is selling well in Victoria, B.C., and starting to move south. Keel and rudder are both deep to assist to windward, often a problem with boats this light. The running backstays are unusual. The manufacturers feel that they are needed for shaping the sail, not for keeping the rig up.

In the main cabin, there are two berths that extend aft. To starboard, the galley with stove and sink is kept under the cockpit and slides forward for use. On the opposite side, the chart table is stored the same way. The head and the vee berths are forward of the bulkhead. The head is on the port side.

Some of the standard sailing equipment, such as all spinnaker gear, the outboard-motor bracket, and a compass, are unusual, as is the headfoil. There are two primary winches and two halyard winches. An outboard can be mounted in the starboard lazarette. When it is not in use, the motor swings up and a hinged flap covers the hull opening. The outhaul is internal and four to one. The vang is eight to one and has double leads, and the backstay is adjustable. All controls lead to the cockpit.

Hotfoot 27

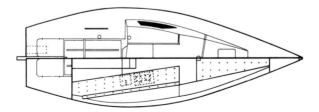

Dana 24

Length: 27 ft. 3 in. LOA;
   24 ft. 2 in.LOD,
   21 ft. 5 in. LWL
Draft: 3 ft. 10 in.
Displacement: 7,200 lbs.
Sail area: 358 sq. ft. (100% FT)
Hull: FRP
Spars: Painted aluminum
Berths: 4

Engine: Yes, size unknown
Fuel: Unknown
Beam: 8 ft. 7 in.
Head: Standard, shower
Galley: 2-burner kerosene
Water: Unknown
Rating: None
Designer: W.I.B. Crealock

Cutter. Main leads to stern. Bowsprit. Masthead rig.

This cruiser incorporates some ingenious interior details that help provide more space. The vee berth forward is not separated from the cabin, but has storage under. In addition, the table for the opposing settees is stored under the vee berth and slides out and around the compression post supporting the cabin-top mounted mast. The setees double as berths, and additional length is attained by extending the foot of the berths under the forward berth.

The galley has a gimbaled, stainless two-burner stove, with oven. The sink is also stainless and has hand operated water. Additional counter space is available from a swing-up table just in front of the galley, which drops and stows when seating space is at a premium. The head and adjacent hanging locker are to starboard. Engine access is under the companionway ladder, as well as through the cockpit sole. The cabin interior is teak, and the sole is holly.

On deck, bronze ports open, and there is a large hatch over the cabin. A chain locker lies just aft of the bowsprit platform, and there are stainless steel bow and stern pulpits. The cockpit is 6 feet 3 inches long, with storage under the seats. The coaming is relatively high. The main sheet leads to a traveler across the transom. Jib sheet winches are island mounted.

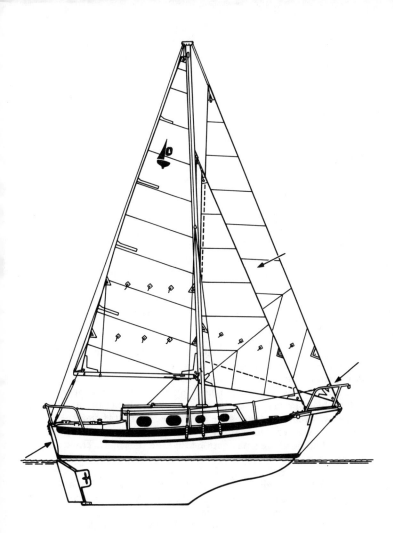

Dana 24

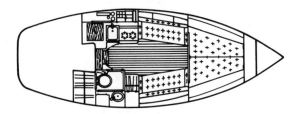

Express

Length: 27 ft. 3 in. LOA;
  23 ft. 9 in. LWL
Beam: 8 ft. 1 in.
Draft: 4 ft. 6 in.
Displacement: 2,450 lbs.
Sail area: Main and jib, 276 sq.
  ft. total
Hull: Vinylester, S-glass, foam,
  balsa core

Spars: Hard-coated aluminum
Berths: 4
Engine: Outboard
Head: Portable
Galley: Optional
Water: Not stated
Rating: PHRF 130 average
Designer: Carl Schumacher

*Reverse sheer. Aspect ratio almost 3 to 1. Reverse transom.
Flare forward.*

The Express is designed for racing and perhaps for overnighting.
The bow is fine, but there is a flare forward to prevent digging in
downwind. The waterline is long. V-sections allow for planing;
and because this is an ultra-light-displacement boat, the large
rudder helps prevent skittering.

Below, accommodations are for the racing crew of four.
There is a vee berth forward with chemical toilet beneath. Aft of
the full bulkhead are a navigation table and the galley. The seats
in the main cabin are not convertible to berths, but two additional quarter berths are aft. The sole is teak and holly.

All lines lead to the cockpit. There is lots of mechanical advantage with the mainsheet four to one, traveler two to one,
outhaul four to one, backstay sixteen to one, vang twelve to
one, and Cunningham three to one. There are two single-speed
winches. A good part of the rig design evolved from these
winches, as most of the power is intended to be in the main,
where it can be dumped quickly. There is a foredeck hatch.

Express

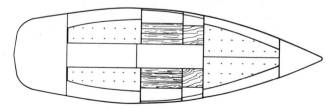

Orion 27 MK II

Length: 27 ft. 4 in. LOA,
  22 ft. 2½ in. LWL
Beam: 9 ft. 3 in.
Draft: 4 ft.
Displacement: 10,000 lbs.
Sail area: 428 sq. ft. sloop;
  452 sq. ft. yawl;
  508 sq. ft. cutter
Hull: FRP, deck has
  plywood core

Spars: Painted aluminum
Berths: 4-6
Engine: Yanmar 27 HP
Fuel: Diesal, 20 gal.
Head: Standard
Galley: 2-burner kerosene
Water: Not given
Rating: None
Designer: Pacific Seacraft

Bowsprit. Rectangular cabin profile, three small, two large ports. May be sloop, cutter, or yawl.

This small cruiser has three options for rigs, and two for cabin plans. The keel is long, with the forefoot cut away. Hull sections are the traditional wine glass shape. The first cabin plan has a U-shaped dinette, and the navigation station is just aft of the galley. The second plan is for longer cruises, and the dinette is smaller, allowing for a wet locker at the bottom of the companionway steps. In addition, extra space forward may be used either for stowage or for installation of a cabin heater. In either event, the enclosed forward cabin has a double vee berth, a hanging locker, and a standard head with shower. As noted, the dining area and the opposing galley are just aft. To port is a quarter berth.

The teak bowsprit is set on a platform, and there are two oak sampson posts. The deck is enclosed with bulwarks, capped with teak, and there are full stainless rails. Other fittings are bronze. On the cutter model the jib is self-tending. The main sheet leads to a traveler on the coach roof. There are two sheet winches and two halyard winches. A hatch over the cabin and two Dorade vents provide ventilation. Ten ports open and are screened. The cabin has long seats and high coamings, with pedestal-wheel steering. Access to the engine is through the cockpit sole. Handrails and trim are teak.

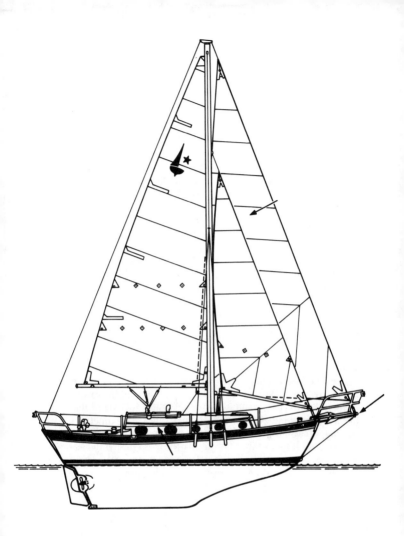

Orion 27 Mark II

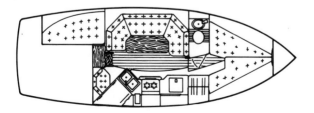

Sea Sprite 27

Length: 27 ft. 11 in. LOA
20 ft. LWL
Beam: 8 ft. 10 in.
Draft: 4 ft. 3 in.
Displacement: 7,600 lbs.
Sail area: Main, 183 sq. ft.; jib
149 sq. ft.; 150% genoa, 233
sq. ft.; spinnaker, 540 sq. ft.
Hull: FRP

Spars: Anodized aluminum
Berths: 5
Engine: Universal 11 HP
Fuel: Diesel, 12 gals.
Head: Standard, shower
Galley: 2-burner alcohol
Water: 45 gals.
Rating: PHRF 232 average
Designer: A. E. Luders, Jr.

Seven-eighths rig. End-boom sheeting. High bow. Note transom.

There are three Sea Sprites. The others are the 23 and the 34. Luders designed the 34, Carl Alberg, the 23. All are displacement boats with full keels.

The vee berth occupies most of the forward cabin, but there is storage. The head lies across the boat and has a hanging locker, storage locker, and optional pressure water. In the main cabin the double berth is to starboard. Shelves are behind both berths. At the companionway the stove and sink are to port; the icebox doubles as a table for navigation. Pressure water is also available for the galley. Bulkheads and trim are teak. There is a translucent forward hatch and four opening ports. A second midships hatch is also an option.

Deck trim, handrails, toe-rails, coamings, and taffrail are teak. The traveler is just aft of the cockpit, and there are genoa tracks. The boom has jiffy reefing and a topping lift. One winch is mounted on the mast and two for genoas at the cockpit. The tiller is laminated wood. Options include a vang, spinnaker gear, main halyard winch, wheel steering, and roller furling gear.

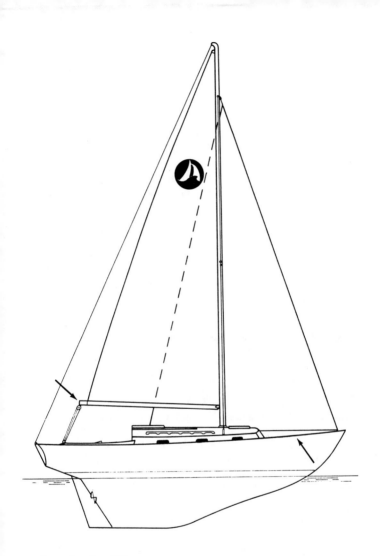

Sea Sprite 27

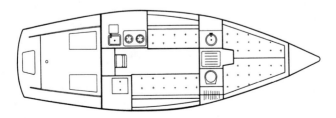

Albin Cumulus

Length: 28 ft 1 in. LOA;
22 ft. 3 in. LWL
Beam: 9 ft. 3 in.
Draft: 5 ft. 3 in.
Displacement: 7,055 lbs.
Sail area: Main, 172 sq. ft., jib,
193 sq. ft.; genoa, 285 sq. ft.;
spinnaker, 645 sq. ft.
Hull: FRP
Spars: Polyurethane-coated
aluminum

Berths: 5
Engine: Yanmar 12 HP
Fuel. Diesel, 9.24 gals.
Head: Standard
Galley: 3-burner alcohol
Water: 25 gals.
Rating: PHRF 197 average
Designer: Peter Norlin

Straight bow. Reverse transom, with rudder following same line.
Very high-aspect main; ⁷/₈ rig.

Cumulus has a sharp bow, short keel, and rudder mounted well aft.

The companionway leads directly into the galley. To conserve space, the galley work area is behind the stairs. To starboard is a quarter berth. Just forward is the saloon. Settees on both sides double as bunks, and the table folds for passageway. The head crosses the boat, with a hanging locker to port. Forward is a vee berth and a well for foresails, anchors, or fenders. A bulkhead with door is just forward of the saloon. There are 24 lockers, drawers, and storage areas. Finish is teak. There is an acrylic hatch over the vee berths and the two ventilators.

The deck has a nonslip surface and bow and stern pulpits. The spinnaker, main, and genoa halyards are internal and lead to jam cleats and two winches. There are also two self-tailing primary winches. Both the mainsheet and the boom vang are four-part. The spinnaker has a track and car, as does the genoa. There is jiffy reefing with a dual track. A tiller is used. The cockpit has two storage lockers as well as compartments for sheets and winch handies.

Albin Cumulus

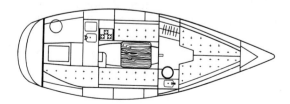

Sabre 28

Length: 28 ft. 5 in. LOA;
   22 ft. 3 in. LWL
Beam: 9 ft. 2 in.
Draft: 4 ft. 8 in. (Standard) or
   3 ft. 10 in. (shoal)
Displacement: 7,800 lbs.
Sail area: Main, 168 sq. ft.;
   jib 234 sq. ft.;
   150% genoa, 351 sq. ft.
Hull: FRP

Berths: 6
Engine: Westerbeke 13 HP
Fuel: Diesel, 20 gals.
Head: Standard
Galley: 2-burner alcohol
Water: 20 gals.
Rating: D-N 92.1 suspect;
   PHRF 200 average
Designer: Sabre Design Team

Straight bow, vertical stern. Ports generally increase in size moving aft. Sheeting is to coach roof. Normal sheer.

A modern performance cruiser, Sabre has low wetted surface and a fin keel. A shoal-draft model is offered.

There are berths for two in the forecabin, a single and a double to port in the main cabin, and a quarter berth. Storage in the bow cabin is in two drawers, two lockers, and storage bins. The head has a hanging locker. The forecabin has a translucent hatch, the head has a Dorade (self-draining) ventilator. A door separates the forecabin from the head. The table folds against the bulkhead. In the galley the stove is recessed. A cutting board fits above. Galley stowage is in four drawers and lockers and a cabinet.

The cockpit is over seven feet long. There are two lockers and a storage bin. There is a control pedestal with wheel. Teak is used for toe-rails, handrails, coaming caps, and other trim. The foredeck has an anchor well. In addition to the foredeck hatch, there are four opening ports, four fixed ports, and a hatch over the main cabin. Halyards for the main and genoa are internal and lead to mast winches. The genoa track is on the toe-rail and leads to two-speed winches on the coaming. The traveler is on the cabin top. There is a winch for the mainsheet, two sets of jiffy-reefing gear, and an internal outhaul and topping lift.

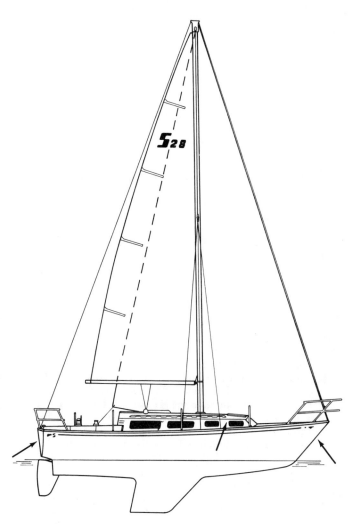

Sabre 28

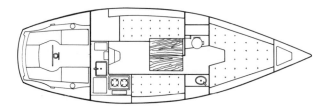

C & C 29

Length: 28 ft. 6 in. LOA;
 22 ft. 4 in. LWL
Beam: 9 ft. 6 in.
Draft: 5 ft. 3 in.
Displacement: 6,500 lbs.
Sail area: Main, 176.72 sq. ft.;
 100% foretriangle, 218.5 sq. ft.
Hull: FRP
Spars: Aluminum

Berths: 6
Engine: Yanmar 12 HP
Fuel: 20 gals.
Head: Standard, shower
Galley: Variable, to be chosen
Water: 32 gals.
Rating: D-PN 88.0 suspect;
 PHRF 174 average
Designer: C & C Design Group

Aspect ratio over 3 to 1. Some counter, reverse transom. Single trapezoidal port.

The hull is long and narrow, with volume carried into the ends of the boat. Design is modern. The keel is quite large and the rudder has no skeg. Displacement is quite light.

The quarter berth, while large, is a single. Across, the galley has a sink and top-loading icebox. There are several stove options, and the layout can be varied. The dinette table folds against the forward bulkhead, allowing room for a double berth to port. The settee opposite is also a berth. The head has a dual-purpose door that can isolate either the entire area or just the head. The vee berth is a double and has a hatch over.

All halyards lead back to the cabin top. The coaming around the T-shaped cockpit is high. The cockpit, with pedestal steering, has a seat locker to starboard. The traveler is recessed into the bridge deck. Genoa tracks are inboard for narrow sheeting angles. A second hatch over the main cabin, four fixed lights, and a vent admit light and air below. There is an anchor locker.

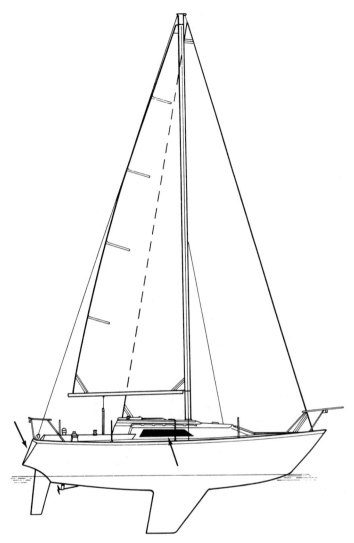

C & C 29

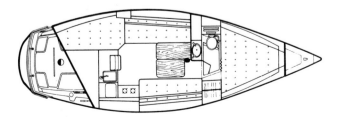

Triton

Length: 28 ft. 6 in. LOA;
  20 ft. 6 in. LWL
Beam: 8 ft. 3 in.
Draft: 4 ft.
Displacement: 8,400 lbs.
Sail area: Sloop with 100%
  foretriangle, 362 sq. ft.;
  yawl with 100% foretriangle,
  400 sq. ft.
Hull: FRP

Spars: Anodized aluminum
Berths: 4
Engine: Universal Atomic 30 HP
Fuel: 15 gals. gas, some diesels.
Head: Standard
Galley: 2-burner LPG
Water: 15 gals.
Rating: D-PN 97.9 (sloop);
  PHRF 246
Designer: Carl Alberg

Yawl or sloop. Double jumper stay. Long spoon bow. Counter. Two-level coach roof. Yawl has boomkin.

Originally built in 1950, the Triton was one of the first — if not the first — stock FRP boats. It is popular, with more than 700 boats found all over the country. The design is displacement, with a full keel.

Cabin layout is traditional. The galley spans the hull at the companionway. The icebox is to port and is front loading. The sink can be covered and its top used for a chart table. There are berths port and starboard, with shelves behind and drawers under. Access to the forward cabin is through the head, which can be closed off from both cabins. There are shelves, hanging locker, and a linen locker. The vee berths in the forward cabin have shelves behind, stowage under, and a hatch above. Trim is teak below, mahogany above.

The cockpit has tiller steering, two seat lockers, and a lazarette. Coamings and rails are wood. There is a genoa track and roller reefing. In the forepeak is a large anchor locker.

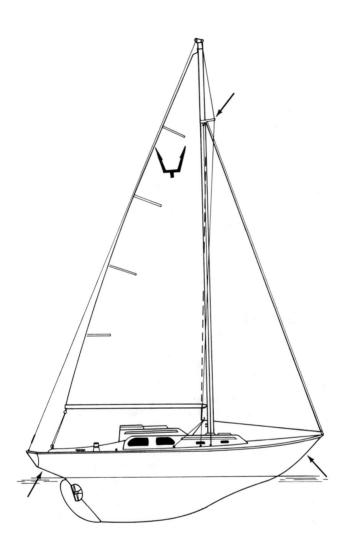

Triton

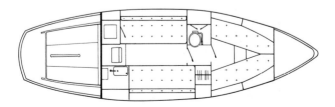

Alberg 29

Length: 29 ft. 3 in. LOA;
22 ft. 3 in. LWL
Beam: 9 ft. 1½ in.
Draft: 4 ft. 6 in.
Displacement: 9,000 lbs,
Sail area: Main, 196 sq. ft.; jib
160 sq. ft.; genoa, 326 sq. ft.
(150%), 208 sq. ft. (110%)
Hull: FRP

Spars: Aluminum
Berths: 6
Engine: 2-cylinder 15 HP
Fuel: Diesel, 15 gals.
Head: Standard
Galley: 2-burner propane
Water: 30 gals.
Rating: None
Designer: Carl Alberg

Counter. Spoon bow. Two-level cabin roof. Three and two port-hole arrangement.

While the Alberg 29 has a full keel, it is not long. The bow and counter combine to give a short, 22-foot 3-inch waterline. The bow is fine, the keel cut away. Bilges are firm, and the wide beam gives stability. Like other full-keel boats, she tracks well. The rig is high aspect and there is a large foretriangle for windward performance.

Below, a quarter berth and navigation station are to port, with a galley to starboard. There is an insulated icebox. The main cabin has a double berth to port, a permanently mounted table, and a single berth to starboard. The head is to port, and the counter and sink are to starboard. The optional shower would be located amidships. Forward is the chainlocker and two vee berths. Trim is teak; the sole is teak and holly. There are six opening ports, a forward Plexiglas hatch, and four fixed portholes.

On deck, the T-shaped cockpit has wheel steering. There are jib and genoa tracks and winches. Pulpit, rail stanchions, and stern rail are stainless. Cleats and chocks are bronze.

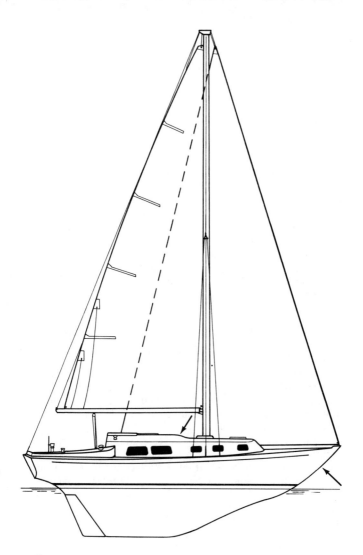

Alberg 29

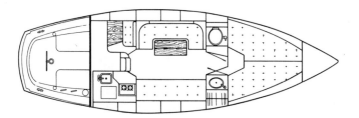

Annie

Length: 29 ft. 5 in. LOA;
24 ft. 6 in. LWL
Beam: 9 ft. 6 in.
Draft: 4 ft. 6 in.
Displacement: 11,027 lbs.
Sail area: Main, 186 sq. ft.; jib,
100% foretriangle, 279 sq. ft.;
genoa, storm, working jibs
Hull: FRP
Spars: Aluminum

Berths: 4
Engine: Westerbeke 2 cylinder
Fuel: Diesel, 18 gals.
Head: Standard
Galley: 2-burner kerosene, and
oven
Water: 37 gals.
Rating: None
Designer: C. W. Paine

Strong sheer. Cutter. High aspect ratio to main. Transom-mounted rudder. Cabin vertical fore and aft.

Annie is a heavy-displacement boat, but she has a very tall rig and much greater sail area in the jib than older boats. In addition, freeboard is low, the bow is sharp, and the keel is quite narrow. The forefoot is cut away. With the long keel and the heavy displacement, Annie should track well. The tall rig will assist in light air.

Two options are available for the cabin, both providing berths for four. As shown, the head is forward, but it can also be aft in the location of the chart table. Both configurations have a wet locker draining into the bilge. A curtain separates the two cabins. If the head is aft, the forecabin has a dresser. A stove is optional. Main cabin berths are fitted with lee boards. Installation of a shower is optional; it involves modification of the freshwater engine cooling to obtain hot water. Cabin trim is teak. There are nine opening ports.

There are the necessary winches, a genoa track, traveler, and jiffy reefing with winch. Sails and electronics are extra.

Annie

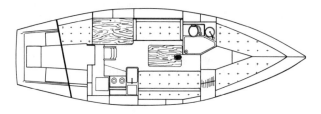

Leigh 30

Length: 29 ft. 7 in. LOA;
  23 ft. 4 in. LWL
Beam: 9 ft. 7 in.
Draft: 4 ft. 7 in.
Displacement: 9,100 lbs.
Sail area: Main, 195 sq. ft.;
  100% foretriangle, 225 sq. ft.
Hull: FRP
Spars: Anodized aluminum

Berths: 4 or 5
Engine: Westerbeke 13 HP
Fuel: Diesel, 18 gals.
Head: Standard
Galley: 2-burner kerosene
Water: 37 gals.
Rating: PHRF 192
Designer: C. W. Paine

Double-ended. Curves of bow and transom remarkably similar. Cutter. Long water line, moderate beam.

The Leigh is moderate displacement, but the ballast/displacement ratio is 48 percent and she is stiff. The high freeboard is extended by bulwarks, making for a dry boat. The keel is moderately long, the forefoot cut away, and the sail plan balanced, so she should steer easily.

The accommodation plan shown can be varied, with the most noticeable differences a balanced settee-berth arrangement in the main cabin, a smaller head, and the sink and icebox moved aft of the stove. As shown, there are berths for four and a very short berth on the port settee. Surprisingly, the starboard main-cabin berth is a pilot and the settee does not convert. The galley has a top-loading ice chest and manual water. Kerosene, relatively inflammable, is used for fuel. Opposite the head is a large hanging locker. The cabin interior is finished in mahogany, pine, and painted wood. There are lots of lockers and bins. Nine bronze ports open and there are hatches over the main and forecabins.

The deck plan shows a small cockpit sole surrounded by seats. There is a locker, and there is tiller steering, with a wheel optional. The cockpit has two primary winches, and there is a halyard winch and a sheeting winch on the cabin roof. The side decks have inboard tracks. A roller for the CQR anchor is in the bow. Teak is used for the companionway hatch, rails, cap rails, and coamings. Pulpits and lifelines are standard.

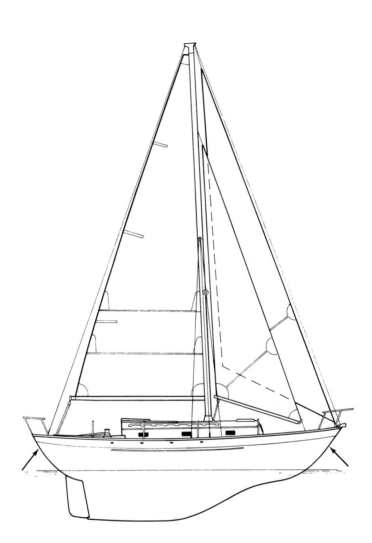

Leigh 30

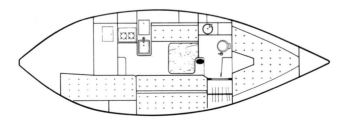

Bahama 30

Length: 29 ft. 11 in. LOA;
  24 ft. 7 in. LWL
Beam: 10 ft.
Draft: 5 ft. (standard)
  4 ft. (shoal)
Displacement: 8,230 lbs.
  (standard); or 8,322 lbs. (shoal)
Sail area: Main, 194 sq. ft.;
  100% foretriangle, 255 sq. ft.;
  genoa, 383 sq. ft.

Hull: FRP
Spars: Painted aluminum
Berths: 5
Engine: Volvo 13 HP
Fuel: Diesel, 20 gals.
Head: Standard, with shower
Galley: 2-burner alcohol
Water: 25 gals.
Rating: None
Designer: Bob Finch

Unusual main-boom sheeting. Clipper bow. Aspect ratio about 3 to 1. Very slight reverse transom.

This Bahama model is available in shoal draft, when to maintain stiffness it is slightly heavier. In either case the keel is quite short and the rudder is mounted well aft.

Below-decks layout is typical. There is a large quarter berth to starboard; the galley, with insulated icebox, is to port. The icebox can be loaded from the cockpit. Forward, the settee to starboard converts into a double berth. The head is placed across the boat and has a midships shower. There are two hanging lockers and a double berth forward. Ventilation is by four opening ports and a forward translucent hatch. The bulkheads are teak, the sole holly and teak, and the headliner vinyl.

Storage above deck is in a forepeak locker and in two under-seat lockers and a lazarette locker. Toe-rails are aluminum. The genoa track is inboard and is recessed. Main sheeting is to a traveler. There are winches for the main and jib, and two winches for the jib sheets. Slab reefing is provided. Halyards are internal and there is a topping lift.

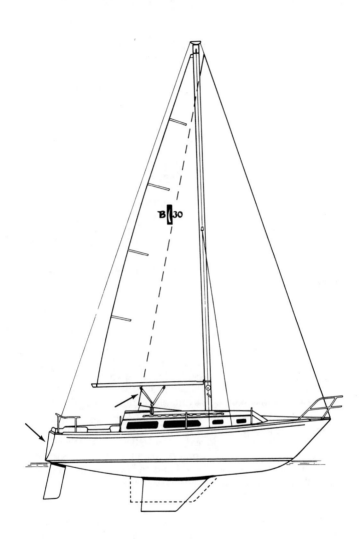

Bahama 30

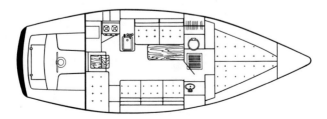

Bristol 29.9

Length: 29 ft. 11 in. LOA;
  24 ft. LWL
Beam: 10 ft. 2 in.
Draft: 4 ft. 4 in.
Displacement: 8,650 lbs.
Sail area: Main, 180 sq. ft.,
  jib 138 sq. ft.;
  150% genoa, 311 sq. ft.
Hull: FRP
Spars: Anodized aluminum

Berths: 6
Engine: Yanmar 15 HP
Fuel: 19 gals.
Head: Standard
Galley: 2-burner
Water: 63 gals.
Rating: PHRF 193 average;
  D-PN 85.5 suspect
Designer: Halsey C. Herreshoff

Spoon bow. Slight reverse transom. Ventilator just forward of mast. Skylight.

The Bristol 29.9 was designed for racing under the MORC and IOR rules. The water line is long compared to overall length. The hull is balanced, the rudder and its skeg are well aft, and the short keel has a centerboard. Beam is quite wide.

There are two cabin plans available, with the main difference lying in galley arrangement. To port of the ladder is a navigation station with a quarter berth behind. Immediately forward is a seat convertible to a double berth. The galley and another seat/berth lie to starboard. A bulkhead and door isolate the forward cabin, vee berth, head, and hanging locker. Above the central table is an operating skylight-hatch, and there is a second hatch above the forecabin. Trim is mahogany and the sole is teak.

The cockpit has wheel steering and a locker under the starboard seat. There is forepeak stowage. A traveler for the mainsheet is on the cabin roof immediately forward of the companionway hatch. There are genoa tracks and jiffy reefing. Four winches are standard.

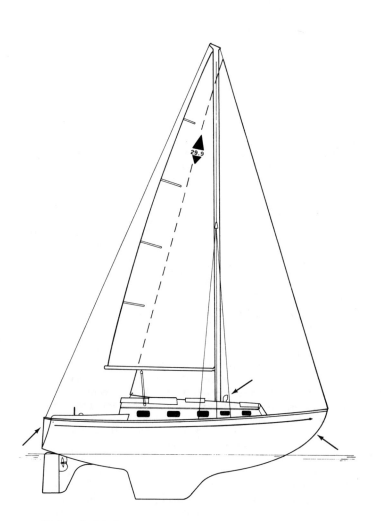

Bristol 29.9

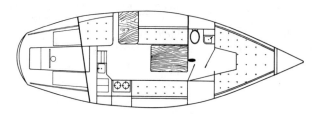

O'Day 30

Length: 29 ft. 11 in. LOA;
25 ft. 5 in. LWL
Beam: 10 ft. 9 in.
Draft: 4 ft. 11 in. (keel); or 7 ft. 2 in. (keel/centerboard)
Displacement: 10,150 lbs. (keel); or 10,600 lbs.
Sail area: Main, 173 sq. ft.; (keel/ centerboard)
100% foretriangle 268.3 sq. ft.
Hull: FRP

Spars: Painted aluminum
Berths: 6
Engine: Universal 16 HP
Fuel: Diesel, 26 gals.
Galley: 2-burner alcohol, oven
Water: 25 gals.
Rating: PHRF 178 average (keel); PHRF 177 average (keel/ centerboard)
Designer: C. Raymond Hunt Associates

Maximum beam well aft. Split backstay. Straight bow. Sheeting to cockpit.

The 30 is not designed solely as a racer, but she has modern lines. The skeg-mounted rudder is high aspect. Either a fixed keel or a combination keel/centerboard is available. Beam is widest aft, just at the center of activity. With the wide beam and a ballast/displacement ratio of 39 percent she should be stiff.

The galley extends under the cockpit floor, with the counter crossing under the ladder. Fresh water is manual, but hot and cold pressure water is optional throughout the boat. A quarter berth and a chart table are to starboard. The saloon seats five around the octagonal table, which drops for conversion into a double berth. A straight settee-berth is opposite. Forward is the head with molded sink and hand-held shower. The hanging locker is to port and has louvered doors. With a filler, the vee berths become a double. All berths have storage bins beneath.

There are two halyard winches on the mast. Two more are on the cockpit coaming for genoa sheets, and two more will be required for the spinnaker. The main is sheeted to a traveler on the bridge deck and a vang is available. Teak is used for the cap and handrails. There are two fixed portlights for the vee berth and four fixed and four opening ones elsewhere.

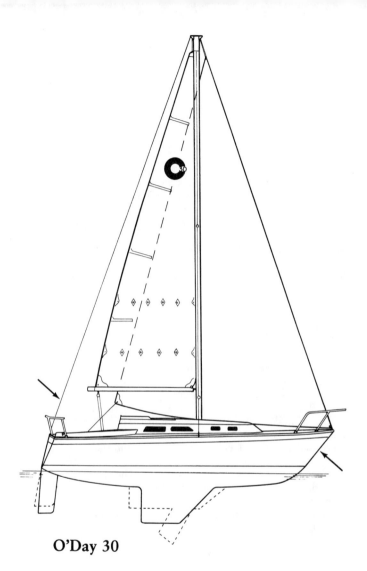

O'Day 30

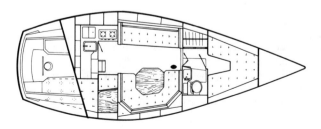

S2 9.2C

Length: 29 ft. 11 in. LOA;
25 ft. LWL
Beam. 10 ft. 3 in.
Draft: 3 ft. 11 in. (shoal);
or 4 ft. 11 in. (deep keel)
Displacement: 9,800 lbs.
Sail area: Total, 468 sq. ft.
Hull: FRP, balsa core
Spars: Hard-coated aluminum

Berths: 5
Engine: Yanmar 15 HP
Fuel: Diesel, 18 gals.
Head: Standard, shower, tub
Galley: 2-burner alcohol
Water: 37 gals.
Rating: PHRF 187 average
Designer: Arthur Edmunds

*Center cockpit. Aft-cabin port. Aspect ratio almost 3 to 1.
Straight bow.*

The raised deck indicates that this S2 is intended primarily for
cruising. For a boat of this size, there is a lot of space below. The
ballast/displacement ratio of 41 percent indicates that she will
be stiff and, with her center cockpit, dry.

The 9.2C sleeps five, and there is a short settee that can be
used for a child's berth. A passageway aft leads from the companionway to the master cabin, where there is a double berth, a
vanity, and a hanging locker. A hatch above and four opening
ports provide light and ventilation. In the passageway are three
hanging lockers and the navigation station. The chart table lifts
to provide access to the engine. The galley has pressure water.
To starboard is the head with a shower and a small tub. There is
pressure water here as well. In the main cabin the table folds.
The bulkhead separating the main and forward cabins is partial,
and there is no door. A second hatch is above the vee berths. In
addition to the aft-cabin ports, four opening ports are in the forward part of the main cabin and ports from the cockpit serve
the chart table area and the head. The large ports indicated on
the drawing are fixed.

The center cockpit has pedestal-wheel steering, and all running rigging is accessible. There are two halyard and two sheeting winches. Halyards, the four-to-one outhaul, and the reef system are internal. The Cunningham is two to one and leads to the
cockpit. Forward is an anchor locker. The topping lift is fixed,
and the four-to-one main sheet system leads to the roof of the
aft cabin. Trim above and below is teak. The jibs sheet to a full-
length toe-rail.

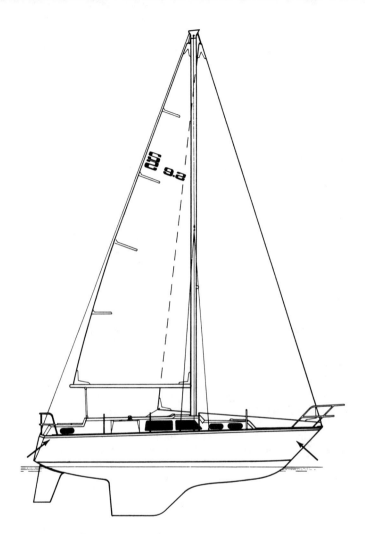

S2 9.2C

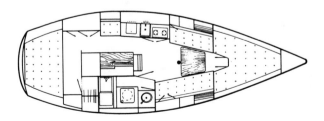

Santana 30/30

Length: 29 ft. 11 in. LOA;
25 ft. 5 in. LWL
Beam: 10 ft. 3 in.
Draft: 5 ft. 6 in.
Displacement: 6,500 lbs.
Sail area: Main and 170%
foretriangle, 637 sq. ft.
Hull: FRP
Spars: Epoxy on aluminum
Berths: 6

Engine: Volvo 13 HP
Fuel: Diesel, 20 gals.
Head: Standard
Galley: 2-burner alcohol, oven
Water: 20 gals.
Rating: PHRF 141 average; IOR
26.2; MORC 26.9
Designers: Bruce Nelson and
Bruce Marek

*Tall masthead rig. Straight bow. Moderate transom overhang.
Long smooth curve of cabin roof. Two spreaders.*

This Santana was designed to the MORC rule. Displacement is
moderate. The bow is fine and the transom broad. The overhanging transom reduces length and wetted surface in light air,
increasing water line as heeled. She is a performance cruiser,
with the emphasis on performance.

Interior design is intended to keep weight amidships and the
ends light. To preserve the settees for use, the quarter berths are
large and can be used for doubles. Another racing consideration
is the location of large bins for the crew's gear and safety equipment outboard of the settees. The galley is split and the ice-box
cover doubles as a navigation station. The head has a hanging
locker. In the forward compartment the large acrylic hatch facil-
itates sail handling.

On deck, controls lead to the cockpit. The traveler is amidships. Halyards are internal and lead to the coach roof, where
there are four winches. The three-to-one Cunningham and a
two-to-one foreguy are also led aft. The vang is twelve to one.
The boom has an internal topping lift and combination outhaul
and two flattening reefs. The toe-rail and the genoa tracks are
aluminum. There is tiller steering.

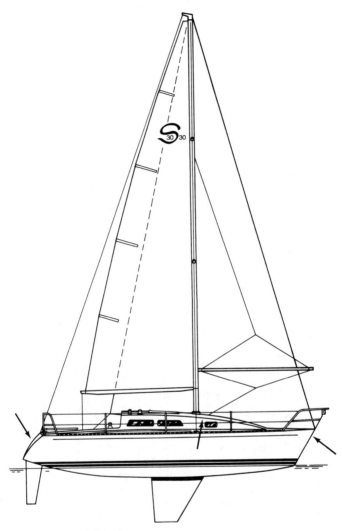

Santana 30/30

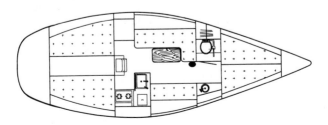

Cal 9.2

Length: 29 ft. 11½ in. LOA;
  25 ft. 5 in. LWL
Beam: 10 ft. 4 in.
Draft: 5 ft. 7 in. or 4 ft. 7 in.
Displacement: 7,000 lbs.
Sail area: Main, 162.5 sq. ft.;
  100% foretriangle, 225.6 sq. ft.
Hull: FRP
Spars: Painted aluminum

Berths: 6
Engine: Universal 11 HP
Fuel: Diesel, 11 gals.
Head: Standard
Galley: 2-burner alcohol
Water: 21 gals.
Rating: D-PN 85.8
Designer: Ron Holland

Straight bow, curved reverse transom. Very long fixed portlight. Transom triangular from aft.

After the many Cals designed by William Lapworth, this Cal is one of a new type called "CalMeter Editions." The series is intended to be high performance. The hull is a descendent of the Holland Half Tonner. The boat is made with two keels — "deep and deeper."

The two cabins are separated by a door, and a curtain further separates the forecabin from the head. A hanging locker is behind the W. C. The seating is directly opposed, with a drop-leaf table between. The mast is mounted on the cabin roof, but an interior stainless steel support is forward of the table. The galley and the chart table are at the foot of the companionway ladder. Seating for the chart table is on the starboard quarter berth. Racing, the forecabin would be used for sail storage.

Definite signs of the racing intent are above deck. There are four internal halyards, all leading to the cockpit. The outhaul and two reefs are also internal, and there is a topping lift. The backstay is adjustable and there is a vang and a Cunningham. Genoa sheeting is to a track or to the toe-rail and from there to either of two winches. The halyard winches are mounted on the cabin. One translucent hatch is over the forecabin and one over the main cabin. A ventilator is over the head. Storage includes an anchor locker, a cockpit locker, and coaming stowage.

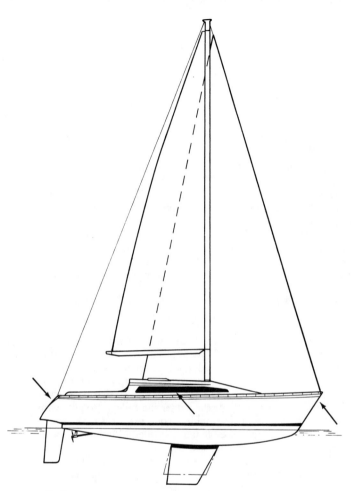

Cal 9.2

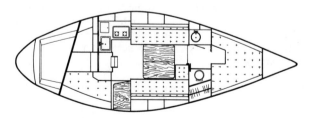

Seafarer 30

Length: 29 ft. 11½ in. LOA;
  25 ft. 7 in. LWL
Beam: 10 ft.
Draft: 4 ft. 9 in. (keel); or
  3 ft. 6 in. (centerboard up)
Displacement: 8,600 lbs.
Sail area: Main, 155 sq. ft.;
  100% foretriangle, 234 sq. ft.
Hull: FRP

Spars: Aluminum
Berths: 7
Engine: Yanmar or Westerbeke
Fuel: Diesel, 20 gals.
Head: Standard
Galley: 3-burner alcohol
Water: 43 gals.
Rating: PHRF 181 average
Designer: McCurdy and Rhodes

*High bow. Aspect ratio 3.25 to 1. Cabin forward of mast high
and long. Three-and-two port arrangement.*

The Seafarer is available in a standard rig or in a racing design
with 521 square feet of sail. Two hulls are available, one with
keel and one with centerboard; the keel version is shown.

Berths, and especially the quarter berths, appear large. Both
main-cabin settees convert to double berths, so that conceivably
the boat can sleep eight. At the ladder the galley is to port with
the two-by-three-foot chart table across. Just forward of the galley is a hinged drop-leaf table that provides additional counter
space and a service table for the main dinette table. The latter
folds against the bulkhead forward. The head spans the hull and
has two doors for privacy. There are two hanging lockers. Forward, the vee berth converts to a double. Wood is teak. There
are fixed ports for light and eight opening ports. There are
hatches above both the forward and the main cabin. In addition,
there are two Dorade cowl ventilators.

Two sheet winches are on the coaming, and the internal halyards lead to two more on the cabin roof. The traveler is on the
bridge deck. There are a boom lift, jiffy-reefing gear, and outhaul. Storage on deck is in two seat lockers and an aft cockpit
locker. Coaming lockers are optional.

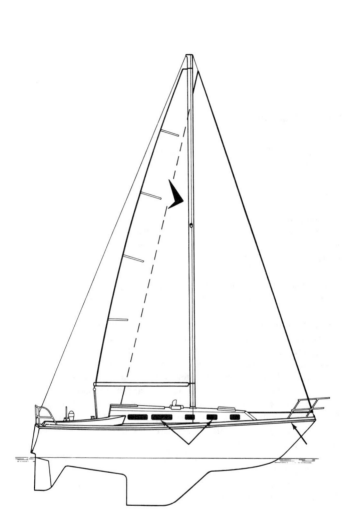

Seafarer 30

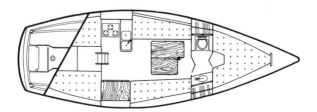

Island Packet 27

Length: 30 ft. LOA;
24 ft. 3 in. LWL
Beam: 10 ft. 6 in.
Draft: 3 ft. 8 in. (keel);
or 6 ft(centerboard)
Displacement: 8,000 lbs.
Sail area. Main, 200 sq. ft.; jib,
220 sq. ft.; genoa, 300 sq. ft.
Hull: FRP
Spars: Anodized aluminum

Berths: 5
Engine: FWC 18 HP
Fuel: Diesel, 19 gals.
Head: Standard
Galley: 2-burner alcohol
Water: 31 gals.
Rating: None
Designers: Robert Johnson,
Walter Scott

Broad beam. Cutter. Bowsprit. Aspect ratio deceptive at about 2.4 to 1. End-boom sheeting.

The keel model is standard, the centerboard version available at additional cost. The Packet is a cruiser, not intended for racing. The broad beam gives an unusually spacious interior.

Forward, the vee berth is full width. The head is just aft, on the starboard side. Pressure water system is available. In the main cabin there is a settee to port, forward of the galley. It may be used as a berth. The starboard settee converts to a double. The folding table in between stores against the W. C. bulkhead. There are six opening ports and a foredeck hatch. Wood is teak; the sole, teak and holly.

The cockpit will seat eight adults. The icebox is located in the cockpit, which also has two seat lockers. There is wheel steering. The traveler is on the taffrail. Two winches are provided for the halyards and two for the jib sheets. The bowsprit has an anchor roller.

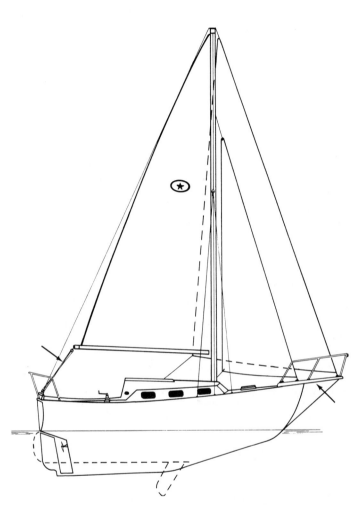

Island Packet

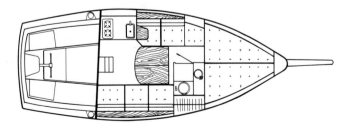

Pearson 303

Length: 30 ft. 3½ in. LOA;
  25 ft. 4 in. LWL
Beam: 10 ft. 1 1 in.
Draft: 4 ft. 4 in.
Displacement: 10,400 lbs.
Sail area: Main, 187 sq. ft.;
  100% foretriangle, 269 sq. ft.
Hull: FRP, balsa core
Spars: Painted aluminum

Berths: 6
Engine: Yanmar 13 HP
Fuel: Diesel, 22 gals.
Head: Standard
Galley: 2-burner alcohol
Water: 38 gals.
Rating: None
Designer: William Shaw

Straight bow. Vertical transom. High freeboard. Ports almost identical size.

Almost all Pearsons are rated, but the 303 is new. Design intent was for a spacious cruising boat that would sail at low angles of heel, have a shallow draft, and perform well. Design was not to any rule.

Pearson claims that the quarter berth is an honest double. With that the case, including the two in the main cabin and the two in the forecabin, there are berths for six. The two in the forecabin have an insert for conversion to a double, and they are isolated from the main cabin by a folding door. There is also a bureau. Just aft is a hanging locker with a shelf top, and the head to starboard. Optional hot and pressure water may be installed. Both settees convert to berths and have stowage behind. The folding table is over a teak and holly sole. In the galley the five-foot icebox has urethane insulation. Pressure water and an oven are optional.

Above deck there is stowage in the anchor well and in cockpit seats, with the locker to port especially large. Steering is wheel, and there is an emergency tiller. Eight ports open, as do the translucent hatches over the main cabin and forecabin. The main sheets to a traveler on the bridge deck, and the genoa has tracks. Shrouds are inboard. Companionway and other trim is wood. There are two genoa winches and two for halyards. Jiffy reefing is internal.

Pearson 303

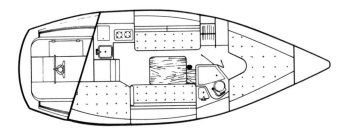

Nonsuch 30

Length: 30 ft. 4 in. LOA;
  28 ft. 9 in. LWL
Beam: 11 ft. 1 0 in.
Draft: 4 ft. 11½ in. or
  3 ft. 11½ in.
Displacement: 11,500 lbs.
Sail area: 540 sq. ft.
Hull: FRP, balsa core
Spars: Aluminum

Berths: 5
Engine: Westerbeke 29 HP
Fuel: Diesel, 30 gals.
Head: Standard, shower
Galley: 2-burner propane, Oven
Water: 80 gals.
Rating: D-PN 84.5
Designer: Mark Ellis

Cat. Cambered cabin roof. Strong sheer, plumb bow, wishbone boom.

The Nonsuch is typical of this type of boat. Although recently popular, there is nothing really new about either the cat rig or the wishbone boom. The mast is unstayed. The wishbone eliminates the need for vangs or travelers, and it imparts a draft to the sail. The sail can be raised, lowered, sheeted, and reefed from the cockpit. The catboat hull has been modified. Maximum beam is farther aft, entry is finer, aft lines are flat, there is a spade rudder, and the fin keel is available with two depths.

With no mast in the cabin and with wide beam, the cabin is roomy. Aft are three bunks, with the double quarter berth to starboard. The galley and the head are opposite. The head has cold pressure water. The galley has ample storage and manual water. The saloon is normal, with two settees, a drop-leaf table, and a hatch above. Forward are a bureau and two hanging lockers with louvered doors. There is access to the forepeak and the mast structure. Dorade vents are located over the head and galley, and there are nine opening ports.

In the cockpit are seat hatches and wheel steering. As below, trim is teak. There are four winches. Two are for reefing, one is for the mainsheet, and the last is for the halyard. A cradle of light lines is between two booms, and dropping the sail into the cradle reefs the sail.

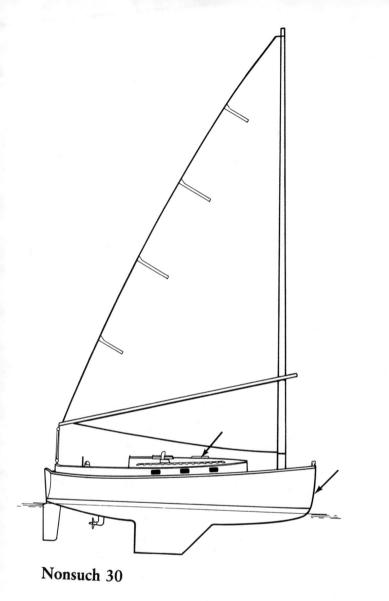

Nonsuch 30

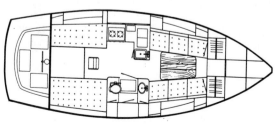

Southern Cross 28

Length: 30 ft. 5 in. LOA;
   20 ft. 2 in. LWL
Beam: 8 ft. 6 in.
Draft: 4 ft. 8 in.
Displacement: 8,500 lbs.
Sail area: Main, 164.5 sq. ft.;
   100% foretriangle, 198 sq. ft.
Hull: FRP and Airex core
Spars: Aluminum

Berths: 5
Engine: Universal 11 HP
Fuel: 15 gals.
Head: Standard, manual shower
Galley: 2-burner alcohol
Water: 47 gals.
Rating: PHRF 230 average
Designer: Tom Gillmer

Bowsprit. Double-ended. Inner forestay runs almost to bow. Coach roof continues past curved coaming.

The keel is modified full, and the rudder skeg is substantial. Forward, the hull flares. Displacement is moderate. With a self-tending staysail, single-handing is simple. As with all cutters, the amount of sail carried can be varied significantly. As the manufacturer says, the Southern Cross "looks like a sailboat."

The forecabin is standard, with vee berths and shelves. The head is split across the boat and isolated from the main cabin, and it includes storage and a hanging locker. The starboard settee pulls out to form a double berth, and the port berth extends under the lavatory in the head. The galley is quite large. Sink and burners are to port, as is food storage. The icebox, to starboard, serves as a large navigation table. Interior trim is teak. There are Dorade boxes, three cowl ventilators, a forward hatch, and six opening ports. A midships opening hatch is optional.

All deck hardware is either epoxy or hard-coated. Companionway, weather boards, seahood, Dorade boxes, and bowsprit are teak. Two winches are included for the halyards, and there are two genoa winches. The boom has jiffy reefing and a topping lift. In the cockpit are two seat lockers and tiller steering. Options include roller-furling gear, vang, spinnaker gear, and genoa tracks.

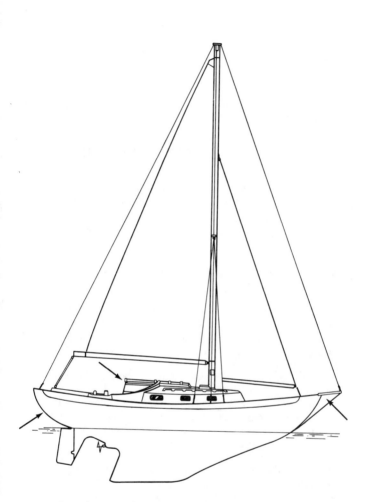

Southern Cross 28

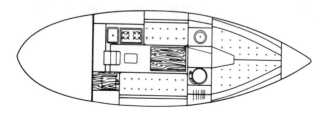

Allmand 31

Length: 30 ft. 9 in. LOA;
  27 ft. 11 in. LWL
Beam: 11 ft. 4 in.
Draft: 4 ft.
Displacement: 12,850 lbs.
Sail area: Main and 100%
  foretriangle, 461 sq. ft.
Hull: FRP
Spars: Aluminum

Berths: 7
Engine: Universal 20 HP
Fuel: Diesel, 40 gals.
Head: Standard
Galley: Type not stated
Water: 50 gals.
Rating: D-PN 85.5
Designers: Walter Scott and
  T. R. Allmand

Three and two port arrangement. Note bow. Long curve to coaming. Long water line.

The Allmand is claimed to have a tacking angle of 84 degrees. Because beam on deck is 11 feet 4 inches and 8 feet 6 inches at the water, after initially heeling she picks up a large amount of buoyancy and is stiff. The long water line allows for additional internal volume.

There is a private cabin aft with a double berth, fold-down chart table, overhead hatch, and hanging locker. The galley is at the bottom of the ladder, has pressure water, and has a toploading eight-cubic-foot icebox. In the saloon the dinette seats seven. The settee to port converts to a double, with storage below. There is a settee-berth across. The head is forward to port and also has pressure water. Two hanging lockers are opposite, and the forward cabin, with vee berths, has a door for privacy.

Shrouds are inboard, but sheeting is to the toe-rail. The main sheets to a traveler forward of the hatch and has a winch. There are also winches for the jib and main halyard, with the latter mounted on the mast. A sail locker and a lazarette may be reached from the cockpit. In addition to the aft-cabin hatch there are hatches over the main cabin and forecabin, and seven opening ports. The large ports shown are fixed. Steering is wheel.

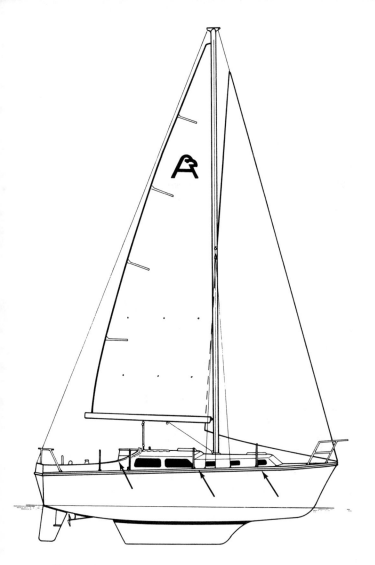

Allmand 31

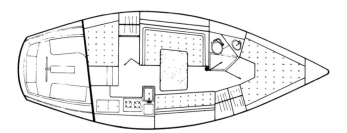

Herreshoff 31

Length: 31 ft. LOA;
27 ft. 6 in. LWL
Beam. 10 ft. 4 in.
Draft: 4 ft.
Displacement: 8,640 lbs.
Sail area: Main and mizzen,
393 sq. ft. total
Hull: FRP, polyurethane over
wood

Spars: Not stated
Berths: 6
Engine: Outboard
Head: Standard, shower
Galley: 2-burner
Water: Not stated
Rating: None
Designer: Halsey C. Herreshoff

*Cat-ketch. Wishbone booms. Main larger than mizzen. Curved
tiller.*

The popularity of cat-ketches is due to the ease with which they
can be sailed. Masts are usually unstayed and running rigging is
simple. Tacking does not have to involve sail handling. Many of
these boats have a fairly high ballast/displacement ratio, are
good (though not excellent) sailers on all points, and have a lot
of room below.

The Herreshoff 31 looks bigger below than it is. There is no
bulkhead between the forecabin and main cabin; instead, the
two are separated by a hanging locker and a bureau. The spaces
merge visually. The forecabin has widely separated vee berths,
ports, and shelves. Except for upholstery, the cabin is finished in
wood. The main cabin has two berths, one convertible to a double, and a central stowable table. There are drawers under the
berths. At the companionway the head is located to port and the
galley to starboard.

The rig is designed for simplicity. There are no stays. The
only running rigging consists of outhauls, halyards, downhauls,
and sheets. Either sail may be reefed, or the boat may be sailed
on one alone. The masts are designed to flex automatically for
various wind loads. Sails are loose-footed. Sheets may be adjusted by hand, and there are no winches. A mizzen staysail is
common.

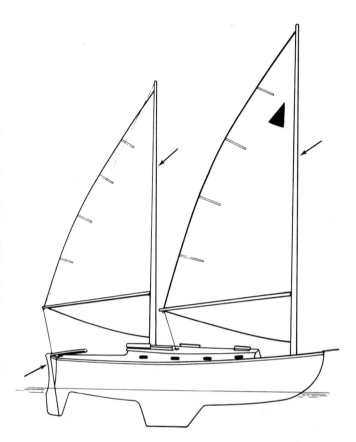

Herreshoff 31

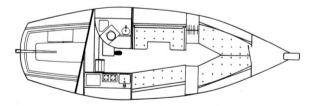

Niagara 31

Length: 31 ft. 3 in. LOA;
  24 ft. 3 in. LWL
Beam: 10 ft. 3½ in.
Draft: 5 ft.
Displacement: 8,500 lbs.
Sail area: Main, 225 sq. ft.;
  100% foretriangle, 267 sq. ft.
Hull: FRP
Spars: Aluminum

Berths: 5
Engine: Westerbeke 21 HP
Fuel: Diesel, 22 gals.
Head: Standard, shower
Galley: 2-burner propane
Water: 40 gals.
Rating: D-PN 84.0
Designer: German Frers

Aspect ratio 3 to 1. End-boom sheeting to cockpit. One and two port arrangement. Slight transom, straight bow.

Beam is moderate and the hull is V-form. Design is modern, with a fin keel and semibalanced rudder. While this is a tall rig, the foretriangle is not excessively large, and handling of foresails is reduced.

The galley is to starboard, except that the icebox is in the after portion of the navigation station, across. In the nav station the chart table lifts up and the seat swings away. Space is provided for electronics. The double berth is to port and makes up when the dinette table is lowered. A settee-berth is across. Both have storage under and above. A folding door isolates the head; and a second, the forward cabin. The head has a freshwater footpump and a teak grating over the shower sump. Opposite are a hanging locker and a bureau. In the forward cabin is a double vee berth with filler panel. There is a translucent hatch above, as in the main cabin. Two of the ports open and four are fixed. Teak is used in the main cabin and there is varnished pine trim.

The bulwark has sheeting tracks. The cockpit has wheel steering, seat lockers port and starboard, a separate compartment for propane, and a traveler with four-part mainsheet. Two winches are provided for sheets on the coaming and one for the main halyard on the aft cabin roof. There are also two winches for outboard reef lines, Cunningham, and outhaul. There is a topping lift and a four-part boom vang. Trim topsides is teak.

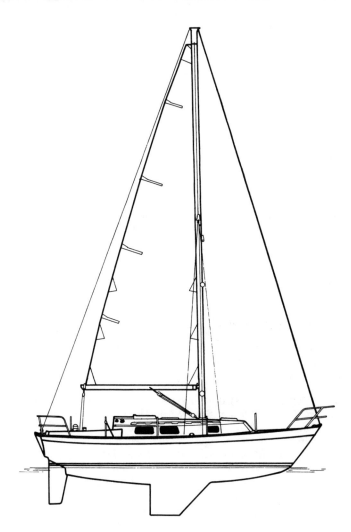

Niagara 31

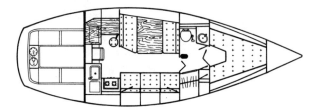

Contest 32 CS

Length: 31 ft. 10 in. LOA;
  24 ft. 7 in. LWL
Beam: 10 ft. 11 in.
Draft: 4 ft. 3 in. (shoal);
  or 5 ft. 3 in. (deep)
Displacement: 14,300 lbs.
  (shoal); or 13,860 lbs. (deep)
Sail area: Main, 225 sq. ft.; jib,
250 sq. ft.; genoa, 404 sq. ft.;
  spinnaker, 918 sq. ft.

Hull: FRP
Engine: Volvo 25 HP
Fuel: Diesel, 62 gals.
Head: Standard
Galley: 3-burner LPG
Water: 92.5 gals.
Rating: None
Designer: Dick Zaul

Sloop or center-cockpit ketch. Standard sheer. Curved transom.

The Contest is built in Holland to Lloyds rules and was designed to the IOR rules. The boat is available either ketch- or sloop-rigged, and with either a shallow or deep keel. Teak or mahogany is available for the interior.

The aft cabin, reached from a starboard passageway, is unusual with its double and single berth. There is also a hanging locker and a sink just aft of the door. In the passageway is the galley and additional storage. A partial-height bulkhead separates the galley from the main cabin. The head is to port and has a shower. Hot and pressure water are available options. In the main cabin are a drop-leaf table and two settees. A navigation table is aft of and above the port berth. Forward the vee berth is full width. Storage bins are below, and a hatch is above. There are also hatches in the main and aft cabins.

The cockpit has wood seats and wheel steering. A second, small wheel can be located on the forward port bulkhead; and with a dodger, the Contest becomes a motor sailer. Gas for cooking is kept in a lazarette hatch, and there is an anchor well. The boom has slab reefing. Two winches are provided for sheets and a mast winch for halyards. Some of the many options include vang, additional winches, refrigeration, and hot air heating.

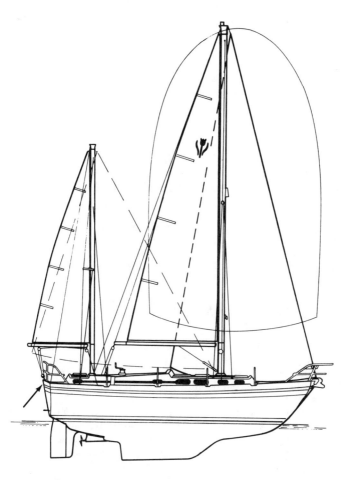

Contest 32 CS

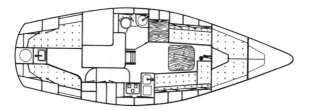

Morgan 32

Length: 31 ft. 11 in. LOA; 25 ft. LWL	*Spars:* Aluminum
Beam: 11 ft. 6 in.	*Berths:* 6
Draft: 4 ft. (shoal); or 5 ft. 4 in. (deep)	*Engine:* Yanmar 22.5 HP
Displacement: 11,000 lbs. approx.	*Fuel:* Diesel, 27 gals.
Sail area: Main, 207 sq. ft.; foretriangle, 277 sq. ft.	*Head:* Standard
Hull: FRP	*Galley:* 2-burner alcohol, oven

Length: 31 ft. 11 in. LOA;
   25 ft. LWL
Beam: 11 ft. 6 in.
Draft: 4 ft. (shoal);
   or 5 ft. 4 in. (deep)
Displacement: 11,000 lbs.
   approx.
Sail area: Main, 207 sq. ft.;
   foretriangle, 277 sq. ft.
Hull: FRP

Spars: Aluminum
Berths: 6
Engine: Yanmar 22.5 HP
Fuel: Diesel, 27 gals.
Head: Standard
Galley: 2-burner alcohol, oven
Water: 35 gals.
Rating: D-PN 86.0
Designers: Ted Brewer and
   Jack Corey

Masthead rig. Aspect ratio about 3 to 1. Straight bow. Main sheets to bridge deck.

This Morgan is offered in either a shoal or a deep-keel model. The drawing shows the shoal version. She will sleep six, but as with most boats this size, five is better and four is best. The design is scaled down from the Morgan 38. An updated model, the 323, is available.

Cabin layout is normal. The galley is to port and has a seven-cubic-foot icebox and single sink with foot-operated pump. The quarter berth opposite serves as the seat for the chart table. There are Dorade vents above both. The lounge area seats convert to berths, with the double to starboard. Here there are six opening ports. The ceiling has ash strips, with other trim teak. There is a full head with manual water, one opening port light, and a hanging locker to port. The forward cabin has a door. Storage is in drawers, in lockers, and under berths. A louvered door gives access to the chain locker, and there is an overhead hatch.

Sheeting is mid-boom with a six-to-one purchase to the bridge-deck traveler. In the cockpit are two seat lockers, teak-covered seats, and a wheel steering pedestal. There is a genoa track that may be mounted inboard. There are two winches for sheets and two for halyards. Options include jiffy reefing, a bow roller chock, and pressure water.

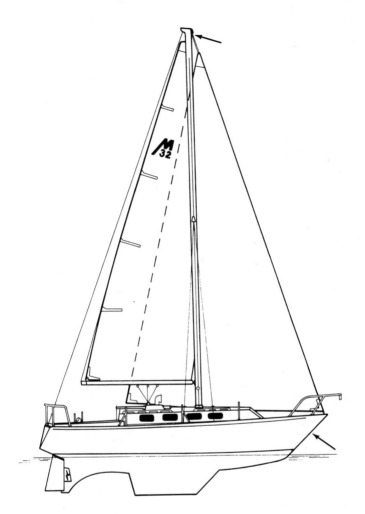

Morgan 32

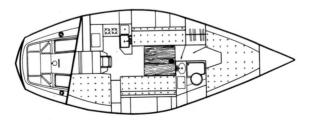

Bayfield 32

Length: 32 ft. LOA;	*Berths:* 5
23 ft. 3 in. LWL	*Engine:* Yanmar 15 HP
Beam: 10 ft. 6 in.	*Fuel:* Diesel, 20 gals.
Draft: 3 ft. 9 in.	*Head:* Standard
Displacement: 9,600 lbs.	*Galley:* 2-burner alcohol, oven
Sail area: 525 sq. ft.	*Water:* 20 gals.
Hull: FRP	*Rating:* None
Spars: Aluminum	*Designer:* H. Ted Gozzard

Very unusual bow. Cutter. Model C has four-foot-taller mast, longer bowsprit. Masthead rig.

This Bayfield is a cruiser. The long, full keel and the clipper bow, which has inlaid ornamentation, are traditional. Maximum beam occurs amidships.

Forward there is a vee berth with filler. The door will isolate either the head, to starboard, or the entire forward section. There is a hanging locker here. The shower grating is teak. Head ventilation is by porthole and Dorade ventilator. In the main cabin there are three berths, with the pull-out double to starboard. Beside the ladder, the chart table stows flush in the ceiling panel. Converted, there is a quarter berth. The galley is to starboard. It has pressure water, a four-foot icebox with teak ice grate, and a stainless steel sink.

The bow and stern pulpits are also stainless. There is a forward translucent hatch, five fixed ports, and the opening in the head. Staysail tracks are inboard; the genoa tracks are mounted on the bulwarks. Steering is wheel. There are two primary two-speed and two secondary one-speed winches in the cockpit. Three halyard winches and cleats are on the aft coach roof. The main sheet is on a traveler, which has a car.

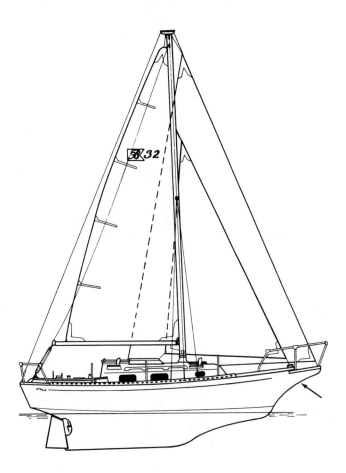

Bayfield 32

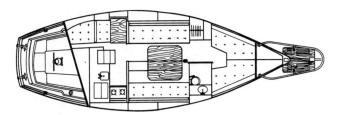

Gougeon 32

Length: 32 ft. LOA; 32 ft. LWL
Beam: 8 ft. 4 in.
Draft: 4 ft. 3 in. boards down
Displacement: 1,100 lbs.
Sail area: Main, 187 sq. ft.;
  Jib, 109 sq. ft.
Hull: Epoxy over balsa and
  foam cores
Spars: Aluminum

Berths: 2 adults & 2 children
Engine: 8 HP outboard
Fuel: 6 gals.
Head: Portable
Galley: Propane
Water: Unknown
Rating: —
Designer: Jan Gougeon

Catamaran. Masthead float and antenna. Teardrop cabin window.

The Gougeon 32 is a big, fast, stable catamaran that can be sailed by one or two and will sleep two adults and two children. In addition, you can camp out in the cockpit. Six hundred pounds of water ballast may be placed in each hull for stability, but may be drained for trailering.

Accomodations below are quite spartan, but everything necessary for short cruises is there. The stove is one burner, and there is a small sink. The floor is padded and probably could serve as a berth. Seats and the rest of the interior are fiberglass.

The normal crew is two, but the cockpit is big enough for more. The mast is stepped with a hinge and rotates forward over the towing vehicle when being trailered. The mast also rotates. Shrouds are single, but a pair of running backstays provide additional support.

The backstays are also used in a procedure to right the boat. The jib is roller furling, and the main may be reefed or furled on the boom. The traveler is full width, and the mainsheet has a purchase of eight-to-one. A trampoline across the bows holds down spray. Forward of the jib there is provision for a drifter, used in light winds.

Gougeon 32

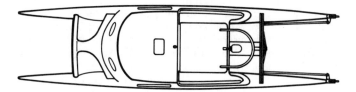

Island Packet 29

Length: 32 ft. LOA;
  25 ft. 7 in. LWL
Engine: 27 HP
Draft: 4 ft. 3 in.
Displacement: 10,900 lbs.
Sail area: 571 sq. ft. (100% F.T.)
Hull: FRP
Spars: Aluminum

Berths: 27
Beam: 10 ft. 10 in.
Fuel: Diesel, 23 gals
Head: Standard, with shower
Galley: 2 burner LPG
Water: 45 gals.
Rating: None
Designer: ??

Cutter. Twin headsails. Bowsprit. Vertical transom. High freeboard.

The sleeping, fuel, and water capacity are indicators of the cruising capability of the 29, as is the full keel. Vee berths are forward, with the head to port and storage lockers across. Seating is conventional, and the galley and a large quarter berth lie aft. The forward berths may be isolated. There are nine opening ports, two Dorade ventilators, and five deck hatches, so lighting and ventilation are unusually good. Water is heated and pressurized. Trim is teak and holly. The navigation station has a hinged table, and the AC/DC electrical panel is built in. Locker doors are louvered. The galley is U-shaped, with fiddles on all horizontal surfaces. The stove is gimbaled, and the sink is stainless.

Above, halyards are internal, with winches. There are also winches for the jib sheets. The genoa has Harken furling, and the main has a auto reefing system with a winch. The main sheet leads to a traveler, with car. A boom vang/preventer system is included. There are twin backstays and a topping lift. The rubrail is teak, as is the bowsprit cap. The cockpit seating is 7 feet long and has storage boxes under locking hatches. Steering is rack and pinion wheel, with a pedestal. The boat is remarkably complete, with few options shown, but you may expect to supply the electronics. A shoal draft version, with a keel and centerboard, may be purchased at no extra charge. Sails normally supplied with the boat include the double-reefing main and a 125 percent roller furling genoa — the cutter package of staysail, hardware, boom, and roller furling are optional.

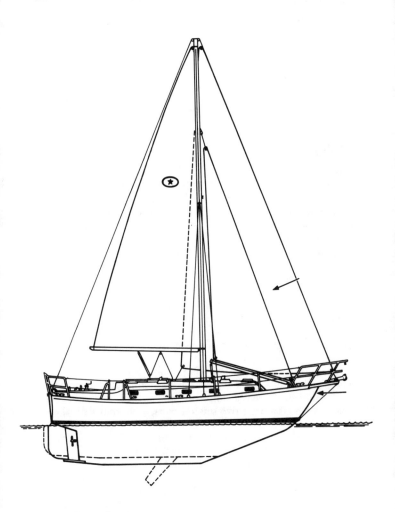

Island Packet 29

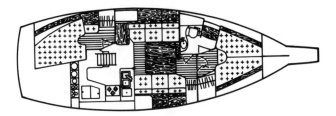

Aloha 32

Length: 32 ft. 5 in. LOA;
  25 ft. LWL
Beam: 10 ft. 10 in.
Draft: 4 ft. 9 in.
Displacement: 9,800 lbs.
Sail area: Main, 213 sq. ft.;
  genoa, 305 sq. ft.
Hull: FRP
Spars: Aluminum

Berths: 5
Engine: Atomic 16 HP
Fuel. Diesel
Head: Standard, shower
Galley: 2-burner kerosene
Water: Tank provided
Rating: None
Designer: Mark Ellis

Short counter. Straight bow. Bowsprit, bobstay. Very high aspect ratio.

The Aloha is light and should accelerate well. It is primarily a cruiser.

The starboard quarter berth is a double. Amidships are the galley and the head. The former has footpumps, while the latter is pressurized. There is a single sink and a two-burner stove with oven. In the saloon are two settee-berths, table, and six lockers. Forward are two hanging lockers and further storage in the bow. The main-cabin ceiling has teak battens. The sole is teak and holly and lockers have cane doors. Trim is teak. Two large and two small translucent hatches and six opening ports with screens provide ventilation.

The Aloha comes with sails. An Ulmer main, number 3 genoa, and number 1 genoa are provided. The main has a cover. Two halyards are internal, as are the reefing and outhaul. There is an anchor roller and locker. On-deck rails and coaming caps are teak and there is wheel steering.

Aloha 32

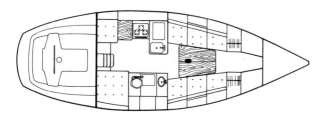

Watkins 32

Length: 32 ft. 6 in. LOA;
26 ft. 7 in. LWL
Beam: 10 ft. 2 in.
Draft: 4 ft.
Displacement: 10,800 lbs.
Sail area: Main and lapper,
470 sq. ft.
Hull: FRP
Spars. Aluminum

Berths: 6
Engine: 15 or 22 HP
Fuel: Diesel, 30 gals.
Head: Standard, shower
Galley: 2-burner, alcohol, oven
Water: 40 gals.
Rating: None
Designer: Watkins Yachts

High freeboard. Medium aspect ratio, masthead rig. Portholes evenly spaced. Slight angle to transom, rudder partially visible.

While the freeboard is high, the cabin is kept low to reduce windage. Both the keel and the rudder are medium in depth, and with a draft of four feet, the Watkins can be used for gunkholing.

The forepeak has vee berths and access to the anchor locker; a hatch overhead is standard. (The hatch in the main cabin is optional.) Just aft, there are two hanging lockers opposite the full head. Main-cabin arrangement is normal, and the U-shaped settee converts to a double. The galley is to starboard and can be modified with a propane stove and refrigeration. A combination nav station and quarter berth are to port. Internal doors are louvered teak.

On deck all halyards and the outhaul are internal. There is a topping lift and internal jiffy reefing. Two sheet winches are supplied, with the halyard winches optional. Six ports open. There is a perforated toe-rail and an anchor locker on the foredeck.

Watkins 32

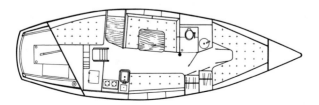

Hans Christian 33

Length: 32 ft. 9 in. LOA;
29 ft. 2 in. LWL
Beam: 11 ft. 8 in.
Draft: 5 ft. 6 in.
Displacement: 18,500 lbs.
Sail area: Main, 258 sq. ft.;
jib, 181 sq. ft.;
staysail, 159 sq. ft.
Hull: FRP

Spars: Aluminum
Berths: 5
Engine: 30-35 HP
Fuel: Diesel, 80 gals.
Head: Standard, shower
Galley: 3-burner, oven
Water: 120 gals.
Rating: D-PN 95.0
Designer: Harwood S. Ives

*Cutter. High bow, bowsprit. Double-ended. Three high vents.
Strong conventional sheer. Note taffrail.*

This is a small ocean cruiser that evolved from the Hans Christian 38 and 42. The design emphasizes appearance and cruising accommodations. The rudder is very large and, for a full-keel boat, far aft. Allowance has been made in the design for a generator and air conditioning.

Below, the two double berths present a strikingly different appearance. They are both well elevated and semimasked from the cabin by a partial bulkhead with curved cutouts. The galley at the bottom of the ladder is almost a part of the main cabin. The settee-table to port does not convert, but the settee across becomes a single. Forward of the main cabin there is a large hanging locker to starboard and an elevated double berth to port, with storage drawers under. The forward part of the boat has a head and more storage.

The cockpit, decks, and cabin roof are teak. In addition to the three pairs of vents, there is a forward hatch and a second over the main cabin. Four bronze ports on each side open, as do two into the cockpit. Steering is wheel. Winches are mounted on the mast and the cockpit coaming. The bowsprit shown is optional.

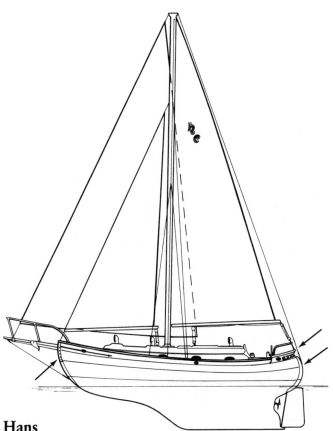

**Hans
Christian 33**

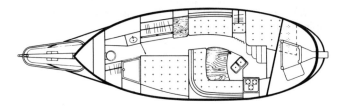

BB 10 Meter

Length: 32 ft. 10 in. LOA;
  23 ft. 11 in. LWL
Beam: 7 ft. 6 in.
Draft: 4 ft. 10 in.
Displacement: 4,956 lbs.
Sail area: Main, 216 sq. ft.; jib
  136 sq. ft.; genoa, 211 sq. ft.
  (155%); spinnaker, 545 sq. ft.
Hull: FRP, foam core

Spars: Aluminum
Berths. 4
Engine: Optional, or outboard
Fuel: Diesel, 10 gals.
Head: None
Galley: 2-burner alcohol
Water: No tank provided
Rating: PHRF 120

Long deck aft of cockpit. Very long bow. Smooth curve from coach roof to coaming. Very narrow beam.

The BB is a boat for racing, not cruising. Its very narrow beam sacrifices interior volume for speed. The narrow beam and light displacement also are penalized by the IOR. However, BB is claimed to beat at 6 knots in 6 knots of wind, reach at 8, and semiplane at 13 in 18 knots of wind.

There are two sea berths doubling as settees and a forward vee berth. The galley slides out from beside the companionway. Finish is wood. There is no standing headroom.

Rigging is stainless rod. The cockpit is big and deep. The deck is wood and toe-rails are aluminum. There is a hatch just forward of the forestay. There are two lazarette lockers. Steering is by tiller. There is a table for the cockpit. All lines lead to the cockpit, including spinnaker-boom control. There is a translucent hatch just forward of the mast. Four deck winches handle the spinnaker and genoa.

BB 10 Meter

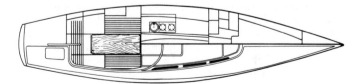

Hobie 33

Length: 33 ft. LOA; 31 ft. LWL
Beam: 8 ft.
Draft: 5 ft. 6 in.
Displacement: 3,800 lbs.
Sail area: Main, 219 sq. ft;.
  jib 210 sq. ft.;
  155% genoa, 325 sq. ft.;
  spinnaker, 838 sq. ft.
Hull: FRP, foam core

Spars: Aluminum
Berths: 5
Engine: Outboard 9 HP
Head: Chemical, portable
Galley: Alcohol, optional
Water: 5 gallons
Rating: D-PN 73.0
Designer: Hobie Alter

Narrow beam. Low profile. Ports combine to form long triangle. Boom is low. Straight sheer, long straight runs.

This boat is Hobie Alter's first venture into monohulls and off-shore boats. She is ultra-light-displacement and designed for one-design racing, but will sleep two couples. The 33 tends to sail well heeled. The narrow beam is required so the boat can be trailered. The keel is lifted for trailering, and it is bolted down for sailing.

Below, accommodations are for four or five. There are two quarter berths, a double vee berth, and a settee to starboard. The central table folds down. The other settee converts to a galley when the back is folded down. There is a dish locker and space for a stove. The portable ice chest goes beneath the ladder. There is a vanity with sink and water pump, and room for a portable toilet. The six windows are fixed, but there is a large forward hatch with an acrylic panel.

There is tiller steering and two sheet winches in the cockpit. All halyards lead aft and serve the main, genoa, and spinnaker. The ⅞ rig has a headfoil and four internal halyards. The mast step is hinged. Rigging also includes a concealed backstay adjuster, four-to-one mainsheet purchase, four-to-one vang purchase, topping lift, and internal boom outhaul. The outboard well is designed so that the motor can be tilted up and a plug inserted to close the opening. Accessories available include a marine head, spinnaker and gear, and a bridle to use with the spinnaker pole raising the mast.

Hobie 33

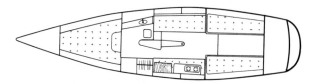

San Juan 33

Length: 33 ft. LOA;
  27 ft. 9 in. LWL
Beam: 7 ft. 11 in.
Draft: 5 ft. 11 in.
Displacement: 6,000 lbs.
Sail area: Main, 263 sq. ft.;
  100% foretriangle, 201 sq. ft.
Hull: FRP
Spars: Aluminum

Berths: 4
Engine: Optional
Head: Optional (portable
  or marine)
Galley: Optional 2-burner
Water: 9 gals.
Rating: D-PN 76.2
Designer: David Pedrick

Rudder may be visible. Reverse transom. Aspect ratio over 3 to 1. Jumper stay. Almost flush deck.

This San Juan is designed for racing, and accommodations are somewhat austere. She is ultra light. The fractional rig allows for a larger-than-normal mainsail; the smaller foresails are easier to handle. The unusually narrow beam means that initial stability is limited, but the ballast/displacement ratio of 60 percent is very high. The designer claims that the only need for a genoa to replace the self-tending jib is in very light airs.

There are four berths below, stowage for sails, and space for the optional head, galley, and engine.

Halyards lead to the cockpit, which has two primary, two secondary, and two spinnaker winches. There are also winches for the jib and the main. The main has jiffy reefing and a flattening reef. There is a vang and an internal outhaul. The main sheets to a traveler. Because the boat is so narrow, sheeting the jib to the toe-rail is at a narrow angle. Rigging is rod, and a headfoil is optional. The split backstay allows adjustment of the very flexible mast.

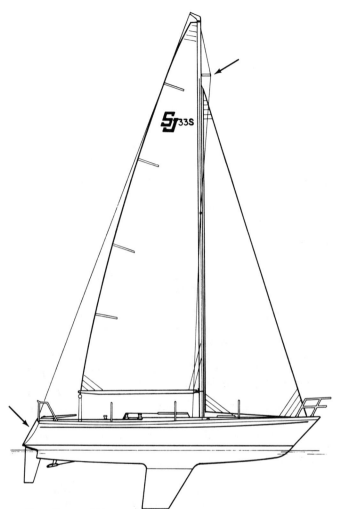

San Juan 33

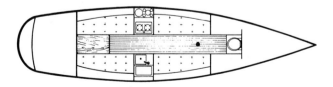

Cape Dory 33

Length: 33 ft. ½ in. LOA;
   24 ft. 6 in. LWL
Beam: 10 ft. 3 in.
Draft: 4 ft. 10 in.
Displacement: 13,300 lbs.
Sail area: Main, 259 sq. ft.;
   100% foretriangle, 280 sq. ft.
Hull: FRP
Spars: Aluminum

Berths: 6
Engine: Volvo 23 HP
Fuel: 21 gals.
Head: Standard, shower
Galley: 3-burner alcohol, oven
Water: 84 gals.
Rating: PHRF 186 average
Designer: Carl Alberg

Long spoon bow. Significant counter. Wide beam. Wood coamings, with winch islands outboard.

Like all Cape Dory boats, the 33 is designed by Carl Alberg, has a full keel, and has a medium-aspect rig. Ballast is 42 percent of displacement. Beam is wide and is extended well aft.

There is no vee berth forward; instead, there is a single to port, a seat, and a bureau. The berth will extend, converting to a double. A hatch is overhead. In the main cabin the settee converts to a double and there is a third berth to starboard. There are hanging lockers ahead to starboard and the head has a grate. The sole is teak and holly. Aft there is a hanging locker beside the ladder, a quarter berth, and the chart table. The galley is opposite.

The deck is balsa-cored, and teak is used for the taffrail, coamings, and grab rails. There are two sail lockers, a lazarette, and wheel steering. The traveler is mounted on the bridge deck. Five winches serve the main halyard, the genoa halyard, the jiffy reefing, and the genoa sheets. Hatches are above the forward and main cabins, and 10 bronze ports open. There are Dorade ventilators.

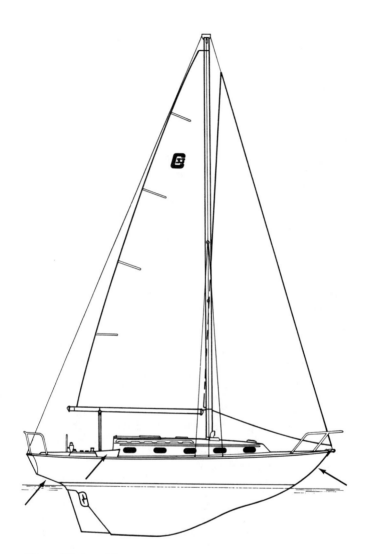

Cape Dory 33

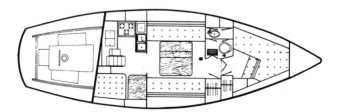

Tartan Ten

Length: 33 ft. 1¾ in. LOA;
  27 ft. LWL
Beam: 9 ft. 3 in.
Draft: 5 ft. 10½ in.
Displacement: 6,700 lbs.
Sail area: With 100%
  foretriangle, 486.72 sq. ft.
Hull: FRP
Spars: Aluminum

Berths: 6
Engine: Farymann 9 HP
Fuel: Diesel
Head: Standard
Galley: Sink
Water: 19 gals.
Rating: PHRF 126 average
Designer: Sparkman and
  Stephens

*Flush deck. Bow and stern parallel. Narrow beam. ⅞ rig.
Spreaders swept back.*

While the Tartan Ten was not designed to any rule, she was designed primarily for racing. The flush deck leaves little room in the cabin; and while there are six berths, the general cabin appointments are for weekends and overnights, not extended cruising. The Ten is a one-design and is delivered complete. No hull or rig alterations are allowed.

There are two quarter berths aft. Forward to port and centered in the boat is the galley, with sink and manual water. The ice chest is portable. A counter to starboard doubles as a galley surface and chart table. Forward are two berths with the head under. There is a privacy curtain.

Above, the mast can be bent by both shroud and backstay adjustment. The latter has a four-to-one purchase. All halyards and the reef lines are internal. The outhaul, also internal, has a 4:1 ratio. There are two cockpit winches for sheets and two halyard winches mounted on the cabin top. The boom vang is 4:1 and leads either to the mast base or, when used as a preventer, to the rail. On the foredeck is a large hatch for both sail handling and ventilation. The perforated toe-rail is full length and a genoa track is optional.

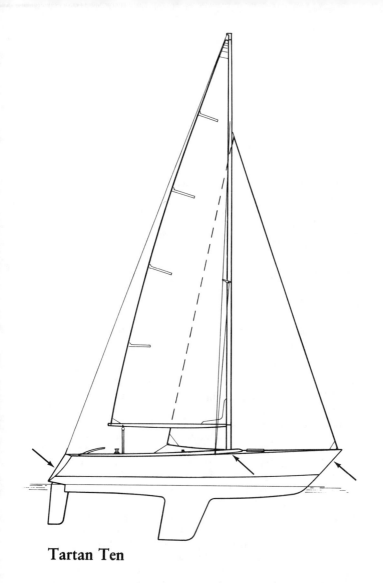

Tartan Ten

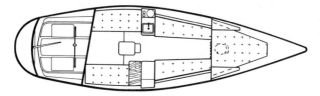

db

Length: 33 ft. 2 in. LOA;
  26 ft. 7 in. LWL
Beam: 11 ft. 2 in.
Draft: 6 ft. 2 in.
Displacement: 7,275 lbs.
Sail area: Main, 341 sq. ft.;
  genoa, 328 to 156 sq. ft.;
  spinnaker, 716 sq. ft.
Hull: Aluminum frame,
  Kevlar and FRP skin

Spars: Anodized aluminum
Berths: 6
Engine: 30 HP
Fuel: Diesel, 11.9 gals.
Head: Standard
Galley: 2-burner
Water: 19.8 gals.
Rating: PHRF 129
Designer: E. G. Van de Stadt

Curved reverse transom. Continuous port covering. Note running backstays.

The db is claimed to be the fastest one-design production ¾-tonner in the world, and she has won at Cowes, at Kiel, and in the Southern Ocean Racing Circuit. The emphasis is on racing rather than cruising.

Below, the forecabin has only a head. There is no vee berth, and the space is available for storage. Brighton (the manufacturer) lists 11 different sails, so space will be needed. In the main cabin there are two settee-berths, two pilot berths, and two quarter berths. The chart table is to starboard and has storage. Teak is used extensively. There is a galley, but no icebox is shown or mentioned.

Above decks there is lots of gear. All running rigging leads to the cockpit, which has a tiller and under-sole and transom storage. There are standing and running backstays. There are winches for the running backstays and two halyard and two genoa winches. The traveler mounts across the cockpit. Halyards are internal, as are the outhaul and reefing lines. Both the jib and the genoa have barber haulers mounted on tracks. The boom vang is tubular and there is a Cunningham. Options are primarily safety equipment and instrumentation.

db

Coast 34

Length: 34 ft. 4 in. LOA;
29 ft. 4 in. LWL
Beam: 12 ft.
Draft: 5 ft. 6 in.
Displacement: 15, 750 lbs.
Sail area: Main, 265 sq. ft.;
staysail 140 sq.
ft.; jib, 225 sq. ft.,
spinnaker, 815 sq. ft.
Hull: FRP, foam core
above waterline

Spars: Anodized aluminum
Berths: 4, and saloon may
also be used
Engine: Yanmar or Volvo
Fuel: 60 gals.
Head: Standard, shower optional
Galley: 3 burner propane
Water: 110 gals.
Rating: None
Designer: Grahame Shannon

Double ender. Rounded stern. High bow. Cutter.

Randle offers the Coast 34 in either a trunk cabin or pilothouse version. The latter has a second, interior steering station. Both are designed primarily for cruising. Forward there is a private cabin with a double berth to port, and a hanging locker. Aft to port is the head, with a grating floor for shower drainage. Drawers and a second hanging locker are across. The saloon is large, with U-shaped seating, and three additional seats to starboard. The galley has double sinks, which are located as close to the boat's centerline as possible, for drainage on either tack. The stove is gimbaled. Space is provided for optional wood or diesel cabin heating. There is a large chart table with an electrical panel for navigation equipment. The wet locker is under the companionway stairs, and there is a quarter berth to starboard.

Above are a pulpit and pushpit, double lifelines, and gates port and starboard. The bow is provided with a double anchor roller, and the anchor is stowed in a self-draining locker. There are opening hatches above the forward berth, the head, and the passageway, and there are an additional ten opening ports in the main saloon, as well as four Dorade vents. Self-tailing winches on the cabin roof handle the internal halyards. Sails for the cutter rig are provided, as are tracks for the genoa, the staysail, and a traveler in the cockpit for the main. Steering is pedestal mounted.

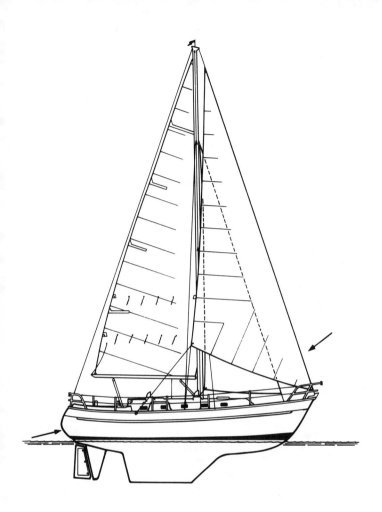

Coast 34

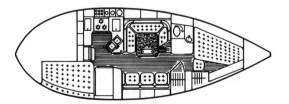

Tanzer 10.5

Length: 34 ft. 5 in. LOA;
  27 ft. 6 in. LWL
Beam: 11 ft. 6 in.
Draft: 6 ft. 6 in.
Displacement: 13,000 lbs.
Sail area: Main, 245 sq. ft.;
  jib, 270 sq. ft.;
  150% genoa, 481 sq. ft.;
  spinnaker, 1300 sq. ft.
Hull: FRP

Spars: Painted aluminum
Berths: 6
Engine: Yanmar 30 HP
Fuel: Diesel, 35 gals.
Head: Standard, shower
Galley: 3-burner propane, oven
Water: 70 gals.
Rating: None
Designer: Dick Carter

Pilothouse with wraparound window. Straight bow. Rudder mounted on both transom and skeg.

With its lifting keel fully up and fully housed, the 10.5 draws 2 feet 1 inch. The lifting mechanism is hydraulic. The housing for the keel is in both the pilothouse and the main cabin. In the main cabin it impinges very slightly on the settee. In the pilothouse it is beside the galley sink.

From the deck, access to the pilothouse is down a short ladder. A steering position is to starboard with the chart table outboard. Just aft is the head, and across is the galley. Two more steps descend to the aft cabin and its double berth. There is a long seat on the port side, a hanging locker, and a vanity. The coach roof extends over the main cabin area, and the result is that the helmsman and the cook, while two steps above the main cabin, are not isolated from it. Note that the helmsman's position is partially in the main cabin. Here the dinette seats eight and converts to a double berth. To starboard are a seat and a hanging locker. Up forward is a vee berth. The head of the starboard berth is above and crosses over the berth to port.

The deck steering position has a wheel. A locker for propane is aft and there is a seat locker for sails. There is a total of seven deck hatches and there are also three opening ports. Two winches are mounted on the coaming. There are two reef lines, a traveler, topping lift, and outhaul. All are internal. The boom vang is four-part. The jib sail area noted is for a self-tending jib, but a 110 percent lapper is available. The spinnaker is for cruising and is poleless.

Tanzer 10.5

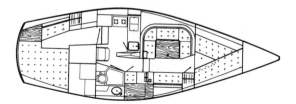

Cal 35

Length: 35 ft. LOA;
  28 ft. 9 in. LWL
Beam: 11 ft. 3 in.
Draft: 6 ft.
Displacement: 13,000 lbs.
Sail area: Main, 247 sq. ft.;
  100% foretriangle, 360 sq. ft.
Hull: FRP sandwich
Spars: Aluminum

Berths: 5
Engine: Universal 32 HP
Fuel: 37 gals.
Head: Marine, shower
Galley: 3-burner alcohol, oven
Water: 84 gals.
Rating: PHRF 136
Designer: William Lapworth

Straight bow, reverse transom. Long water line.

In order, Cal designs have been the 40, 36, 39, and the 35. All are moderately light displacement and have fin keels, long water lines, and high-efficiency rudders. The hulls are balanced. Since these designs, there have been many more.

Cabin layouts may vary. A design not shown has a distinct separation between living and working areas, with dining and berths forward, and the galley, large head, and navigation station aft. The layout shown is quite normal, with the galley aft to port and navigation area to starboard. Here they are part of the main cabin, which has a double and a single berth. The head is large, and there are two hanging lockers. The vee berth forward is full width. There are four opening ports in the main saloon, two opening ports in the forward cabin, four fixed ports in the cabin house, and a Dorade ventilator over the head.

In the cockpit there is pedestal steering. Flush deck deadlights are mounted over the galley and forward berths. The mainsheet has a cabin-mounted traveler and there are genoa tracks mounted on deck. There are two-speed sheet winches, a winch for the mainsheet, and two halyard winches. The boom has a topping lift, double internal reef, internal outhaul, and a 4:1 boom vang.

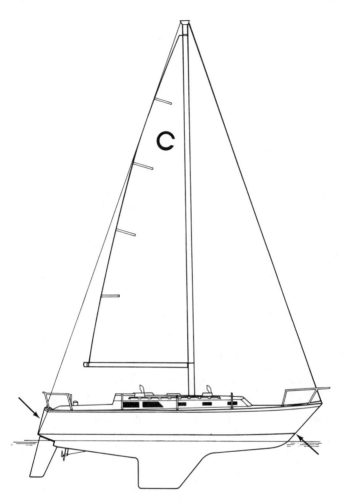

Cal 35

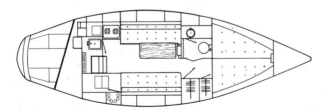

Niagara 35

Length: 35 ft. 1 in. LOA;
   26 ft. 8 in. LWL
Beam: 11 ft. 5 in.
Draft: 5 ft. 2 in.
Displacement: 15,000 lbs.
Sail area: Main, 238 sq. ft.;
   100% foretriangle, 360 sq. ft.
Hull: FRP, balsa core
Spars: Aluminum

Berths: 5
Engine: Westerbeke 29 HP
Fuel: Diesel, 20 gals.
Head: Standard, shower
Galley: 3-burner propane, oven
Water: 80 gals.
Rating: PHRF 144 average
Designer: Mark Ellis

Tall, with aspect ratio over 3 to 1. Masthead rig. High freeboard. Straight bow cuts away at forefoot.

This Ellis sloop was designed for cruising, but the forward cabin arrangement is planned to facilitate sail handling. The entire cabin layout is unusual.

The companionway does not lead to the saloon but aft to the master cabin, which sleeps three in a single to starboard and a double to port. There is a hanging locker and the chart table. There are two passageways forward to the saloon: to port through the galley and to starboard through the head. The galley has the stove and icebox outboard, the sink inboard. The head is reached from either the aft or the main cabin and has a teak grating over the shower sump. Because of the companionway location, both head and galley would be dark if it were not for the hatch provided above each. The standard saloon layout has the double berth to starboard, and there are two hanging lockers and other storage. The folding table has a skylight above it. The forward cabin is designed for sail handling and does not have a vee berth. There are bins, a workbench, and a large hatch above. The bench and its seats serve as the ladder to the foredeck. There is a single folding berth stored overhead to port.

The bulwark has sheeting tracks and a toe-rail cap. There are also sheeting leads inboard. Trim is teak. The four-part main halyard has its own winch on the mast. Two more winches are on the cabin roof and two on the coaming. There are slab-reefing control lines, four-part vang, a topping lift, and an internal clew outhaul. In addition to the hatches, there are four fixed windows and six opening ports, two of which are between the cockpit and the aft cabin.

Niagara 35

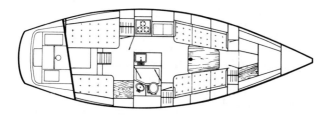

Southern Cross 35

Length: 35 ft. 3 in. LOA;
28 ft. LWL
Beam: 11 ft. 5 in.
Draft: 4 ft. 11 in.
Displacement: 14,461 lbs.
Sail area: Main, 245 sq. ft.;
150% genoa, 587 sq. ft.;
staysail, 171 sq. ft.;
spinnaker, 1371 sq. ft.
Hull: FRP sandwich hull and
deck

Spars: Anodized aluminum
Berths: 5 or 6
Engine: Yanmar 30 HP
Fuel: Diesel, 35 gals.
Head. Standard, shower
Galley: 3-burner propane
Water: 90 gals.
Rating: None
Designer: Tom Gillmer

*Masthead cutter. Fine bow. Curved coaming. Cockpit way aft.
Canoe stern.*

The Southern Cross 35 was new in 1982. The forefoot is cut
away and entrance is fine. The keel is raked. Many other sails
are available, including other genoas, storm sails, jibs, and jib-
topsails. The optional sixth berth is a quarter berth. Construction is sandwich, with an Airex core for the hull and balsa used
for the deck.

The forecabin has vee berths with a filler. There is a seat in
front of the hanging locker and a hatch above. The galley has
pressure water, an opening hatch, and an opening port. The
fiberglass shower pan has a teak grate. In the main cabin are a
bureau and a hanging locker. The settee to port converts to a
double berth. The drop-leaf table mounts on the mast. There is
a grate in the sole, which is teak-planked. The galley has three
burners and an oven, a footpump for the fresh water, and four
inches of insulation for the icebox. There is a wet locker at the
navigation area opposite. The main cabin also has a hatch, and
there are eight opening ports.

Above, the cockpit has two seat lockers. A traveler crosses
just in front of the pedestal-wheel steering. Hardware is epoxy-
coated or hard-anodized. Halyard winches are mounted on the
coach roof, and there are two genoa winches. The genoa track
allows for close sheeting, and there is jiffy reefing and a topping
lift. The staysail is normally self-tending. On the foredeck is a
well for the anchor and a locker for the rode.

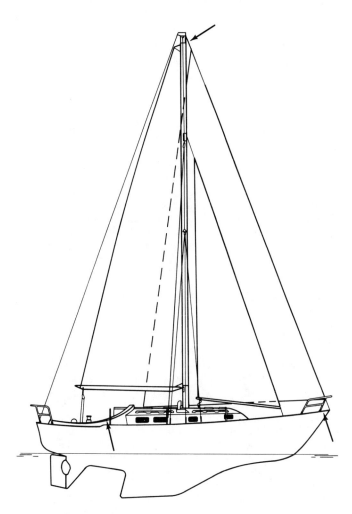

Southern Cross 35

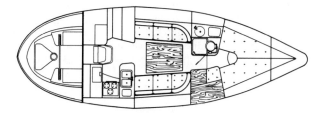

Freedom 35

Length: 35.35 ft. LOA;
  29.86 ft. LWL
Beam: 12 ft.
Draft: 6.5 ft., wing keel 4.5 ft.
Displacement: 13,000 lbs.
Sail area: Main, 511.5 sq. ft.;
  jib, 228.60 sq. ft.
Hull: FRP, balsa core
Spars: Carbon fiber

Berths: 6
Engine: Yanmar 27 HP
Fuel: 30 gals.
Head: Standard
Galley: 2 burner propane
Water: 82 gals.
Rating: None
Designer: David Pedrick

Fully battened main with high roach. Unstayed mast. Reverse transom.

Freedom Yachts was the first to emphasize free-standing rigs for cruising and continues with this design by David Pedrick. This design, however, is intended for faster sailing than other Freedom designs, such as the 38. The wing keel is designed for shallow-water cruising, and the deep keel for racing. There are racing sail options, such as overlapping jibs, spinnakers, and running backstays for mast control.

Berths for six are in a stateroom forward, saloon berths, and a separate stateroom aft, with an athwartships berth. This fairly unusual placement of the berth provides more room in the galley and saloon and also, because it tends to push the maximum beam aft, makes the cockpit quite wide. The interior has a hatch and two skylights. Trim is cherry. There are various storage spaces, including two dry and one wet hanging lockers. The galley has two burners, a large icebox, and twin sinks. The nav station is across and is designed for use standing up. The head has a separated shower, and hot and cold pressure water is optional.

All sheets and halyards lead aft along the cabin roof, as does the main sheet. There are two winches, both located here. The cockpit is T-shaped, and as noted, large. A swimming platform is incorporated in the transom, and the boat may be boarded without a ladder.

C & C 34/36

Length: 35 ft. 6 in. LOA;
   30 ft. LWL Berths: 5
Engine: Yanmar 27 HP
Draft: Fin keel, 7 ft. 3 in.
   Wing keel, 4 ft. 11 in.
Displacement: fin, 12,000 lbs.
   wing, 12,525 lbs.
Sail area: 636 sq. ft.
Hull: FRP and balsa core

Spars: Painted aluminum
Beam: 11 ft. 7 in.
Fuel: 44 gals.
Head: Standard, shower
Galley: 3 burner propane
Water: 90 gal.
Rating: None
Designer: C & C

Masthead rig. Straight bow. Double angle in transom.

There are two berths midships, and an aft cabin for two. The head is just aft of the forward cabin, and there is a hanging locker across. This hull has three versions — the 34/36, the 34/36 XL; and the 34/36 R. This drawing shows the R version, which has a galley with two-burner propane, double sinks with a cutting board cover,and an icebox. There is pressure hot and cold water. A navigation station is across from the galley. The interior is varnished teak, and the sole is holly. Trim is oiled teak. There is a forward hatch, four vent hatches, and five opening ports.

Rigging varies depending upon the model. The mainsheet traveler may be on the coach roof, at the pedestal, or on the transom. Winches also vary and may be either on the coach roof or on the coaming. In any event, there are leads to the mast, and there are stoppers. The genoa track is inboard, with cars. The stays are rods. The spreader may be double or triple. Reef lines are in the boom, and there is a two-part Cunningham with a cam. There may be either running backstays or a single stay leading to the bottom of the transom.

There are bow and stern pulpits, and double lifelines, with gates port and starboard. The above-deck bilge pump is manual — the one below, electric, with a float switch. The spinnaker pole chocks on deck.

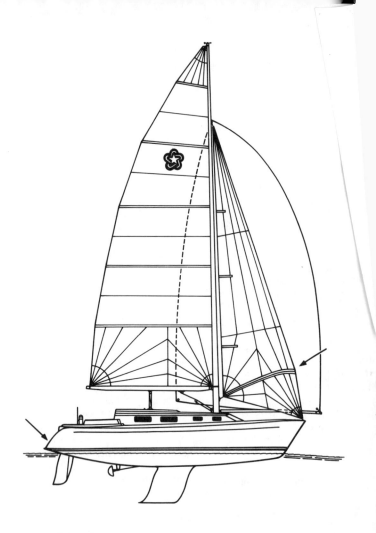

Freedom 35

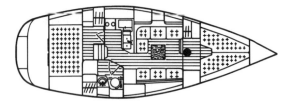

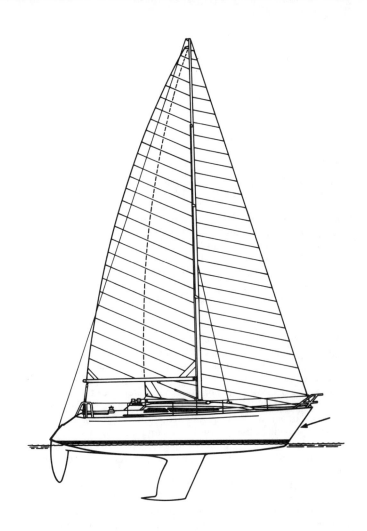

C & C 34/36

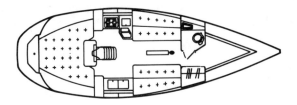

J/35

Length: 35 ft. 6 in.	*Berths:* 6
Beam: 12 ft.	*Engine:* Yanmar 30 HP
Draft: 6.9 ft.	*Fuel:* Diesel, 20 gal.
Displacement: 10,500 lbs.	*Head:* Standard
Sail area: 636 sq. ft.; I, 46.6 ft.;	*Galley:* Alcohol
J, 14.8 ft.; P, 41.6 ft.; E, 14.0 ft.	*Water:* 35 gals.
Hull: FRP, balsa core	*Rating:* PHRF 72
Spars: Tapered aluminum	*Designer:* Rodney Johnstone

Notice combination backstays. Masthead rig. Bow and stern almost parallel.

When you consider the J series of boats, the J stands for the designer, Rodney Johnstone, and the number is usually the length in feet. The series originated with the now famous J/24. There are racing associations for almost all. The J/35 was first built in 1983, and over 300 have been built to date. Since the emphasis is on racing, below decks the amenities are sparse and conventional. There is a vee berth forward, with a head just aft. The settees provide berths for two more, and there are two quarter berths. The galley has a two-burner alcohol stove, and there is an icebox. Water is hand pumped. Eight ports open and there are two hatches.

On deck there are two primary two-speed winches, two secondary, and two halyard.

The main sheet has a rough four-to-one purchase, with a fine tuning system that is sixteen to one. The main leads to a traveler, and the car has a four-to-one adjustment. The vang is eight to one. Leads for the jib are adjustable, with cars on an anodized track. The head, back, and cap stays are rod. Bow and stern rails are stainless, and the stern rail has an opening for a swim ladder. The cockpit is self-bailing and has teak footrests.

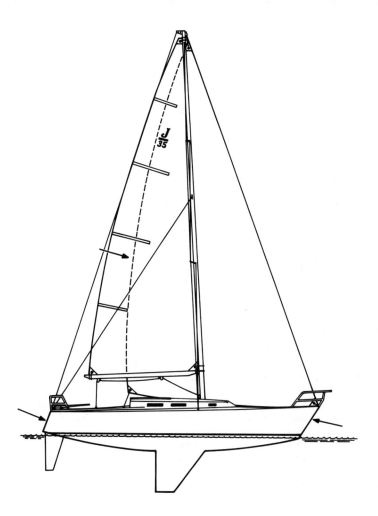

J/35

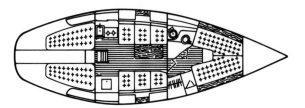

Ericson 36

Length: 35 ft. 7 in. LOA;
  29 ft. LWL
Beam: 11 ft. 10 in.
Draft: 6 ft. 3 in.
Displacement: 11,600 lbs.
Sail area: Main, 252 sq. ft.;
  100% foretriangle, 346 sq. ft.
Hull: FRP
Spars: Coated aluminum

Berths: 7
Engine: 24 HP
Fuel: Diesel, 50 gals.
Head: Standard, shower
Galley: 2-burner alcohol, oven
Water: 70 gals.
Rating: PHRF 108 average
Designer: Ron Holland

*Straight bow. Curved reverse transom. Sheer quite straight.
Note angles in portlights. Aspect ratio 3.6 to 1.*

This Ericson is a racing boat, but the construction technique minimizes weight, allowing for a full cruising interior. Ballast constitutes 45 percent of the total displacement, so she should be stiff.

The forward cabin has a double berth with removable insert, storage under, shelves, and an access door to the anchor locker. Just aft, there is storage for an outboard and a hanging locker to port, and the full head, with pressure water, to starboard. In the main cabin, the port berth is a double, and there is a pilot berth across. The folding table is teak, and the sole is teak and holly. The galley has pressure water and also footpumped fresh and salt water. A wet locker is adjacent to the companionway, and a double quarter berth and the navigation station are to starboard.

In the cockpit, pedestal steering is optional and seats are teak with storage under the port seat. The traveler is mounted on the bridge deck. Genoa tracks are located both inboard and outboard. Two primary, two secondary, and four cabin-roof winches are shown. The optional staysail stay is fixed to an adjustable track. There are hatches over both the main and forward cabins.

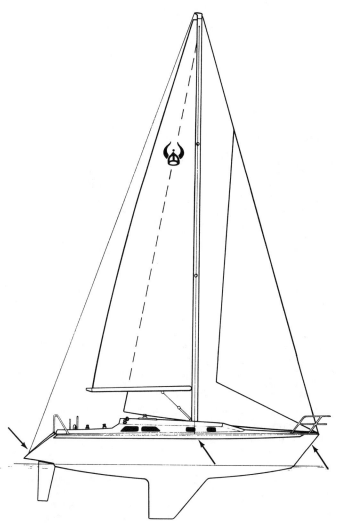

Ericson 36

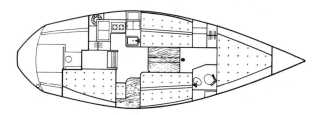

Goderich 35

Length: 35 ft. 7½ in. LOA;
28 ft. 4 in. LWL
Beam: 11 ft. 5 ½ in.
Draft: 4 ft. 9 in.
Displacement: 16,900 lbs.
Sail area: Main, 314 sq. ft.; jib,
219 sq. ft.; staysail, 126 sq. ft.;
genoa, 515 sq. ft.
Hull: Steel
Spars: Aluminum

Berths: 6
Engine: Volvo 24 HP
Fuel: Diesel, 80 gals.
Head: Standard, shower
Galley: 3-burner
Water: 80 gals.
Rating: None
Designer: Brewer, Walstrom and
Assoc., Inc.

Wide beam. Cutter, no bowsprit. Steel hull. High bow, standard sheer. Club-foot staysail, if used.

This steel cutter is built in Canada. Stiffness comes from the beam, as the ballast is moderate. The ballast/displacement ratio is 37 percent. To minimize sweating, the hull is insulated with urethane foam.

Cabin layout is standard, but there are interesting details. At the ladder the area under the cockpit is put to use. A galley locker is located aft of the 14-cubic-foot icebox. There is a shelf inboard of the quarter berth. Seating for the navigation station is on the quarter berth, and there is chart storage under. A locker for oilskins is just forward of the table. In the main cabin the table folds. Settee-berths are on both sides, and a pilot berth is to port. The head may be reached from either the forecabin or the main cabin. Opposite, there is a large hanging locker in the main cabin and a second in the forward cabin. This cabin also has a seat, a bureau, another locker, and a hatch overhead.

Deck storage includes a locker in the forepeak, a cockpit sail bin, and three smaller bins. The hull finish is urethane paint and the decks are nonskid. Steering is by tiller. There are five opening portlights and four opening ports.

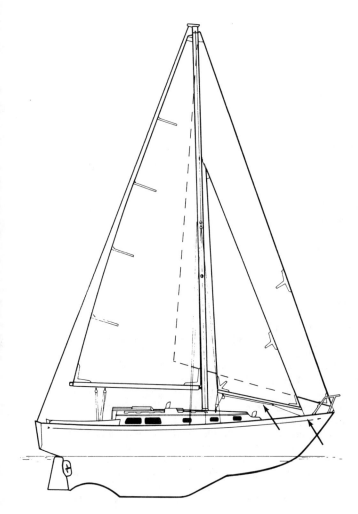

Goderich 35

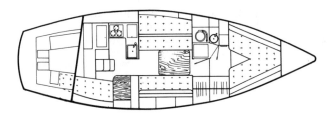

Pilot 35

Length: 35 ft. 9 in.
Beam: 9 ft. 6 in.
Draft: 5 ft.
Displacement: 13,500 lbs.
Sail area: Yawl, 553 sq. ft.;
  sloop, 554 sq. ft.
Hull: FRP
Spars: Aluminum
Berths: Varies: 4 – 6

Engine: Universal 30 HP
Fuel: Gas or diesel, 35 gals.
Head: Standard
Galley: Two-burner alcohol or
  propane
Water: 70 gals.
Rating: D-PN 81.0
Designer: Sparkman and
  Stephens

Yawl. Long counter. Classic bow. Long, low coach roof.

For years Hinckley has said that they build wooden yachts in-side fiberglass hulls. And for many years — since 1945 — they have produced Pilots, first in wood, then in FRP. The first was in wood and was 32 feet 11 inches. The second was designed in 1955, and LOA was 35 feet 2 inches. In 1962 the design was converted to fiberglass, and 117 boats 35 feet 9 inches were built, of which 25 were yawls. Forward, a private cabin has two berths, a hanging locker, and the head. The saloon is just aft, with opposing settees. The table swings down from beside the mast. On some models there are two berths above the settees. The galley is split port and starboard. To port is the stove, oven, and sink. The flush-topped refrigerator opposite doubles as the navigation station. There is pressure water for both the head and the galley. Woodwork is Philippine mahogany, and the sole is holly.

Above deck spars are aluminum. There are winches for the jib and main, for the jib sheets, and, on the cabin roof, for the main sheet. Genoa tracks are stainless steel and have slides. Standing rigging is also stainless. The cockpit is large, sunken, and has two sail lockers. There is pedestal-wheel steering. Toe-rails, handrails, the coaming, and other trim are teak.

Pilot 35

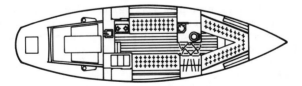

S2 11.0

Length: 36 ft. LOA;
28 ft. 3 in. LWL
Beam: 11 ft. 11 in.
Draft: 4 ft. 8 in.
Displacement: 15,000 lbs.
Sail area: Main and 100%
working jib, 625 sq. ft.
Hull: FRP
Spars: Aluminum

Berths: 6
Engine: Pathfinder 42 HP
Fuel: Diesel, 70 gals.
Head: Standard, shower-bathtub
Galley: 2-burner alcohol, oven
Water: 80 gals.
Rating: None
Designer: Arthur Edmunds

Center cockpit. Shrouds inboard. Long straight bow. Counter, transom.

This is the 11.0 C model, and it has the same underwater lines as the 11.0 A. There is substantial weight and a broad beam for stability. The deep keel and rudder help track off the wind. The center cockpit has become very popular for cruisers, and the 11.0 has a big one.

Because of the center cockpit there is a private cabin aft reached by a passageway to port. Outboard are the galley, a hanging locker, and a drawer unit. Inboard is access to the engine. In the cabin are storage cabinets, another hanging locker, a double bunk, and a drawer unit. Behind the companionway to starboard is a large head with a shower and tub. Head and galley both have pressure water. In the main cabin is the remainder of the galley, to port, with the navigation station opposite. In order to obtain the maximum working space, there is no fixed seat. Instead, the seat swings away to stow over the starboard settee-berth. The large cabin table hinges down. Sliding louvered doors isolate the full-width vee berths forward. Cabin light and ventilation are via two large windows, two Dorade vents, ten opening ports, and two acrylic hatches faced with teak strips.

There are two aft-deck lockers and a self-draining anchor locker. The traveler is mounted just aft of the cockpit. Two primary winches are on the cockpit coamings, and there are two halyard winches on the coach roof forward. The genoa track is mounted on the rail. The boom has a 5: 1 outhaul and internal double reef. The rig is masthead and has a moderate aspect ratio.

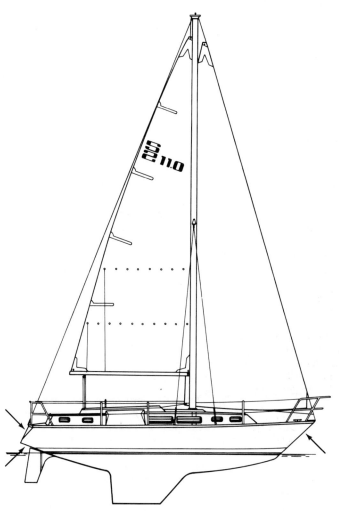

S2 11.0

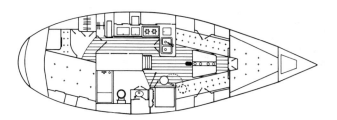

Vancouver 36

Length: 36 ft. LOA;
  27 ft. 11 in. LWL
Beam: 11 ft.
Draft: 5 ft.
Displacement: 18,000 lbs.
Sail area: Total 700 sq. ft.
Hull: FRP
Spars: Aluminum

Berths: 4
Engine: Volvo 35 HP
Fuel: Diesel, 65 gals.
Head: Standard, shower
Galley: 3-burner
Water: 140 gals.
Rating: None
Designer: Robert Harris

Cutter, double-ended, rudder inboard. Aft ports higher than those forward. Upper jumper faces forward.

Robert Harris also designed the Vancouver 27, 32, and 42, but the first two are produced in England and the latter in Taiwan. The 36 has an unusual cabin layout. With a large space but only four bunks, she is designed for long-range cruising. Entry is fine, bilges are hard, and the maximum beam is well aft. Ballast/displacement ratio is 42 percent.

Cabin plans may vary. One particularly interesting design is shown. Behind the ladder to port are a locker for oilskins and a very large locker for sails. Entrance to the engine is through the larger locker. The navigation station is unusually large, as is the galley, which has a 12-cubic-foot icebox. There are two steps down into the main cabin, which gives it very high headroom. Layout here is more normal, with a berth to port and a pilot berth to starboard. Note, however, that there is a fireplace. The large forward cabin is also unusual. Across from the large double berth is a workbench with storage both below and above. The head is also large, with cabinets and lockers. Another large sail locker is located forward, but aft of the chain locker.

Some of the space below came out of the cockpit. It is small, seating four, which in view of the boat's purpose is adequate. There are two cockpit lockers. Deck plans indicate four deck hatches and two cowl vents. The traveler is on the coach roof. Shrouds are inboard, while the genoa sheets to the toe-rail.

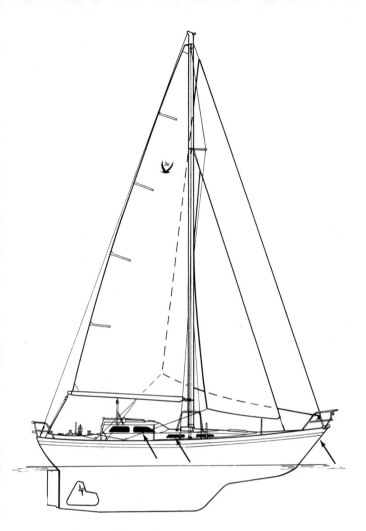

Vancouver 36

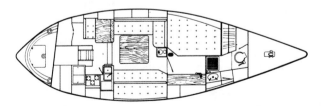

F 3

Length: 36 ft. 3 in. LOA; 29 ft. 6 in. LWL	*Berths:* 6
Beam: 11 ft. 10 in.	*Engine:* Westerbeke 29 HP
Draft: 6 ft. 9 in.	*Fuel:* Diesel, 25 gals.
Displacement: 10,900 lbs.	*Head:* Standard
Sail area: Main, 280 sq. ft.; jib, 350 sq. ft.; genoa, 525 sq. ft.; spinnaker, 650 sq. ft.	*Galley:* 3-burner propane
	Water: 40 gals.
	Rating: IOR 28.5 estimated; PHRF 96 average
Hull: FRP, balsa core	*Designer:* German Frers
Spars: Aluminum	

Running backstays. Long, sloping coach roof. Aspect ratio over 3 to 1. Sharply reversed transom. Masthead rig.

This boat has been designed for both racing and cruising. The hull and rig give a lot of consideration to the IOR without completely succumbing to it. Neither is radical. While the boat is suited for cruising, the interior has certain features that are meant for racing. Balance, in particular, has been emphasized.

Actually, there are berths for eight. When the boat is raced the forepeak is used for sail storage. The berths for racing are the two quarter berths, two pilot berths, and the converted settee. For cruising, or in port, the pilot berths can be augmented by the forward vee berth. The intent is quite deliberate. The vee berths can be folded up out of the way or removed. If there are two watches of four people each, the pilot and quarter berths may still be used leaving the settees available. The galley can be equipped with refrigeration. Water is from a foot-operated pump. The navigation station has its own seat. The head, opposite two hanging lockers, has pressure water and a teak grating over the shower pan. Ventilation is from a forecabin hatch, a port in the head, and opening ports for the quarter berths.

There are long, inboard genoa tracks that allow for very close (8 degree) sheeting. The cockpit is T-shaped and has a wheel. All halyards and reefing controls lead to the cockpit. The toe-rail is slotted its full length. There are four winches on the coach roof for halyards and spinnaker topping lift, and two primary and two secondary winches. The traveler is recessed into the deck just forward of the cockpit. There are two cockpit lockers and a special locker for propane stowage.

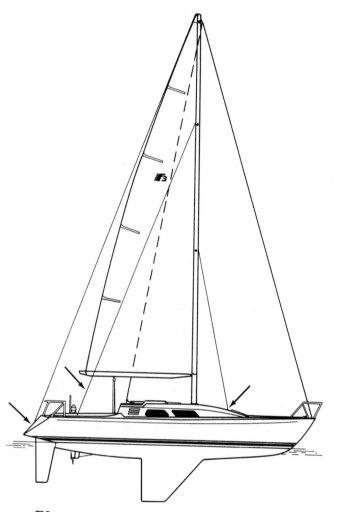

F3

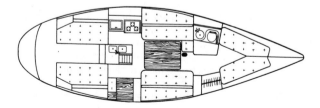

Swan 371

Length: 36.84 ft. LOA;
    29 ft. 9 in. LWL
Beam: 11.32 ft.
Draft: 6.8 ft.
Displacement: 15,400 lbs.
Sail area: Main, 246 sq. ft.;
    100% foretriangle, 351 sq. ft.
Hull: FRP
Spars: Aluminum

Berths: 79
Engine: BUKH 20 HP
Fuel: Diesel, 37 gals.
Head: Standard, shower
Galley: 3-burner propane, oven
Water: 66 gals.
Rating: PHRF 112 average
Designer: Ron Holland

Reverse transom. Running backstays. Very flush deck. Straight bow, high freeboard.

Swans are built by Nautor in Finland; and as might be expected, wood is featured both in the cabin and on deck. The basic design intention was for a racing boat with a large master cabin. The racing intent may be seen in the running backstays, which are not strictly required for mast support but give a steadying effect in rough water and may be used to shape the mainsail.

Also indicating an intention for serious racing is the forward cabin layout. It is designed for sail stowage but has two pipe berths. There is a hatch overhead, and doors lead to the forepeak. Aft to port are drawers and a hanging locker. The head has a hand-held shower over a fiberglass shower pan. The drop-leaf table in the main cabin is removable. There are two transom berths and either one or two pilot berths. In the galley, refrigeration for the ice chest is optional. The chart table is opposite and has space for charts under the tabletop. There is a partial bulkhead, with cutouts, between the galley and navigation area and the main cabin. Going aft, a door provides privacy to the master cabin. Aft of the master cabin are a double and a single quarter berth, stowage, and access to the steering gear and the batteries. For light and air there are the foredeck hatch, two opening ports in the main cabin, a light prism over the head, and an opening port from the cockpit to the aft cabin.

Halyards lead to two winches on the coach roof. On the coaming are two genoa-sheet winches and two more for the spinnaker. The main sheets to a winch on the bridge deck, and there is a traveler. Genoa tracks and shrouds are inboard. An eye for a staysail is provided on the foredeck. There is stowage for a life raft and for a propane bottle. The decks, trim, and cabin woodwork are teak.

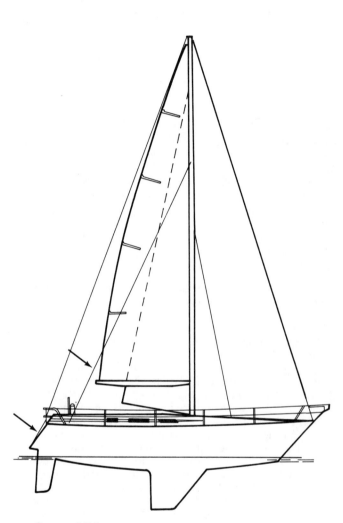

Swan 371

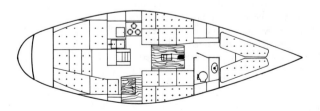

Seidelmann 37

Length: 36 ft, 10 in. LOA;
29 ft. 6 in. LWL
Beam: 12 ft.
Draft: 5 ft. 11 in. (deep);
or 4 ft. 11 in. (intermediate)
Displacement: 13,500 lbs. (deep);
or 13,900 lbs. (intermediate)
Sail area: Main and jib,
643 sq. ft. total
Hull: FRP

Spars: Aluminum
Berths: 6
Engine: 24 HP
Fuel: Diesel, 18 gals.
Head: Standard, shower
Galley: 2-burner alcohol, oven
Water: 70 gals.
Rating: PHRF 120 (deep keel)
Designer: Bob Seidelmann

Aspect ratio almost 4 to 1. Slight reverse transom. Sheer sweeps down toward stern. Slight roach. Straight bow.

Like many Seidelmanns, this one has a very tall rig. The beam, however, is wide in relation to length. The result is a spacious interior.

There is a total of five berths, with a sixth pilot berth possible above the double berth-settee. Two berths are forward, two in the main cabin, and there is a quarter berth with stowage under. In the galley there are two sinks, two burners, and a top-loading icebox. The navigation station is opposite. Sections show the table at an angle, but it can be made level for additional counter space. The dinette table folds away against the forward bulkhead. Storage is under all berths, in four drawers near the head, in two hanging lockers, in three lockers in the forward compartment, and elsewhere. Many of the locker doors are louvered. Also louvered are the head door and the door to the forecabin. Wood is teak. There is pressure water. Light and ventilation are from two Dorade vents, forecabin and main-cabin hatches, and four opening ports.

A traveler is mounted on the bridge deck forward of the T-shaped cockpit. Halyards, the topping lift, and the reef line are internal. Two halyard winches are mounted on the mast and there are two cockpit winches. Genoa tracks are inboard. Deck stowage includes two cockpit lockers and an anchor well. Handrails and the companionway are teak.

Seidelmann 37

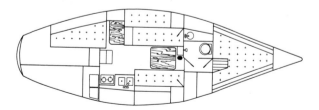

Crealock 37

Length: 36 ft. 11 in. LOA;
  27 ft. 9 in. LWL
Beam: 10 ft. 10 in.
Draft: 5 ft. 4 in.
Displacement: 16,000 lbs.
Sail area: Main, 272 sq. ft.;
  100% foretriangle, 347 sq. ft.
Hull: FRP
Spars: Aluminum

Berths: 7
Engine: 32 HP
Fuel: Diesel, 47 gals.
Head: Standard
Galley. 3-burner, oven
Water: Not stated
Rating: PHRF 174
Designer: Wib Crealock

Sloop, cutter, or yawl, so hull is important for identification. Distinctive stern. Long spoon bow with chin. Two-and-three porthole layout.

Underwater lines show a very normal fin keel, but the canoe stern is unusual. The cutter rig shown does not indicate staysails. Maximum beam is aft.

Below, the main saloon appears spacious. A double berth is to starboard, a single to port. There is unusual storage in the fo'c'sle, with five drawers, a hanging locker, and a vanity to port, and three drawers under the double berth. The head has a grating over the shower drain. Aft is a navigation station, seat, and double quarter berth. The galley is to starboard and has three burners, a double sink, top-loaded refrigerator, and oven.

The cockpit has three seat lockers, and there is a transom locker. Two skylights are over the forecabin and the saloon. A short jib track, a traveler, and three winches are mounted on the coach roof. A genoa track is mounted on deck inboard, with leads to two primary cockpit winches. There is pedestal-wheel steering.

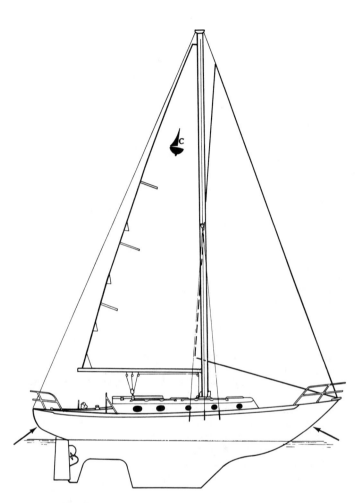

Crealock 37

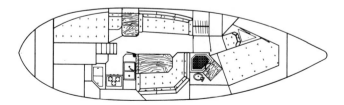

Alajuela 33

Length: 37 ft. LOA;
  27 ft. 6 in. LWL
Beam: 10 ft. 8 in.
Draft: 4 ft. 9 in.
Displacement: 13,500 lbs.
Sail area: Main, 241 sq. ft.;
  genoa, 135%, 450 sq. ft.;
  staysail, 132 sq. ft.; genoas,
  Yankee, trysails, spinnaker
Hull: FRP

Spars: Aluminum
Berths: 6
Engine: Pisces 27 HP
Fuel: Diesel, 50 gals.
Head: Standard
Galley: 3-burner propane, oven
Water: 75 gals.
Rating: None
Designer: Ray Richards

Double-ended. Bowsprit. Cutter. Four oval ports. Dorade ventilators.

There is a long keel for tracking, and the forefoot is cut away for turning. With significant sheer, this boat has a traditional look. The keel is quite thick, as it contains ballast, water, fuel, and the holding tank.

The head is located in an unusual position, amidships on the port side. This tends to separate the cabin into distinct areas, with a small space at the base of the companionway ladder. A hanging locker for wet gear and the navigator's station are located here. The cabin is finished in teak with a vinyl headliner. Ventilation is handled by two Dorade ventilators, three hatches, and eight bronze opening ports.

The decks are wide and the cockpit has 7½-foot-long seats, with two storage lockers and a lazarette for propane bottles. Steering is by wheel or tiller. There are optional running backstays, and the staysail stay can be removed. There are spinnaker, genoa, and staysail tracks. The four-to-one mainsheet has a traveler, and the main has a two-to-one internal outhaul.

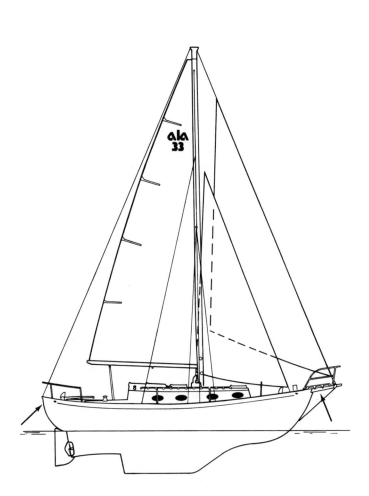

Alajuela 33

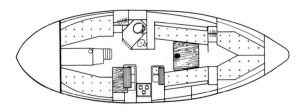

Baltic 37

Length: 37 ft. LOA;
  28 ft. 10½ in. LWL
Beam: 12 ft.
Displacement: 13,600 lbs.
Draft: 5 ft. 9 in.
Sail area: Not given. 1, 49 ft.;
  J, 15.56 ft.; P, 43.5 ft.;
  E, 11.75 ft.
Hull: FRP, balsa core

Spars: Anodized aluminum
Berths: 8
Engine: Volvo 23 HP
Fuel: 21 gals.
Head: Standard
Galley: 3-burner propane
Water: 34.3 gals.
Rating: IOR 27.5; PHRF 113
Designer: C & C Design Group

Sharp clipper bow. Sharp reverse transom, some counter. Low cabin. Tall rig for size.

Baltic has a fin keel with high-aspect spade rudder. With a narrow beam at the water line she is initially tender but gains stiffness as she starts to heel. Aft sections are full to increase sailing length when heeled. C & C wants to maintain speed off the wind without a strong weather helm.

Companionway stairs land amidships. To port is the head; access to the aft cabin is to starboard. The aft cabin has a double berth, seat, stowage, and a hanging locker. Amidships is an L-shaped galley and the navigation area. The former has a stainless steel icebox. Foot-operated pumps deliver fresh water and seawater. There is a hanging locker aft of the navigator's seat and stowage under the stairs. Settees in the main cabin convert to berths, and there are two pilot berths. Forward are berths to port and starboard with stowage under. There are two hanging lockers and shelves. The interior is faced with teak. There are two tinted-glass hatches. The aft cabin and the head have opening portholes; other windows are fixed.

Topsides, rigging, except the midstay, is stainless steel. There are winches for the main halyard and sheet; two for reefing, the Cunningham, the spinnaker pole, and the topping lift; two for the genoa and spinnaker halyards; and two each for the genoa and spinnaker sheets. Equipment is unusually complete and includes such items as turning blocks, bosun's chair, anchor, fenders, etc. The cockpit is T-shaped and has wheel steering. Teak is optional for the deck.

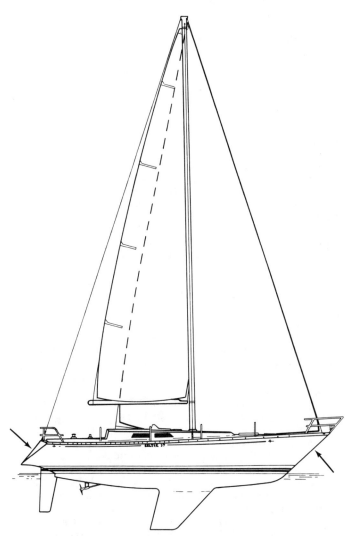

Baltic 37

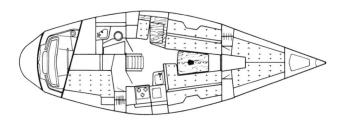

Dickerson 37

Length: 37 ft. LOA;
   28 ft. 10 in. LWL
Beam: 11 ft. 6 in.
Draft: 4 ft. 6 in.
Displacement: 15,950 lbs.
Sail area: Main, jib, and mizzen,
   675 sq. ft. total
Hull: FRP, deck balsa core
Spars: Aluminum

Berths: 6
Engine: Perkins 37 HP
Fuel: Diesel, 45 gal.
Head: Standard, shower
Galley: 3-burner alcohol
Water: 90 gals.
Rating: None
Designer: George Hazen

Center-cockpit ketch. Masthead rig. High aspect ratio. Pulpit platform.

The overhangs and sheer have been deliberately designed for a traditional appearance, but the center cockpit and aft cabin are modern. The Dickerson 37 is designed as a cruiser for two or three couples. Dickerson has specialized in cruising ketches for many years.

The aft cabin may be reached from its own companionway, or through a passage below. There are berths for two and storage. In the passageway to the main cabin are lockers and access to the engine. The galley to starboard has a pressure water system, as does the large head. In the main cabin the L-shaped dinette converts to a double berth. There is an opening hatch above, and all ports operate. The sole is teak and holly, with access panels to the bilge. Forward, the isolated cabin has vee berths, a hanging locker, and a bureau. A second hatch is above.

On deck, handrails and cap rails are teak, as are coamings and the bow platform. There is wheel steering in the center cockpit. The mizzen has a traveler and the main a vang. There are three halyard winches, genoa tracks and cleats, and two genoa winches. Both the main and the mizzen have jiffy reefing.

Dickerson 37

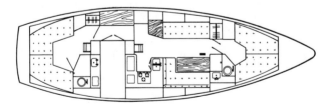

Dockrell 37

Length: 37 ft. LOA; 30 ft. LWL
Beam: 10 ft. 2 in.
Draft: 8 ft. 4 in.
Displacement: 11,500 lbs
Sail area: Main, 220 sq. ft.;
   jib, 224 sq. ft.;
   no. 1 staysail, 131 sq. ft.;
   genoa, 395 sq. ft.
Hull: FRP

Spars: Aluminum
Berths: 7
Engine: Yanmar 30 HP
Fuel: Diesel, 20 gals.
Head: Standard
Galley: 2-burner propane, oven
Water: 40 gals.
Rating: None
Designer: Dockrell Yachts

Cutter. Distinctive rudder shape. Masthead rig. Reverse transom.

This boat, built to Lloyd's specifications, has the beam restricted to 10 feet for use in European canals or for overland transportation. She is light displacement, has a low wetted surface, and combines a fixed with a swing keel. Lines from the keel through the rudder skeg are unusual.

The quarter berth is a double. Its isolation from the main cabin is an unusual feature. This layout indicates the galley backed up to port of the companionway, but other drawings show a plan with the galley parallel to the hull. In both designs there is electric refrigeration and a double sink. The main cabin is finished in teak and mahogany. With the standard layout, three are accommodated for sleeping. Forward is the head and stowage, as well as the forecabin with vee berths for two. Hatches are over the saloon and aft cabin, and there is a forward opening port in the forecabin.

The cockpit is small and self-draining. The water line is relatively long, while overhangs are moderate. The bow has very little flare.

Dockrell 37

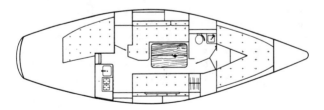

Alberg 37

Length: 37 ft. 2 in. LOA;
  26 ft. 6 in. LWL
Beam: 10 ft. 2 in.
Draft: 5 ft. 6 in.
Displacement: 16,800 lbs.
Sail area: Total, 686 sq. ft.
Hull: FRP
Spars: Aluminum
Berths: 7

Engine: Volvo MD 11C
Fuel: Diesel, 35 gals.
Head: Standard, shower
Galley: 3-burner alcohol, oven
Water: 60 gals.
Rating: PHRF 162, D-PN 83.0
Designer: Not stated; manufact-
  ured by Whitby Boat Works

Yawl. Mainmast backstay split. Mizzen sheets to stern pulpit.

This yawl was derived from the Alberg 37 sloop and is available in that rig. Lines are classic, with a long counter, full keel, and spoon bow. Beam is moderate and the hull quite symmetrical.

The companionway ladder interferes with work at the galley sink, but large counters are to the side and out of the way. One ladder step will fold out of the way when the sink is used. A quarter berth and the navigation station are to port, and there is a wet locker directly below the ladder. In the main cabin the table folds against the forward bulkhead for storage. The port settee makes up into a double berth, and an extension berth and a pilot berth are opposite. The head has pressure water and a grating over the sump. A sliding door closes it off. Across is a large hanging locker. The forward cabin has a door for privacy, lockers, a hanging locker, the vee berths, and storage under.

Teak is used for the inlaid cockpit seats and for the fixed main-cabin skylight. A forward skylight over the forecabin opens. There are winches for both main and jib halyards, one for the mainsheet, and two for the genoa. Genoa tracks have cars and blocks. There is a vented anchor locker in the forepeak.

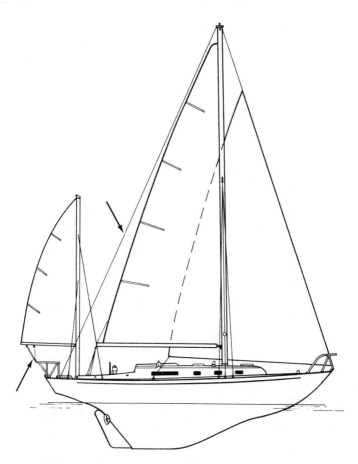

Alberg 37

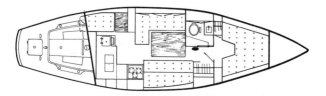

Endeavour 37

Length: 37 ft. 5 in. LOA;
   30 ft. LWL
Beam: 11 ft. 7 in.
Draft: 4 ft. 6 in.
Displacement: 21,000 lbs.
Sail area: Main, 312 sq. ft.;
   100% foretriangle, 414 sq. ft.
Hull: FRP
Spars: Aluminum

Berths: 6
Engine: Perkins 50 HP
Fuel: Diesel, 55 gals.
Head: Standard, shower
Galley: 3-burner alcohol, oven
Water: 101 gals.
Rating: PHRF 186, D-PN 88.0
Designer: Endeavour Yacht Corp.

Cutter. Bowsprit. Curved coaming. Possible ketch rig. High bow. Vertical transom. Aspect ratio 2.4 to 1.

With a private stateroom aft and with a total of six bunks, the Endeavour qualifies as a live-aboard boat with a lot of storage space. With two or four aboard there is no need to use the settees for berths. The keel is long and the displacement hull is heavy. Draft is shallow. When the boat is rigged as a ketch, the mizzen goes through the cockpit just forward of the binnacle. A more conventional cabin arrangement is available.

The aft cabin is to port and has a double berth, seat, and hanging locker. There is direct access to the head. On the other side of the boat there is a double quarter berth and the nav station. The partial bulkhead does not isolate this area from the galley. The galley is U-shaped and has pressure water. There is also a footpump. The ice chest is 10 cubic feet. The main cabin entrance to the head is opposite. The forward area of the cabin is devoted to the dinette and to storage. The central table folds. No bulkhead separates these areas, which contributes to a feeling of spaciousness. Wood is teak and the sole is teak parquet. Ten ports and three hatches open.

On deck, teak is used for the coaming and rail caps as well as for handrails. Main sheeting is to the bridge deck. A winch for the main halyard and one for the genoa are mast-mounted. Two primary sheeting winches are on the coaming. Jibs lead to a track on the rail.

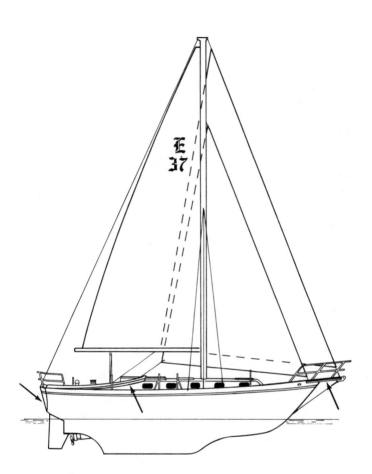

Endeavour 37

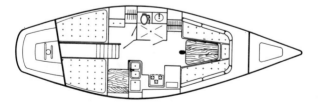

Northeast 37

Length: 37 ft. 6 in. LOA;
  34 ft. LWL
Beam: 13 ft. 8 in.
Draft: 4 ft. 10 in.
Displacement: 18,000 lbs.
Sail area: 686 sq. ft.
Hull: FRP
Spars: Aluminum
Engine: Yanmar 100 HP

Berths: 4
Fuel: Diesel, 150 gals.
Head: Standard
Galley: 3-burner propane
Water: 200 gals.
Rating: None
Designer: Mark Ellis Design
  Group

Large "split level" coach roof, with very large windows.

Motor cruisers are designed for cruising comfort, rather than speed. Note the fuel and water capacities of the Northeast. Range is said to be 800 miles. She can be easily sailed by a couple, but there is a private stateroom to port for visitors. The owner's cabin is forward and has a walk-around double berth. The head is across from the visitors' stateroom. The U-shaped galley lies just aft. Three steps lead to the interior steering station, which has areas for navigation and charting. Just aft is the saloon, with opposing seating and a table. There is standing headroom. The engine is below the cabin floor and well amidships. The deck level is even with the cockpit where there is a second, exterior steering station. The jib is self-furling, and the main sheet leads to the coach roof top, well aft and easily accessible from the cockpit. A bow thruster is optional, as is a transom door, a swim platform, and davits for a dinghy.

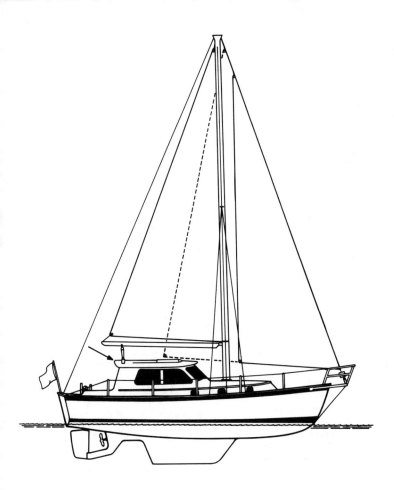

Northeast 37

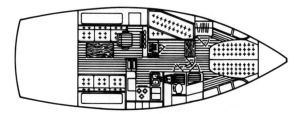

Shannon 38

Length: 37 ft. 9 in. LOA;
  30 ft. 10 in. LWL
Beam: 11 ft. 6 in.
Draft: 5 ft.
Displacement: 18,500 lbs.
Sail area: (Ketch): mizzen,
  169.4 sq. ft.; main, 285.9 sq.
  ft.; total, 751 sq. ft.
Hull: FRP

Spars: Aluminum
Berths: Custom
Engine: Perkins 40 HP
Fuel: Diesel, 70 gals.
Head: Standard, shower
Galley: 3-burner propane, oven
Water: 120 gals.
Rating: PHRF 181.5 average
Designer: Schultz and Stadel

Motor sailer or standard. Ketch and cutter have double fore-sails. Staysail self-tending. Bowsprit.

This Shannon has been designed for long-range offshore cruising. The keel is long and full. Basic options include either a cutter or a ketch rig and either a standard or a pilothouse design. Cabin layout is semicustom and will depend upon the choices above.

As shown, the design is for a standard deck arrangement. The companionway leads directly to the navigation station and the galley. Pressure water is standard in the latter, and there is a nine-cubic-foot icebox located just aft of the stove. A quarter berth serves as the seat for the chart table, which is located just aft of a wet locker. In the layout shown both settees extend, and there is a pilot berth above the port settee. The central table is drop leaf. Forward is the head, with pressure water and an independent pump for the shower sump; a hanging locker; and other storage. The forward cabin is somewhat unusual, with a double berth to starboard and a workbench and sail bin across. Interior surfaces are teak. There are four Dorade vents, hatches over the main and forward cabins, and 12 bronze opening ports.

On deck, the trim, including the coaming and the bowsprit, is teak. There are eight winches, including primary, staysail sheet, mainsheet, genoa, main, staysail halyards, and reefing. Both the main and the staysail have travelers. The propane locker is vapor-proof and has an overboard vent.

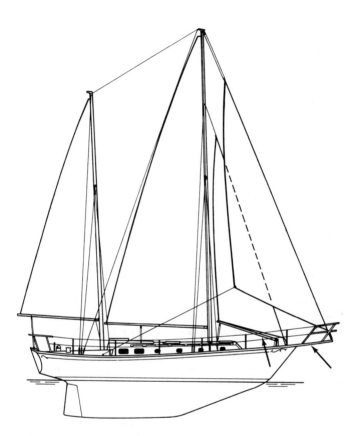

Shannon 38

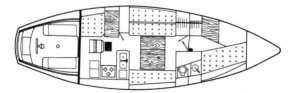

Sabre 38

Length: 37 ft. 10 in. LOA;
  31 ft. 2 in. LWL
Beam: 11 ft. 6 in.
Draft: 6 ft. 6 in. (keel);
  or 8 ft. (keel/centerboard)
Displacement: 15,200 lbs. (keel);
  or 15,600 lbs.
  (keel/ centerboard)
Sail area: Main, 168 sq. ft.
  100% jib, 234 sq. ft.;
  150% genoa, 351 sq. ft.

Hull: FRP
Spars: Aluminum
Berths: 6
Engine: Westerbeke 33 HP
Fuel: Diesel, 10 gals.
Head: Standard, shower
Galley: 3-burner alcohol, oven
Water: 94 gals.
Rating: PHRF 111 (manufacturer)
Designer: Sabre Design Team

Aspect ratio over 3 to 1. Masthead. Sheer almost straight. Straight bow. Long cabin.

The hull and rig are designed for speed, while the cabin arrangement is comfortable for cruising. Fuel and water are adequate for offshore sailing. The keel model is standard, the keel/centerboard is optional. Other Sabres are the 28, 30, and 34.

Both the galley and the head appear quite spacious. Note how the icebox is partially under the cockpit. Refrigeration is available. Water here and in the head is pressure. In the forward cabin are vee berths, drawers, lockers, and storage compartments. Opposite the head are wet and dry hanging lockers. In the main cabin the port settee converts to a double. The table folds forward against a magazine rack. Aft to starboard is the nav station with its separate seat and a large quarter berth. There are hatches over both forward and main cabins.

The traveler is mounted on the coach roof just forward of the companionway hatch. The cockpit is T-shaped and has cockpit lockers and wheel steering. Primary winches are self-tailing, and there are winches for the main and genoa halyards, the mainsheet, and reefing. Eight ports open. A boom vang and spinnaker gear, including winches, are optional.

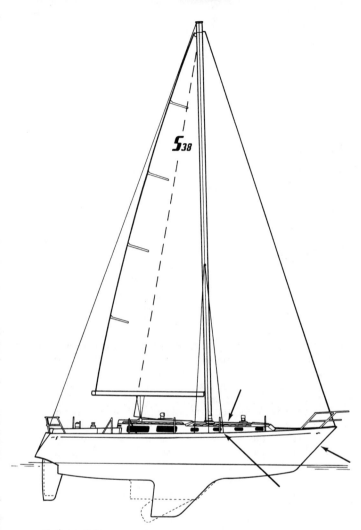

Sabre 38

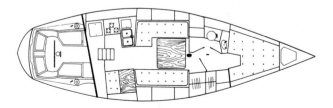

Alajuela 38

Length: 38 ft. LOA;
32 ft. 7 in. LWL
Beam: 11 ft. 6 in.
Draft: 5 ft. 7 in.
Displacement: 27,000 lbs.
Sail area: Main, 366 sq. ft.;
jib, 344 sq. ft.;
staysail, 178 sq. ft.
Hull: FRP

Spars: Aluminum
Berths: 5
Engine: Pisces 40 HP
Fuel: Diesel, 85 gals.
Head: Standard
Galley: 2-burner propane, oven
Water: 100 gals.
Rating: None
Designer: Terry Wells

Cutter. Bowsprit. Cruiser bow. Two backstays, one to each quarter. Double-ended. Square lines to cabin.

This is a passage or cruising boat, not a racer. Long keel gives directional stability, but Alajuela will not turn on a dime. Double-enders offer less area to pooping seas and are intended for cruising. Alajuela has a fast-draining, relatively small cockpit for insurance.

The main cabin is located forward and has a double berth, small settee, vanity, hanging locker, and the head to starboard. There is access to the chain locker. There are two berths and a pilot berth in the main cabin, as well as the U-shaped galley and a chart table. The icebox is top loading. Between the engine room and the galley is a wet locker. The interior is teak with contrasting planked ceiling. The sole is teak and holly.

There are three two-speed halyard winches and five two-speed sheet winches. The tiller may be replaced by a wheel. The nonskid surface is ground walnut shell. Side decks are 22 inches wide, and the pulpit has a teak footwalk. A teak skylight is optional. There are genoa and staysail tracks, a six-to-one mainsheet with traveler, and a two-to-one internal outhaul. There are four teak ventilators, teak coaming, a Samson post, and a lazarette for propane storage.

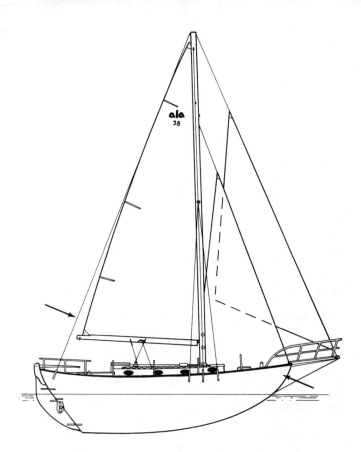

Alajuela 38

Island Packet 35

Length: 38 ft. LOA,
   35 ft. 4 in. LWL
Beam: 12 ft.
Draft: 4 ft. 6 in.
Displacement: 17,500 lbs.
Sail area: Main, 263 sq. ft.;
   jib 377 sq. ft.;
   staysail 95 sq. ft.
Hull: FRP, deck has core

Spars: Anodized aluminum
Berths: 7
Engine: 38 HP
Fuel: Diesel, 48 gal.
Head: Standard, shower
Galley: 3 burner LPG
Water: 90 gal.
Rating: None
Designer: Robert K. Johnson

Cutter. Masthead rig. Pulpit on bowsprit. Vertical stern.

The forward cabin is private and has a vee berth, hanging lockers, an overhead hatch and two opening ports. The trim here, and throughout, is teak, and the sole holly. An additional hanging locker and the head lie just forward of the main saloon. In the saloon, seating to port can be converted to a double settee berth, and the starboard seating to a single. Another hatch is above, and there are opening ports. The large galley lies to starboard. The icebox has a capacity of 12 cubic feet, and pressure hot and cold water serves the double sink. The gimbaled stove has an oven. Just aft of the navigation station is a large, private, double berth cabin, which has its own hanging locker, a seat, two opening ports, and an overhead hatch.

The cockpit has a coldwater washdown connection and a separate icebox. There is storage under the seats, two scuppers, and storage for the propane tanks. Steering is wheel, and there is a pedestal. The bowsprit is actually a platform. Both the jib and the staysail have furling systems, and there is a single-line reefing system for the main. Midboom sheeting for the main keeps the cockpit unobstructed, and there is a traveler. There is a jib halyard winch on the mast, a winch for the main halyard and sheet in the cockpit, and two jib sheet winches. The backstays are twin, and the topping lift is adjustable.

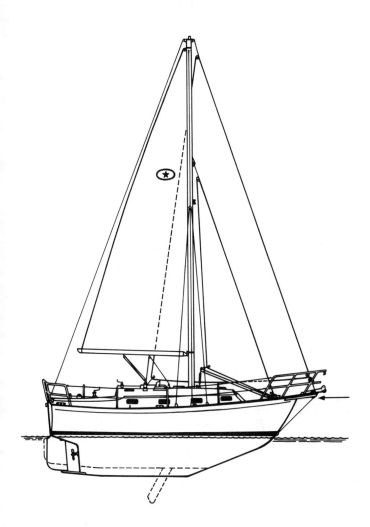

Island Packet 35

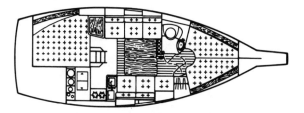

Catalina 38

Length: 38 ft. 2 in. LOA;
  30 ft. 3 in. LWL
Beam: 11 ft. 10 in.
Draft: 6 ft. 9 in. (standard);
  or 4 ft. 11 in. (shoal)
Displacement: 15,900 lbs.
  (standard); or 16,700 lbs.
  (shoal)
Sail area: Main, 253 sq. ft.;
  100% foretriangle, 386 sq . ft.
Hull: FRP

Spars: Aluminum
Berths: 5
Engine: Atomic 30 HP
Fuel: Diesel, 36 gals.
Head: Standard
Galley: 2-burner
Water: 41 gals.
Rating: D-PN 76.8,
  PHRF 116 average, keel
Designer: Frank Butler

Distinctive counter and transom. Boom appears very short, aspect ratio high. Long smooth sheer. Balanced hull.

The Catalina is available with either a standard or a shoal-draft keel. Entry is fine and rig tall, which should assist in going to weather. Maximum beam is amidships.

Photographs, but not the cabin plan, show a quarter berth on the starboard, which would increase berths to six. The cabin finish is oiled teak. There is a skylight over the main cabin and a hatch forward. The galley is U-shaped and has double sinks and an icebox. Pressure water is standard. To starboard is the navigation station. The dinette is U-shaped and has a settee opposite. Just forward of the partial bulkhead there are drawers and lockers to starboard and the head, with teak shower grating, to port. Vee berths are forward.

The cockpit has pedestal-wheel steering and lockers. An anchor locker is in the forepeak. Two halyard winches are on the coach roof, as is a traveler for the mainsheet. There are primary winches indicated for the genoa. Tracks are on the bulwarks.

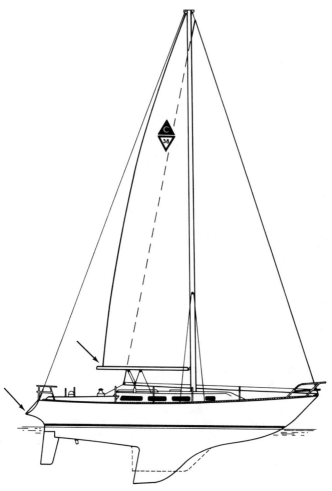

Catalina 38

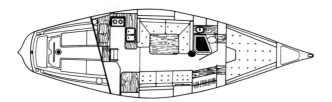

Farr 38

Length: 38 ft. 3 in. LOA;
  31 ft. 2 in. LWL
Beam: 12 ft.
Draft: 6 ft. 4 in.
Displacement: 10,600 lbs.
Sail area: Main, 397 sq. ft.;
  100% foretriangle, 286 sq . ft.
Hull: Epoxy and polyurethane
  over wood structure

Spars. Aluminum
Berths: 8
Engine: Pathfinder 40 HP
Fuel: Diesel, 26 gals.
Head: Standard
Galley: 2-burner LPG, oven
Water: 75 gals.
Rating: PHRF 83 average
Designer: Bruce Farr

Reverse counter. Long, continuous port. Long, sloping coach roof. Spreaders swept back.

Cold-molded wood, unusual in a boat of this size, is used for construction. The hull framing is cedar and the skins, spruce. Planking is thin strips adhesive-bonded in diagonal and longitudinal laminations. The result is a high-performance cruiser that has been successfully raced.

Below decks the layout is fairly standard except for the number of berths. There are two quarter berths, one double and the other single. In the main cabin are a double and a single settee. Vee berths are in the peak. The head with shower is forward to port with hanging lockers opposite. At the bottom of the ladder are the navigation station and the galley.

Above is lots of sail control. There are four halyard, two primary, two secondary, and one general-purpose winch. Halyards are internal, as is the outhaul and the quick reef for the main. The boom vang is four-part and the backstay is adjustable. Spars are painted with polyurethane. There are a traveler, genoa track, and lead blocks. Options include pressure water, refrigeration, wheel steering, and anodized spars. A cedar deck may also be chosen.

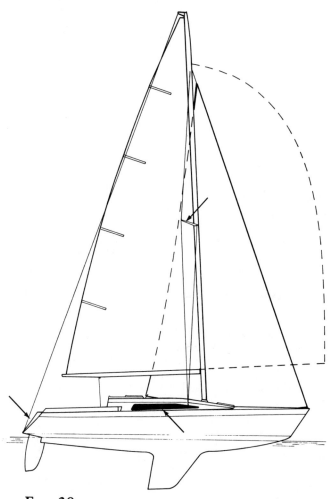

Farr 38

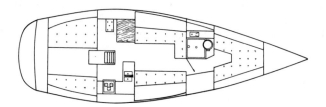

Clark 31

Length: 38 ft. 7 in. LOA;
26 ft. 3 in. LWL
Beam: 9 ft. 3 in.
Draft: 5 ft.
Displacement: 11,800 lbs.
Sail area: Main, jib, and foresail,
579 sq. ft.
Hull: FRP
Spars: Spruce or aluminum

Engine: Volvo 2S HP
Fuel: Diesel, 50 gals.
Head: Standard
Galley: Standard
Water: 45 gals.
Rating: None
Designer: Modified from
L.Francis Herreshoff

*Classic clipper bow. Bowsprit. Spars possibly wood. Boomkin
for backstay.*

When L. Francis Herreshoff designed the H-28 in 1939, it may
have been his most popular boat. This modification has a
counter transom, a taller and more powerful rig, and a higher
ballast ratio; and the hull is deeper and is wider on deck. However, the hull lines, bowsprit, boomkin, and round ports are
classic, as is the rectangular coach roof.

Clark calls the cabin layout "sensible," but it is also somewhat unusual forward. The forecabin, instead of having the
standard vee berths, has a berth to port and a work counter
starboard. Aft, the head is opposite a hanging locker. The starboard berth converts to a double. Farther aft is a navigation
table with the quarter berth serving as the seat. The galley is to
port. The counter beside the seat folds down for storage, and
the four-cubic-foot icebox can be loaded from the cockpit.

The prototype of the Clark was rigged as a yawl. Bronze
hardware such as a boom bail, outhaul, and gooseneck were developed for this boat. Most other hardware and the eight opening ports are also bronze. Hatches are teak, as is the skylight.
The bulwarks are mahogany with a teak cap.

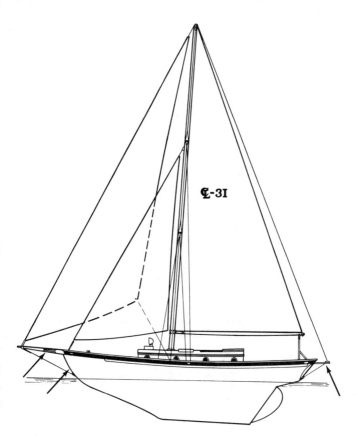

Clark 31

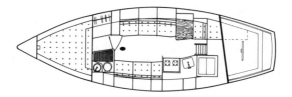

Corbin 39

Length: 38 ft. 9 in. LOA;
  31 ft. 11 in. LWL
Beam: 12 ft. 2 in.
Draft: 5 ft. 6 in.
Displacement: 21,500 lbs.
Sail area: Main, 367 sq. ft.; jib,
  455 sq. ft.; genoa, 709 sq. ft.;
  spinnaker, 1593 sq. ft.
Hull: FRP sandwich
Spars: Aluminum

Berths: 7
Engine: BMW D-35
Fuel: Diesel, 104 gals.
Head: One with shower;
  aft wash basin
Galley: 3-burner, oven
Water: 128 gals.
Rating: None
Designer: Dufour Yacht Design

Rounded stern. Straight bow, pulpit. May be center-cockpit or pilothouse, cutter or ketch. Running backstays on cutter.

The Corbin may be purchased in various stages of completion. Rig may be ketch or cutter, and the cockpit may be aft or amidships for either, although the mizzen will go through the aft cockpit of a ketch. Corbin is pleased that their boat has been termed "overbuilt," as they intend it for cruising. Data is for the tall rig, but a shorter rig is available.

The companionway leads to an aft cabin that has its own wash basin. The main cabin is forward of a bulkhead and has a navigation station to starboard and the galley against the bulkhead and to port. Two hatches are above the galley, with another two over the dinette area. A hanging locker and the head are aft of the forecabin bulkhead. The berths in the forecabin are to starboard, with a settee to port. A hatch is above. Water systems are pressurized. Additional ventilation is through six Dorade boxes.

On deck, trim is teak. Storage includes two foredeck sail lockers, one cockpit locker, coaming lockers, and a locker for the anchor chain. There are two mast winches, two primary winches, a genoa track with a traveler, and a mainsheet traveler. Running backstays are used.

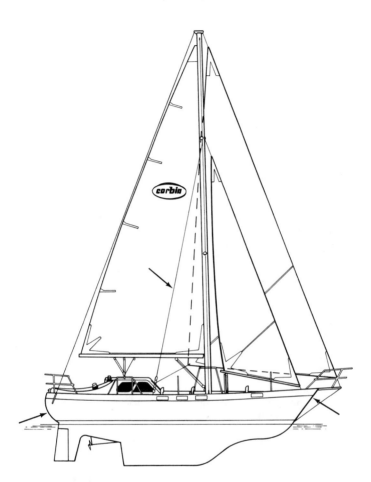

Corbin 39

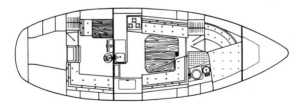

Cal 39

Length: 39 ft. LOA;
   32 ft. 1 in. LWL
Beam: 12 ft.
Draft: 6 ft. 8 in. or 5 ft. 6 in.
Displacement: 19,000 lbs.
Sail area: Standard rig: main,
   303 sq. ft.; 100% foretriangle,
   417 sq. ft. Tall rig: main, 326.6
   sq. ft. Tall rig: main, 326.6
   450 sq. ft.
Hull: FRP

Spars: Painted aluminum
Berths: 6
Engine. Universal 44 HP
Fuel: Diesel, 45 gals.
Head: Two
Galley: 3-burner alcohol, oven
Water: 152 gals.
Rating: D-PN 75.4
   standard, PHRF 114
Designer: William Lapworth

Sloop or cutter, optional tall rig. Either is high aspect. Straight bow. Note reverse transom and line of rudder.

A Lapworth design, this Cal has a long water line, aft-extending rudder, and a substantial sailplan. In addition to the two rigs offered, a shoal-draft keel is available. The fastest boat incorporates the tall rig and the deep keel, with a PHRF of about 106.

The Cal 39 provides privacy for three couples. There is an aft cabin with a double berth entered from portside beside the companionway. In addition to the sink/hanging locker plan shown, an optional full head is available. If selected, it occupies the space shown for the navigation station. The galley is large, with double sinks, three burners and an oven, and an eight-cubic-foot icebox. Forward of the galley is the saloon with two settee-berths and a folding table. A second head is forward and also has pressure hot and cold water. A teak door gives privacy to the forward cabin with its double berth and hanging locker. Light and ventilation are through two translucent hatches, one over the foredeck and one over the main cabin. There are four fixed and eight opening ports, deadlights over the head and the passageway, and a Dorade ventilator over the galley.

The cockpit is T-shaped and has pedestal-wheel steering. Winches include one for the mainsheet, two for halyards, and two for genoa sheets. Halyards are internal, as is the outhaul. The mainsheet is on a traveler and has a five-to-one mechanical advantage. There are tracks for the jib sheets. Stowage includes an anchor locker, a lazarette, and two locking seat lockers.

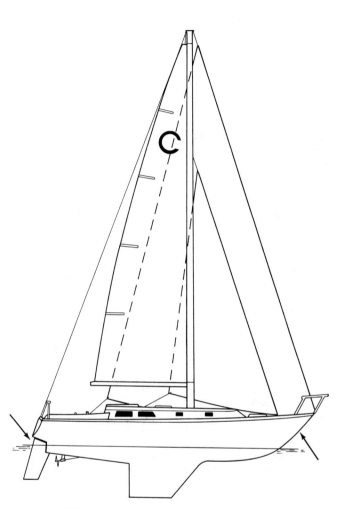

Cal 39

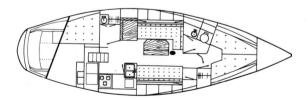

Freedom 39

Length: 39 ft. LOA; 31 ft. LWL
Beam: 12 ft. 10 in.
Draft: 5 ft. 6 in.
Displacement: 18,500 lbs.
Sail area: Main, 456 sq. ft.;
    foresail, 288 sq. ft.
Hull: FRP, balsa core
Spars: Carbon fiber
Berths: 6

Engine: Perkins 50 HP
Fuel: Diesel, 100 gals.
Head: Standard, shower
Galley: 3-burner propane, oven
Water: 160 gals.
Rating: None
Designers: Ron Holland and
    Garry Hoyt

*Pilothouse schooner. Unstayed. Two vangs. Modern hull lines.
Forward port long and low, rear port large.*

This cruiser was designed to offer the advantages of a schooner but with improved windward sailing characteristics. Since there is no forestay it cannot sag, and upwind performance is improved. The pilothouse is very low and does not block vision from the cockpit.

There is a private cabin aft reached from the pilothouse. It has a private head, hanging lockers, shelves, and a double berth. The pilothouse has a settee-double berth to port. Opposite is the below-deck steering position with a captain's chair, the instrumentation, and a navigation station. The galley is large and U-shaped. Opposite is a second head with molded fiberglass shower stall. The forecabin has a double berth, hanging lockers, and a seat. Ventilation is through four hatches and two opening ports. The hatches are over the forecabin, forward head, galley, and main cabin. The ports are in the aft cabin.

Boat control, as in most Hoyt designs, is intended to be from the cockpit. Two winches and sheet stoppers are centrally located for the main and mizzen sheets, halyards, reef lines, and vangs. There is a full-length toe-rail. Both steering positions use wheels.

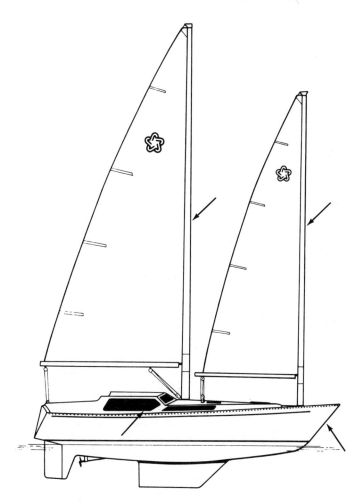

Freedom 39

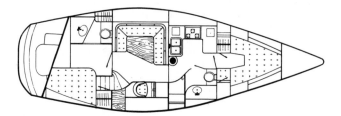

Nautical 39

Length: 39 ft. LOA;
   32 ft. 6 in. LWL
Beam: 12 ft.
Draft: 5 ft. 4 in.
Displacement: 22,500 lbs.
Sail area: Sloop: main, 314 sq. ft.,
   100% foretriangle, 363 sq. ft.
Hull: FRP
Spars: Aluminum

Berths: 8
Engine: 50 HP
Fuel. Diesel, 60 gals.
Head: Two, standard, shower
Galley: 3-burner, oven
Water: 200 gals.
Rating: None
Designers: Charles Morgan,
   Roger Warren

Sloop or ketch. Center cockpit. Aft cabin has raised deck. Transom portlights. Water line long in relation to LOA.

The Nautical 39 is the smallest of the line, with other boats at 56 and 60 feet. With three cabins, two full heads, lots of water and fuel, and a center cockpit, she is designed for cruising. A ketch is also available.

In the forecabin the vee berths can convert to a double with a filler. There is a hanging locker as well as an overhead hatch. Access to the full head is private. Just aft is stowage and a second door to the head. In the main cabin the dinette is fixed, but the port settee converts to a double. All ports open, and there are hatches both here and in the aft cabin. The galley has a 12-cubic-foot icebox, and refrigeration is available. Outboard the passageway is a very large chart table/workbench. A door allows access to the engine room. The aft cabin has a private head and shower, dressing table, hanging locker, and shelves.

In the cockpit, winch bases are molded in, and two can be accommodated on each side. There are genoa tracks and a three-point traveler. Two sheet winches are provided, as is a winch for the mainsheet and two mast-mounted halyard winches. Handrails, toe-rails, and other exterior trim are teak. There is a roller in the bow for the anchor. Steering is pedestal wheel.

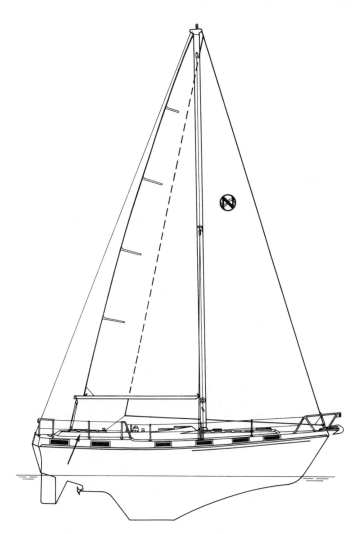

Nautical 39

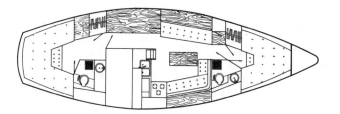

Baltic 40

Length: 39.37 ft. LOA;
 32.73 ft. LWL
Beam: 12.73 ft.
Draft: 7.15 ft.
Displacement: 14,900 lbs.
Sail Area: I is 53.81 ft.;
 J, 15.11 ft.;
 P, 47.90 ft.; and E, 15.63 ft.
Spars: Anodized aluminum

Berths: 4
Hull: FRP, balsa core
Engine: Yanmar 34 HP
Fuel: Diesel, 33 gals.
Head: Standard, shower
Water: 50 gals.
Rating: IOR 25.7
Designers: Judel/Vrolijk and
 Baltic Yachts

Tall mast, sleek design with long, low coach roof. Sharp bow.

Baltic is a Finnish builder, and the 40, with its winged keel, is designed for both racing and cruising. The boat looks fast, and is, but notice that sleeping space is limited in the cruising version shown. A second layout is available for a crew of nine. The racing intent shows in the narrow water line, with a light, shallow hull, but with a significant amount of ballast making the boat relatively stiff, and allowing for a masthead rig.

The cabin plan shown has a stateroom fore and aft, and each may have a separate head if desired. As shown, there is only one head, which places the saloon unusually far forward, and the mast stepping through the middle of the saloon. With a second head forward, the mast is in the more common position, at the forward end of the saloon. With a single head, there are two opposing settees; in the double head version, the navigation station is opposite a U-shaped settee. Just aft is the galley, to starboard, at the bottom of the companionway steps. It has a gimbaled propane stove and oven, a stainless steel icebox, and a stainless sink. A foot-operated pump provides both fresh water and seawater. The owner's cabin has a king-size berth, a hanging locker, seating to port and starboard, and storage space. Note the position of the companionway, well forward, with the head accessible from either the owner's or the main cabin.

Standing rigging is rod. The backstay has hydraulic adjustment. Main sheeting runs forward to the mast, then aft to the winch on the bridge deck. There are genoa tracks, with cars. Winches are provided for the main, genoa, and spinnaker halyards and for the main sheet. Two each serve the genoa and spinnaker sheets, and there is one for the reefing and the Cunningham. The mast has three spreaders, and halyards are internal. Reefing is slab. Windows in the trunk are fixed, but there are a number of opening ports and hatches. The deck is teak.

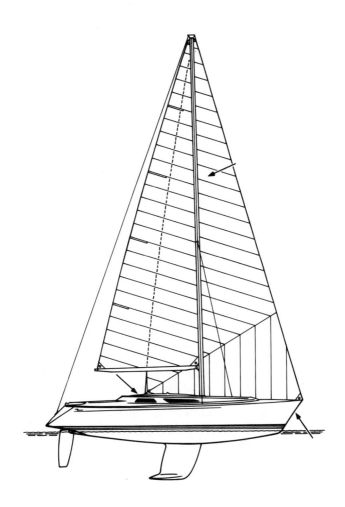

Baltic 40

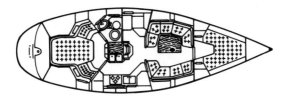

Islander 40

Length: 39 ft. 6½ in. LOA;
 30 ft. 10 in. LWL
Beam: 11 ft. 10 in.
Draft: 7 ft. 2 in.; or 5 ft. 1 in.
 (shoal)
Displacement: 17,000 lbs.
Sail area: Main, 297 sq. ft.;
 100% foretriangle, 437 sq. ft.
Hull: FRP

Spars: Aluminum
Berths: 6
Engine: Pathfinder 42 HP
Fuel. Diesel, 38 gals.
Head: Standard, shower
Galley: 3-burner propane, oven
Water: 48 gals.
Rating: PHRF 82 average
Designer: Doug Peterson

Rudder partially exposed. Reverse transom. Note main sheeting. Straight bow.

The Islander 40 is available with either deep keel or shoal draft. The latter has a 297-square-foot main and a 100 percent foretriangle with a 421-square-foot area.

The forecabin is private and has its own access to the head. There are two berths, which may be converted to sail storage. There are also drawers and a hanging locker. Aft to starboard is a hanging locker with sliding door. The head has hot and cold pressure water and a hand-held shower with teak grating over the sump. In the main cabin is a settee-berth to starboard and a second to port with a pilot berth over. The navigation area is large and has space for electronics. Both pressure water and a footpump serve the galley. To starboard is a large quarter berth. Six ports open and there are both forward and midcabin hatches. Wood is oiled teak.

On deck, stowage includes an anchor well, two seat lockers, and two lazarettes. The main has a traveler on the coach roof. All sheets and halyards lead to the cockpit or to the cabin roof aft of the mast. There are two jib winches, one for the main and one for the jib halyards, and secondary winches are optional. There is a topping lift, internal outhaul, and internal reefing. The vang bale is designed for hydraulics. A baby stay package with track, car, and other necessary gear is included.

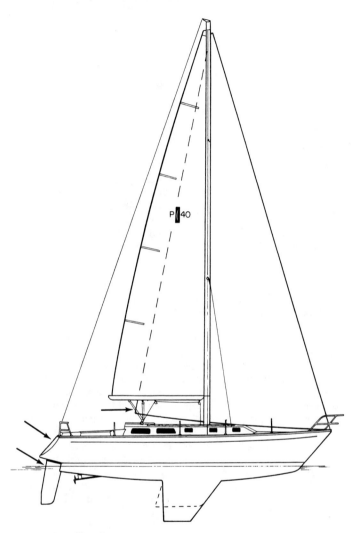

Islander 40

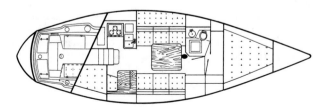

C & C 40

Length: 39 ft. 7 in. LOA;
   31 ft. 4 in. LWL
Beam: 12 ft. 8 in.
Draft: 7 ft. (keel)
Displacement: 17,100 lbs.
Sail area: Main and 100%
   foretriangle, 742 sq. ft.
Hull: FRP, balsa core
Spars: Aluminum

Berths: 7
Engine: Standard
Head: Standard, shower
Galley: 3-burner propane, oven
Water: 60 gals.
Rating: Wide variation
   depending upon keel and rig
   height; PHRF from 84 to 102
Designer: C & C Design Group

Very sharp bow. Maximum beam amidships. Very short counter. Reverse transom. Low cabin profile.

The model shown is aft cabin. Previous C & C 40s had the head forward. The designers obtained space by moving the companionway forward. This necessitated moving the traveler from the cabin roof to the bridge deck. As noted in rating data above, various models are available. Only one mast height is shown, but note the shallow keel, deep keel, and swing keel. In any case, entry is fine and the forefoot is deep. The V forward becomes a U further aft. The spade rudder is high aspect.

The aft cabin has a double berth to port. There is a hanging locker and a seat. There are two doors for the head, one from the aft cabin and one from the main cabin. The galley is to port, and the large navigation station is opposite. A hanging locker is behind the navigator's seat. In the main cabin the double berth is to port. The midships table folds. Pilot berths are available. A double berth, a bureau, and hanging lockers are forward. The forward cabin has a door for privacy. The number of opening ports varies by model, but the minimum is two. Hatches are above the head, the aft cabin, the main cabin (three), and the forward cabin.

The cockpit is T-shaped and has pedestal-wheel steering. Genoa tracks are inboard, but there is also a slotted toe-rail. The deck plan shows six winches just aft of the mast, two secondary at the cockpit. Some photographs show variations. There is a locker for the anchor.

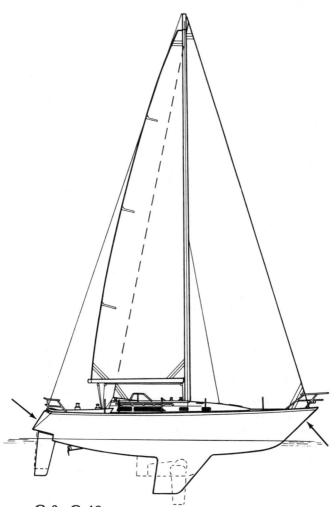

C & C 40

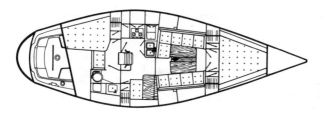

Nordic 40

Length: 39 ft. 8½ in. LOA;
　32 ft. 6 in. LWL
Beam: 12 ft. 5 in.
Draft: 6 ft. 4 in. (deep);
　or 5 ft. 6 in. (shoal)
Displacement: 18,000 lbs.
Sail area: Main, 336 sq. ft.;
　100% foretriangle, 420 sq. ft.
Hull: FRP

Spars: Painted aluminum
Berths: 6
Engine: Universal 32 HP
Fuel: Diesel, 55 gals.
Head: Standard
Galley: 3-burner propane, oven
Water: 130 gals.
Rating: PHRF 105
Designer: Robert H. Perry

Straight bow parallel to reverse transom. Note portlight arrangement. Running backstays.

The Nordic shows many of the hull features that have become popular since the late sixties. The hull is fine forward, has a short underwater length, and flattens aft toward the skeg and the spade rudder. The keel is short, thin, and quite deep. Overhangs are short.

In the forecabin are vee berths and a hanging locker, with a skylight-hatch above. The head is large and has a molded fiberglass shower stall with seat. Opposite are lockers and a shelf. In the saloon the L-shaped settee and folding table are to port with another settee to starboard. Aft is a small private cabin with a double quarter berth, hanging locker, and a chart table with swing-away seat. The U-shaped galley across is also large. There is a nine-cubic-foot icebox. Propane for the stove is kept aft in the lazarette well. Provisions for light and air include three hatches at the companionway, main cabin, and forecabin; four Dorade boxes with cowls; two fixed windows; and six opening portlights.

Control lines are internal and include five halyards, a topping lift, a spinnaker-pole topping lift, and three reef lines. Seven winches are standard. There are two primary, one for the genoa halyard, one for the main halyard, one for the main sheet, and one for reefing and for the outhaul. The toe-rail is slotted and there is an inboard sheeting track. Shrouds are inboard. The traveler is mounted on the cabin roof. Backstay adjustment can be added.

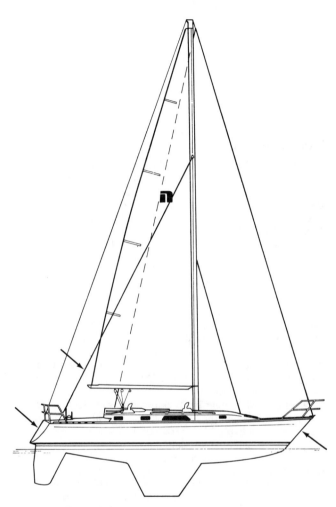

Nordic 40

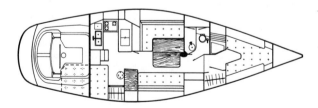

Concordia Yawl

Length: 39 ft. 10 in. LOA;
    28 ft. 6 in. LWL
Beam: 10 ft. 3 in.
Draft: 5 ft. 8 in.
Displacement: 18,000 lbs.
Sail area: Total, 650 sq. ft.
Hull: Mahogany
Spars: Wood

Berths: 4
Engine: Gray 30 HP
Fuel: Gasoline, 20 gals.
Head: Standard, shower
Galley: Alcohol
Water: 60 gals.
Rating: PHRF 168 approx.
Designer: C. Raymond Hunt

Wood hull and spars. Mizzen sheets to transom. Long counter. Jumper stays on both masts.

The Concordia was first built in 1938, but the majority of the boats were built after World War II. On most boats many of the items listed, such as the gasoline engine and wood spars, have certainly changed. While this classic yawl is no longer built, most of the boats are still sailing. "Malay" and "Babe" both won the Bermuda race.

Most hulls were built by Abeking and Rasmussen in Germany and finished in the United States. The cabin plan shown is typical and has two folding berths in the forward cabin with seats under. A sail bin with slatted floor is in the forepeak. There is a door for privacy. Just aft to port is the head, and there are five lockers opposite. In the main cabin the berths fold to form backrests, and the central table folds. The galley lies across the boat, with icebox and sink to port and the stove to starboard.

Decks are canvas-covered. All plank fastenings and hardware are bronze, as are the winches. Two skylights, one over the main cabin and one over the forecabin, provide light. Dinghy chocks are on the cabin roof.

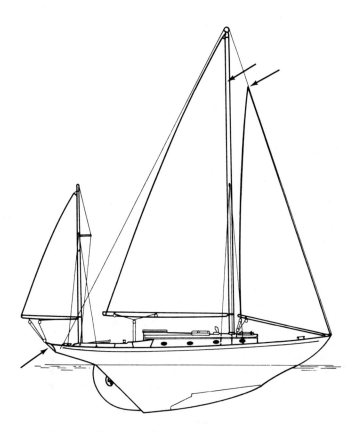

Concordia Yawl

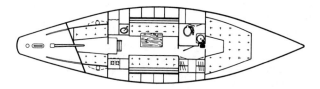

Endeavour 40

Length: 40 ft. LOA; 32 ft. LWL
Beam: 13 ft.
Draft: 5 ft.
Displacement: 25,000 lbs.
Sail area: Sloop: main,
    338 sq. ft.; 100% foretriangle,
    405 sq. ft.
Hull: FRP
Spars: Aluminum

Berths: 6
Engine: Perkins 50 HP
Fuel: Diesel, 75 gals.
Head: Two, standard, shower
Galley: 3-burner alcohol, oven
Water: 135 gals.
Rating: PHRF 126
Designer: Endeavour Yachts

Sometimes a ketch. Center cockpit fairly far aft. Four forward ports rectangular, aft ports more oval. Sweeping sheer, with off-set upwards amidships.

Endeavour is a big, comfortable cruiser intended for extended trips. Note that both fuel and water capacity are high. Ballast/displacement ratio is 36 percent. The cockpit, like most center cockpits, is high and therefore dry.

The galley is set beside the companionway and does not obstruct traffic. It is still close enough to the main seating area to allow the cook to communicate. There is hot and cold pressure water, a freshwater pump, and refrigeration. The navigation station is also aft of the ladder. Here, the table folds down out of the way allowing access to the seat. Going aft there is a step down to the passageway. The central engine room is accessible, and a workbench, hanging locker, and stowage are outboard. The aft cabin is one step up. The aft cabin has a double berth, a chest of drawers, and a private head. The main cabin has a central folding table and two settees. Lockers are suspended and have paneled doors. The head forward has two doors so that it may be entered either from the forecabin or from aft. There is pressure water and a shower. Opposite are hanging lockers and drawers.

Storage on deck includes two lazarette bins, an anchor well, and an insulated locker in the cockpit. There is a traveler, as well as slab reefing and a topping lift. Two winches are for the main and jib halyards, one is for the mainsheet, and there are two for genoa sheets. There are 16 opening ports and 4 cabin-top hatches. Teak is used on deck and below.

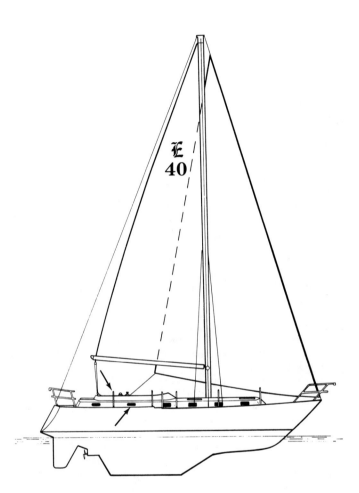

Endeavour 40

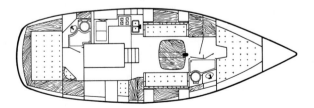

Bristol 40

Length: 40 ft. 2 in. LOA;
27 ft. 6½ in. LWL
Beam: 10 ft. 9 in.
Draft: 5 ft. 4½ in.
Displacement: 17,580 lbs.
Sail area: Main, 317 sq. ft.; jib,
265 sq. ft.; no.1 genoa, 495
sq. ft.; spinnaker, 1189 sq. ft.
Hull: FRP

Spars: Aluminum
Berths: 6
Engine: Westerbeke
Fuel: Diesel, 31 gals.
Head: Standard
Galley: 3-burner alcohol, oven
Water: 130 gals.
Rating: PHRF 166 average
Designer: Ted Hood

Classic lines. Full keel. Long bow. Foredeck ventilators. May be rigged as yawl.

The Bristol 40 is designed as a racer-cruiser. Many options, including a yawl rig, and several interior layouts are available for the owner who favors cruising. This boat, with its long bow and counter and full keel, is not for round-the-marker sailing, but it will do well on longer races.

The layout shown is quite traditional, with the galley aft to port with an opposing navigator's station. Some photographs show this arrangement flipped, and the nav station coupled with a quarter berth. A dinette, used as a double berth, is shown to port. The starboard berth and a pipe berth above are standard. The portside head has a draining floor for the shower. There is a lot of storage, with 10 drawers and 2 shelf compartments. The head has doors to both the forecabin and the main saloon. Note the cross bulkhead at the mast. The forecabin has vee berths and a hanging locker. A hatch above this cabin is double-hinged and will open fore or aft.

There is an Edson wheel. The bow pulpit, stern rail, genoa tracks, and anchor roller on the stem are provided. Two primary, two secondary, and a jib-halyard winch come with the boat. There is jiffy reefing.

Legend 40.5

Length: 40 ft. 2 in. LOA;
  35 ft. 4 in. LWL
Beam: 13 ft. 5 in.
Draft: 4 ft. 10 in. (Bulb-wing)
Displacement: 20,000 lbs.
Sail area: 773 sq. ft. (100% FT)
Hull: FRP, balsa core
Spars: Anodized aluminum
Berths: 6

Engine: Yanmar 50 HP
Fuel: Diesel, 40 gal.
Galley: 3-burner CNG
Head: Two, standard
Water: 105 gal.
Rating: Not given
Designer: Warren Luhrs and
  Hunter Design Group

Tall rig. Curved reverse transom. Spreaders sweep aft. Straight bow.

The boat is designed for cruising, and consideration is given to doing so short-handed.

The main is fully battened, and the headsails are relatively small. Furling and reefing are designed as simplified systems. The interior is light, well ventilated, and spacious. There are nine opening hatches and eight opening ports, as well as large fixed lights. Accomodations are in two staterooms, with a third stateroom aft as an option. The third stateroom is attained by dividing the aft stateroom into two. The forward stateroom has a private head and hanging lockers. The saloon is just aft, and has U seating with an opposing settee. The dinette converts to a double berth. To port is the navigation station, and an L-shaped galley across. The galley has top- and front-opening refrigeration, a freezer, Corian counter tops, and a hot and cold pressure water system. The accomodation ladder sits atop the engine and has two "flights." Just in front, and to starboard, is a second head. The aft stateroom has an athwartships double berth and two hanging lockers. Trim throughout is teak.

The 130% genoa has roller furling. Halyards are internal, with two two-speed self-tailing winches. Genoa tracks are anodized aluminum, as is all aluminum, and there are two more winches, also self-tailing. There is a boom vang, and a traveler for the main. The cockpit is T-shaped, with a walk-thru transom leading to a swim platform with a stowable ladder, a shower, and two storage lockers. The cockpit has a table, three storage lockers, and standard instrumentation, including a compass, knotmeter, depthsounder, engine panel, and VHF radio. There is a well for the anchor, and bow and stern pulpits.

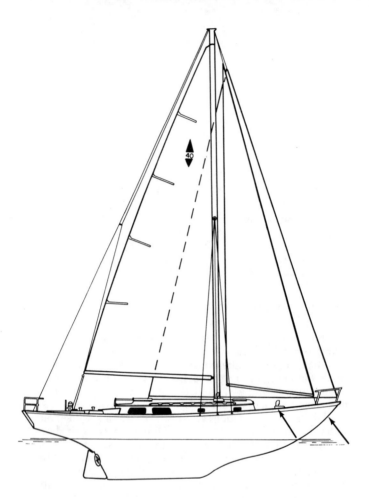

Bristol 40

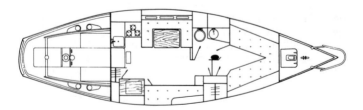

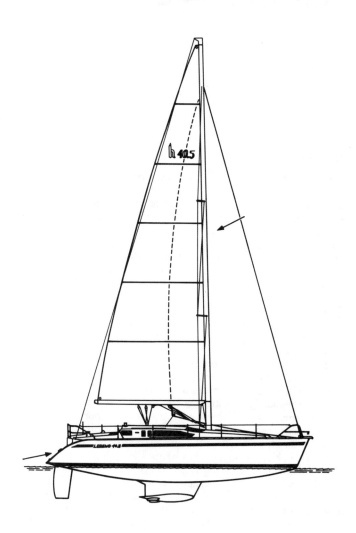

Legend 40.5

Bermuda 40

Length: 40 ft. 9 in. LOA;
27 ft. 10 in. LWL
Beam: 11 ft. 9 in.
Draft: 4 ft. 3 in. (board up);
or 8 ft. 9 in. (board down)
Displacement: 20,000 lbs.
Sail area: Main, 260 sq. ft.;
mizzen, 96 sq. ft.;
100% foretriangle, 427 sq. ft.
Hull: FRP

Spars: Coated aluminum
Berths: 6
Engine: Westerbeke 40 HP
Fuel: Diesel, 48 gals.
Head: Standard, shower
Galley: 3-burner propane, oven
Water: 110 gals.
Rating: PHRF 163 average
Designer: William H. Tripp, Jr.

Also a sloop. Note long curved counter leading to short vertical transom. Mizzen sheets to stern pulpit. Cruiser bow.

The centerboard on this cruiser is bronze and is operated by a worm gear. There is an override for grounding. Cabin layout may be modified, and there is a sloop model available.

The galley-navigation area crosses the boat at the foot of the companionway ladder. The stove and sink are to port. On the opposite side the icebox top serves as the chart table, and there is space allocated for electronics and chart stowage. Refrigeration is available. The main-cabin layout shown has two extension berths with pilot berths over and stowage under. The center table is drop leaf. Other storage space includes a bridge deck and a wet locker aft, shelves, bookcases, and a hanging locker forward to starboard. The head is opposite and has a teak grate over the shower pan. A bulkhead and a door give privacy to the forward cabin, which has vee berths with a seat between, a hanging locker, and stowage under the berths.

The cockpit has wheel steering, sail bins under the seats, and a lazarette. There are two secondary and two primary winches, and winches for the main and jib halyards, the mizzen halyard and sheet, and the mainsheet. Jiffy reefing on the main boom allows for two reef points. Coamings and trim are varnished teak.

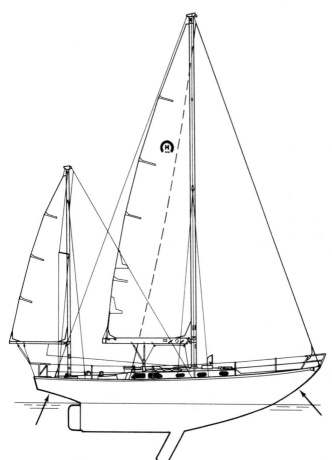

Bermuda 40

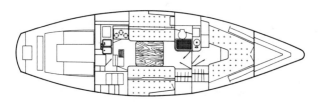

Dickerson 41

Length: 41 ft. LOA;
  31 ft. 6 in. LWL
Beam: 12 ft. 6 in.
Draft: 4 ft. 6 in.
Displacement: 24,500 lbs.
Sail area: Main, mizzen,
  and jib, 791 sq. ft.
Hull: FRP
Spars: Aluminum, epoxy finish

Engine: Westerbeke 50 HP
Fuel: Diesel, 100 gals.
Head: One standard; second
  depending on cabin plan
Galley: 3-burner alcohol
Water: Tank provided
Rating: None
Designer: Ernest Tucker

Aft deckhouse. Clipper bow, bowsprit. Identical ports uniformly spaced. May be rigged as a cutter or a ketch.

The 41 is the intermediate Dickerson. Dickerson also makes a 37 and a 50. All are based on Dickerson's long experience with cruising ketches. The 41 has a number of rig options, such as a cutter or ketch rig, a self-tacking forestaysail, twin headsails, and a roller-furling genoa.

There are also many optional cabin plans. The aft cabin shown has a private head/shower, but a navigation station may be substituted. The two berths may be converted to a double. In place of the workbench shown, storage may be located across from the engine-room doors. In the main cabin the dinette converts to a double. In this view, the navigation station is shown aft of a settee, but there may be two chairs with a table. Pilot berths are available. There is a hanging locker just aft of the forecabin door. The cabin itself has a private head, vee berths convertible to a double, and storage. Both heads have pressure water, as does the galley. Trim is teak; the sole is teak and holly. There are two port lights, three opening ports, and three acrylic hatches.

Teak is used above deck for handrails, toe-rails, hatch covers, and coamings. There are lockers in the coaming and an anchor locker in the bow. The aluminum spars are epoxy-painted. Standard equipment includes three halyard winches, genoa tracks and blocks, and two two-speed genoa winches. The main and mizzen have jiffy reefing.

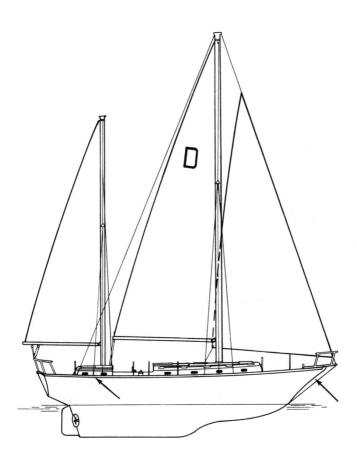

Dickerson 41

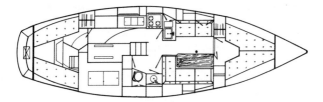

Lord Nelson 41

Length: 41 ft. LOA;
  36 ft. 2 in. LWL
Beam: 12 ft. 10 in.
Draft. 5 ft. 8 in.
Displacement: 30,500 lbs.
Sail area: Main, 395 sq. ft.;
  100% foretriangle, 661 sq. ft.
Hull: FRP
Spars: Painted aluminum

Berths: 58
Engine: BMW 50 HP
Fuel. 120 gals.
Head: Standard, shower
Galley: 3-burner propane,
  oven
Water: 200 gallons
Rating: None
Designer: Loren Hart

Double-ender. Deep sheer with high bow and stern. Pulpit on bowsprit. Boom gallows. Pronounced rub-rail.

The designer must be a navigator, as he has his own berth at the navigation station. This is a big cutter intended for cruising. Hull design is traditional, as are the finishing touches, such as actual belaying pins and a Samson post.

The galley, at the foot of the ladder, has a double sink. Hot and cold water is pressure, as is the case at the head and shower. The settee just forward is large and U-shaped. It converts to a double berth. The navigation station and its berth are opposite. Forward is a private cabin with side-entering double berth, curved settee, and hanging locker. It has its own entrance to the head. A second private cabin is aft. A double berth, seat, hanging locker, and sink are in this cabin. There are louvered doors on lockers and bookcases in each cabin. Three opening hatches and 14 opening portlights are bronze.

The cockpit is large and could be used for sleeping. Two winches are for halyards, one for the main sheet, two for staysail sheets and the halyards, and two for primary sheets. The main sheets to a traveler bridge. Of the two lazarette hatches, one is insulated for use as an icebox.

Lord Nelson 41

Newport 41

Length: 41 ft. LOA;
  32 ft. 3 in. LWL
Beam: 11 ft. 3 in.
Draft: 6 ft. 3 in.
Displacement: 18,000 lbs.
Sail area: Main and jib, 750 sq. ft.
Hull: FRP
Spars: Anodized aluminum

Berths: 7
Engine: Standard
Fuel: Diesel, 35 gals.
Head: Optional
Galley: 3-burner alcohol, oven
Water: 75 gals.
Rating: PHRF 114; D-PN 74.5
Designer: C & C Design Group

Spoon bow. Counter, reverse transom. Tall masthead rig. Mid-boom sheeting to cabin roof. One-and-two port arrangement.

Perhaps the most unusual aspect of the Newport 41 is the cluster of winches around the mast, all located on the cabin roof. There are five winches that almost complete a circle. These are all for halyards and vangs. All sheeting leads to the cockpit. There are two winches on the coach roof and two primary and two secondary winches at normal locations in the cockpit.

Cabin layout is quite normal. The main cabin has a quarter berth, nav station, and settee to starboard. The latter converts to a bunk, and a pilot berth over is optional. The galley to port is U-shaped with sink, icebox, stove, storage, and counter space. A trash bin is accessible from the cockpit. Forward is an L-shaped settee and fold-down table. The settee converts to a double berth. The head is forward to port and has a molded fiberglass shower pan. Water here and in the galley is manual, with pressure optional. The head has an opening port. Across from the head are two hanging lockers. The forward cabin is closed off with a curtain; there are drawers, a double berth, and a hanging locker. The chain locker may be reached from below. Ventilation is through two translucent hatches and two opening ports. There are also four fixed windows.

The traveler is mounted on the coach roof. The hard-anodized toe-rail accepts blocks, and an inside sheet track is optional. Above and below, trim is teak. The cockpit has wheel steering and two lockers. Some options are an internal outhaul, vang, head, saltwater pump in the galley, and spinnaker gear.

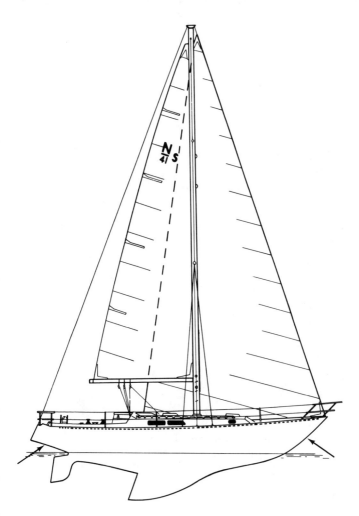

Newport 41

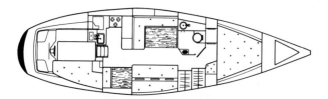

Morgan Out Island 41

Length: 41 ft. 3 in. LOA;
34 ft. LWL
Beam: 13 ft. 10 in.
Draft: 4 ft. 2 in.
Displacement: 27,000 lbs.
Sail area: Main, 312 sq. ft.;
100% foretriangle, 413 sq.
ft.; mizzen, 153 sq. ft.
Hull: FRP

Spars: Aluminum
Berths: 7
Engine: Perkins 62 HP
Fuel: Diesel, 90 gals.
Head: Two, marine; showers
Galley: 2-burner alcohol, oven
Water: 200 gals.
Rating: D-PN 87.0; PHRF 192
Designer: Morgan Yacht Inc.

Ketch. Center cockpit. Semiclipper bow. Only visible ports are aft. Curved coaming.

The Morgan Out Island 41 is one of the world's most popular cruising boats. Over 800 have been built, and the boat is used extensively in the charter industry. There is often roller furling for the jib. There are two double cabins that are really private; a main cabin with a double and a single; and in desperate cases, the nav station and workbench could be used for one person.

The aft cabin has entries through a passageway and through its own companionway. There are hanging lockers, a double berth, a private head, and a seat. Going through the passageway, a workbench is to port and the double-door access to the engine room to starboard. In the main cabin is the chart table, which has a 7-cubic-foot icebox below. The galley is at the foot of the main ladder and has a second icebox with 10-cubic-foot capacity, double sink, and pressure water. The saloon table is mounted on the bulkhead, and it stores. A door isolates the forward cabin with its vee berth, hanging locker, and separate head and shower. Wood is teak. Air and ventilation is through 14 opening ports, 2 transom opening ports, the companionways, aft and galley hatches, and a forecabin hatch. A prism in the cockpit sole admits light to the engine room.

On deck, there are full-length toe-rails for jib sheeting. Winches include two two-speed sheet winches, two halyard winches on the main mast, and one on the mizzen. Both main and mizzen have topping lifts, and there is a roller for the anchor. The cockpit has wheel steering and a seat locker. Teak is used for trim above and below.

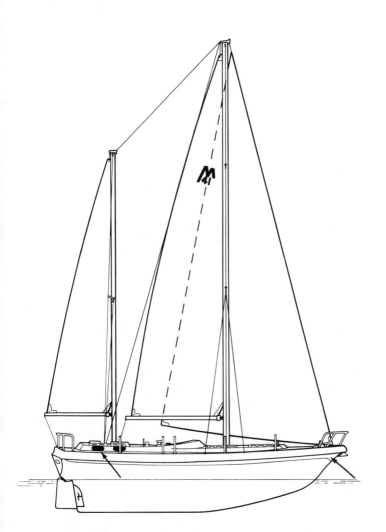

Morgan Out Island 41

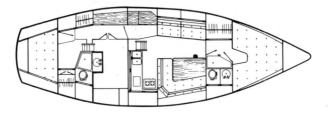

Albin Nimbus

Length: 41 ft. 6 in. LOA;
  34 ft. 2 in. LWL
Beam: 12 ft. 6 in.
Draft: 5 ft. 10 in.
Displacement: 21,500 lbs.
Sail area: Main, 368 sq. ft.; jib,
  486 sq. ft. (100%); various
  genoas and spinnakers
Hull: FRP
Spars: Polyurethane-coated
  aluminum

Berths: 8
Engine: Pathfinder 50 HP
Fuel: Diesel, 60 gals.
Head: Two
Galley: 3-burner propane, oven
Water: 120 gals.
Rating: PHRF 90-99
Designer: Kaufman and Ladd

High-aspect masthead rig. Backstay, running backstays. Cutter or sloop. Low, long ports.

Nimbus is a big auxiliary with three cabins, but with a tall, high-aspect rig for racing. Shrouds are inboard for good windward sheeting angles. The keel is relatively short and the rudder is well aft.

There is an aft master stateroom that will sleep three and has its own settee, vanity, hanging locker, and head with shower. The galley is to port midships and has two sinks and a large icebox. Opposite is the chart table, with chart stowage. Under the companionway stairs is a wet locker. The dinette converts to a double, and to starboard is a settee-berth. A second head with shower, a vee berth, and a hanging locker are forward. In all there are more than 40 drawers and lockers. The cabin and sole are finished in teak and holly. Ventilation is through six translucent opening hatches, two Dorade vents, and four deck cowls. There are also four deck prisms for lighting.

Above, the decks are teak. There are six internal halyards, with one for the main, two for genoas, two for the spinnaker, and one for the staysail. They lead to four halyard winches and four two-speed self-tailing winches. Both spinnaker pole and boom have topping lifts. The genoa and the spinnaker pole have tracks and cars. There is a foredeck anchor storage locker and two aft lazarettes.

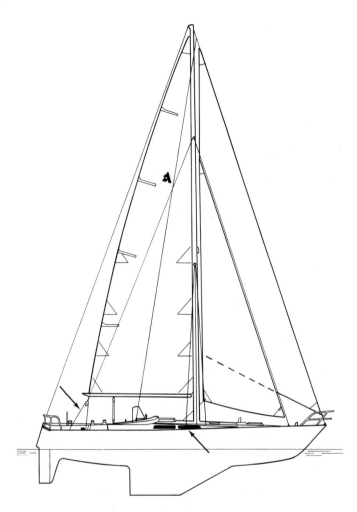

Albin Nimbus

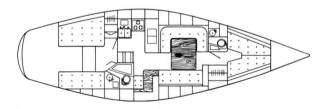

Irwin 41

Length: 41 ft. 8 in. LOA;
33 ft. 4 in. LWL,
Beam: 13 ft. 4 in.
Draft: 4 ft. 6 in. (shoal)
Displacement: 25,000 lbs.
approx.
Sail area: Total, 959.8 sq. ft.
Hull: FRP
Spars: Coated aluminum

Berths: 7
Engine: Perkins 62 HP
Fuel: Diesel, 150 gals.
Head: Two separate with showers
Galley: 3-burner propane, oven
Water: 150 gals. approx.
Rating: None
Designer: Ted Irwin

Ketch. Dinghy may be on davits. Bowsprit with pulpit, two foresails. Main has double backstay.

The Irwin 41 was designed as a blue-water cruiser. The hull is moderate displacement, the keel is long, and the ballast/displacement ratio is 32 percent. Optional hulls are a centerboard/keel and a deep keel. The sail plan is balanced and designed to be handled by two people.

The passageway to the aft cabin passes an optional entertainment center with wet bar, stereo, and television. It continues past the chart table. The cabin itself has hanging lockers, a double berth, and a private head with shower. Forward at the companionway the galley is tucked away to starboard. At this location the sole is tile. The main saloon has a berth to starboard, and the port settee makes into a double with the table dropped. Forward there is storage to starboard and a second full head to port, reached from either the forward or the main cabin. The bow cabin has a vee berth.

The main sheets to the aft coaming, has a winch, and is four-part purchase. There are winches for the main halyard, the genoa sheets, the jib and mizzen halyards, and the mizzen sheets. Both the main and the mizzen have vangs and topping lifts. The main has slab reefing on the boom; both booms have internal outhauls. Handrails, toe-rails, and coaming boards are teak. The bowsprit is aluminum and the pulpits are stainless steel. Seven cabin hatches open.

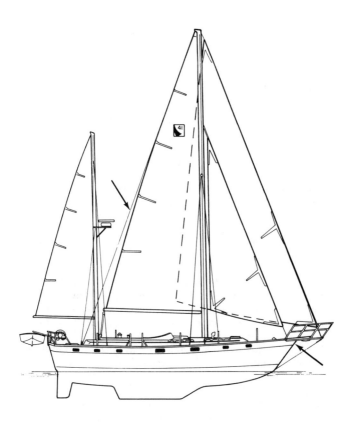

Irwin 41

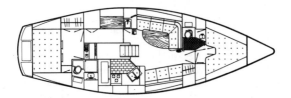

Landfall 43

Length: 42 ft. 1 in. LOA;
   34 ft. 5 in. LWL
Beam: 12 ft. 7-1/2 in.
Draft: 5 ft. 6 in.
Displacement: 24,600 lbs.
Sail area: Total with 100%
   foretriangle, 796 sq. ft.
Hull: FRP
Spars: Aluminum

Berths: 7
Engine. Westerbeke
Fuel: 60 gals.
Head: Two
Galley: 3-burner propane, oven
Water: 130 gals.
Rating: None
Designer: C & C Design Group

Ketch or sloop. Center cockpit. Stanchions at hatches forward and aft of the mast.

The Landfall 43 evolved from her sister ships, the 48 and the 35. Draft is moderate and the fin keel is fairly long. The rudder is semibalanced. The designers claim particular success controlling helm characteristics when the boat is heeled, thus allowing for more sail area in light air.

As might be expected in a boat this large, systems are sophisticated. Refrigeration and hot and cold pressure water are standard; there is optional air conditioning and heating; and space designed to accept a diesel generator is under the workbench. The aft cabin is large and has a hanging locker and a private head. The passageway forward has a workbench outboard and engine access inboard. Entering the main cabin, the large galley is to port and the navigation station just ahead. In the main cabin is a U-shaped dinette that converts to a double and a settee across. There are six lockers behind the berths. Forward is a head, accessible from either the main cabin or the forecabin. The forward cabin berth is a double, and there are lockers, hanging lockers, and other storage.

Sheeting is to a traveler on the aft-cabin roof. Winches are provided for the mainsheet, the genoa and main halyards, the outhaul and reefing system, and the primary foresail sheets. There are hatches over the aft, forward, and main cabins. Steering is pedestal wheel. A ketch rig is optional, as is roller furling.

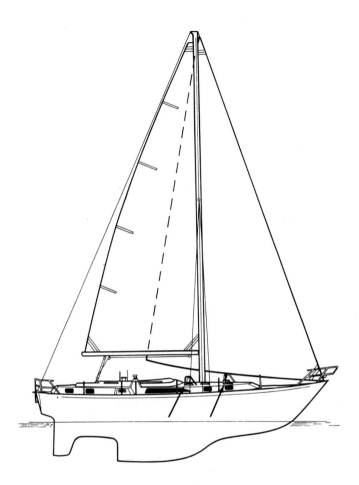

Landfall 43

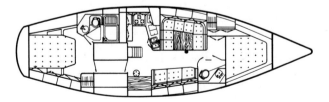

Tayana 37

Length: 42 ft. 2 in. LOA;
   30 ft. 10 in. LWL
Beam: 11 ft. 6 in.
Draft: 5 ft. 8 in.
Displacement: 22,500 lbs.
Sail area: Main, 342 sq. ft.; jib,
   292 sq. ft.; staysail, 230 sq, ft.
Hull: FRP
Spars: Spruce

Berths: 7
Engine: Yanmar 33 HP
Fuel: 90 gals.
Head: Standard
Galley: 3-burner propane, oven
Water: 100 gals.
Rating: PHRF 126
Designer: Robert Perry

Cutter or ketch. Double-ended. Boom gallows. Pilothouse or trunk cabin. Bowsprit with pulpit.

When the Tayana is built with a pilothouse, the quarter berth and chart table are replaced by the interior helm, a seat, and a wet locker. The galley is rearranged to provide another seat to port. Tayana is in many respects — perhaps except for the double-ended design — typical of the many high-performance designs built today that retain a traditional appearance.

In the trunk-cabin version the U-shaped galley, with refrigerator, is to port at the foot of the companionway. The quarter berth opposite serves as the seat for the navigation station. The large settee converts to a double, and the seat opposite is also a berth. There is a pilot berth above the latter. Cabin trim is teak. The head, forward to port, has hot and cold pressure waters and a teak grating over the shower sump. To starboard is a large storage area with drawers, shelves, and two hanging lockers. There are shelves in the forward cabin and storage under the vee berths. Two doors give access to the forepeak. There are 11 bronze opening ports, a teak forward hatch, and a teak skylight.

Decks are teak, as are the coaming top and the cockpit seats. There are two travelers, with the main traveler located just forward of the companionway hatch. Two winches are provided for jib sheets, one for the mainsheet, one for the staysail, and three for halyards. Tracks for the genoa are on the toe-rail, and shrouds are outboard.

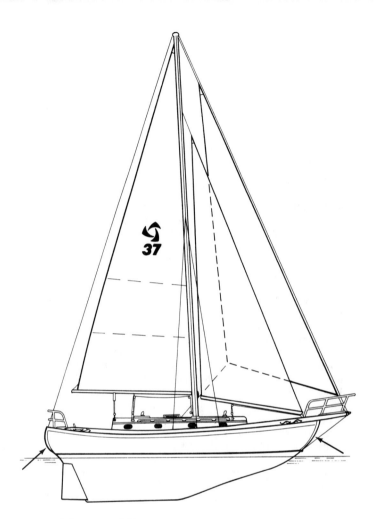

Tayana 37

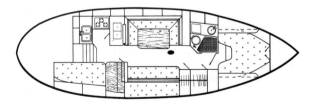

Caliber 40

Length: 42 ft. 6 in. LOA;
   32 ft. 6 in LWL
Beam: 12 ft. 8 in.
Draft: 5 ft.
Displacement: 21,600 lbs.
Sail Area: 739 sq. ft.
Hull: FRP
Spars: Anodized aluminum

Berths: 6
Engine: Yanmar 50 HP
Fuel: 46 gals.
Galley: Two burner LPG, oven
Water: 156 gals.
Rating: None
Designer: Michael McCreary

Masthead rig. Pulpit forward of bow on platform. Reverse transom. Cutter.

A big cutter for cruising, with high displacement, and lots of ballast for stability. There is a quick conversion available to change the cutter to a sloop rig. The forward stateroom has its own head — located in the foremost part of the boat. The shower is separate and is reached throught the head. Both have hot and cold pressure water. Just aft is a double berth, hanging lockers with cedar lining, and a vanity. An L-shaped settee to port converts to a bed for two, and there is a second settee opposite. Just aft, to port, is the galley, with a two-burner stove, an oven, and an 11-cubic-foot icebox. The stainless steel sink is a double. The nav station is located at the aft end of the galley. The second head lies to starboard and has two doors, so that it may be reached either from the aft stateroom or the main cabin. There are 14 opening portholes and seven hatches, as well as two deck cowls. Furnishings are teak.

Main boom sheeting is to a deck traveler, and then aft. Halyards are internal, and there are two backstays. Deck trim such as handrails and coaming caps are teak. Winches are provided for the main sheet, and the halyards, and there are two genoa winches. All are self-tailing and two speed. The topping lift is adjustable, and the outhaul is internal. The main has twin reef points, and the reefing lines are led aft. In the cockpit there is pedestal-wheel steering, and an insulated cold box. The stern is notched to provide a boarding platform, and the boarding ladder swings down for use. A hand shower allows for washing off.

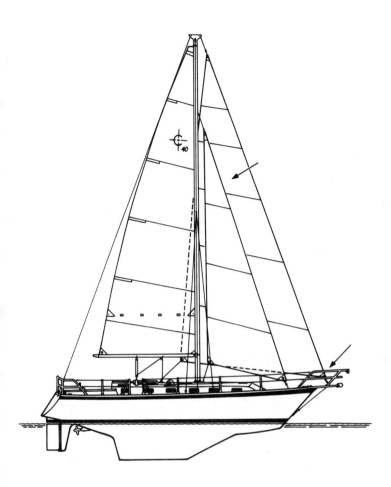

Caliber 40

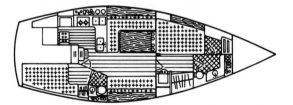

Nauticat 44

Length: 43 ft. 7 in. LOA;
    38 ft. 8 in. LWL
Beam: 12 ft. 1 in.
Draft: 6 ft.
Displacement: 39,700 lbs.
Sail area: Main, 306 sq. ft.;
    staysail, 118 sq. ft.; jib, 296
    sq. ft.; forestaysail, 96 sq. ft.
Hull: FRP

Spars: Aluminum
Berths: 6 or 7
Engine: Ford 120 HP
Fuel: Diesel, 285 gals.
Head: Two standard
Galley: 2-burner gas, oven
Water: 200 gals.
Rating: None
Designer: Nauticat Inc.

Motor sailer rigged as ketch, sloop, or schooner. Slight clipper bow, bowsprit. Stern ports. If ketch, main mounts over third port aft and mizzen over aft deck.

This big motor sailer is shown primarily because of its schooner rig. It is also included because of the wheelhouse and the cabin plan peculiar to a motor sailer. The large quantities of water and fuel give a cruising range under power of 900 nautical miles.

Typical of the breed, there are helms both inside and outside the wheelhouse. Various options are possible in the master cabin. A center berth is shown. In addition to the private head there is a hanging locker, and there are lots of drawers and cabinets. Ports open, and there is a skylight hatch. Passage to the main cabin is up and through the wheelhouse. The main cabin has an L-shaped settee, a navigation table, the helm, and the helmsman's seat. There is a sliding hatch above, and two sliding doors give access to the side decks. Forward and below is the main cabin. To port is a large U-shaped settee that seats eight and converts to a double berth. Another settee is to starboard. The galley is forward and has two stainless sinks and a refrigerator. A second head is across. Two berths, storage, a hanging locker, and an overhead hatch are in the forecabin.

Decks are teak plank, as is the rub strake. An anchor roller and genoa furling gear are forward. There are two halyard winches on each mast and four for the sheets.

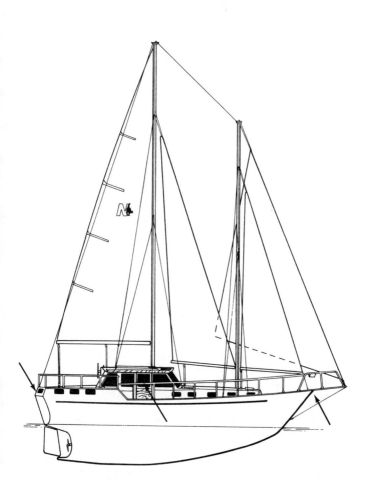

Nauticat 44

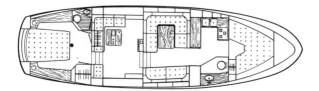

Worldcruiser 44

Length: 43 ft. 11 in. LOA;
  33 ft. 4 in. LWL
Beam: 11 ft.
Draft: 6 ft. 2 in.
Displacement: 23,000 lbs.
Sail area: Main, 280 sq. ft.;
  100% foretriangle, 356 sq. ft.;
  foresail, 136 sq. ft.;
  fisherman, 230 sq. ft.
Hull: FRP

Spars: Painted aluminum
Berths: 5
Engine: Varies; 25-50 HP
Fuel: Diesel, 60 gals.
Head: Standard, shower
Galley: 3-burner, oven
Water: 100 gals.
Rating: None
Designer: Bud Taplin

Traditional schooner. Might have a genoa and a gollywobbler.
Long overhangs. Bowsprit and boomkin.

Worldcruiser feels that the sails on a boat over 40 feet should be small enough to handle without a large crew and that two-masted rigs are the answer. In light weather, flying a genoa instead of the headsails, and with a gollywobbler in place of the foresail and fisherman, the boat has a total sail area of over 2,000 square feet.

Cabin layout is unusual. Aft of the ladder is a double berth to port. In the center, freestanding, is the engine box. To starboard are two desks, a bookcase, storage for charts, and a large hanging locker. Forward, the galley is across from the dinette, which can convert to a single berth. In the galley, water is pressure. A second work area is just forward and has the electrics behind and a bookcase, coffee table, and desk. A second double berth is to starboard, and a very large hanging locker and drawers ahead to port. The head is also very large and crosses the boat. The head has a hamper, linen storage, and general stowage. In the forepeak are separate sail and chain lockers. Trim is ash and teak. Four hatches are shown and all opening portlights are bronze.

The staysails have self-tending booms leading to travelers. The deckhouse may be extended forward of the mast, providing more headroom, or held between the masts. The deck aft of the main mast is flush, except for the distinct scuttle over the aft cabin.

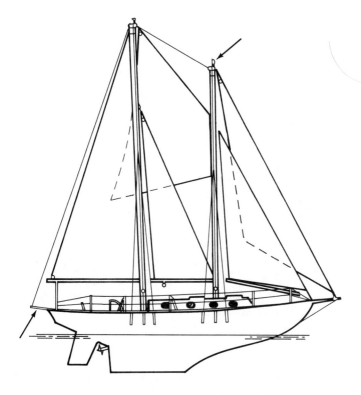

Worldcruiser 44

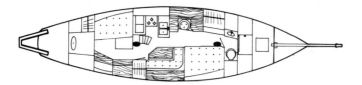

Alden 44

Length: 44 ft. 2 in. LOA; 34 ft. 1 in. LWL	*Berths:* 7
Beam: 12 ft. 6 in.	*Engine:* Perkins 4-108
Draft: 8 ft. 9 in.	*Fuel:* Diesel, 80 gals
Displacement: 24,500 lbs.	*Head:* Standard, shower
Sail area: Rated for IOR with 150% genoa, 1085.7 sq. ft.	*Galley:* Propane oven and stove
Hull: FRP, balsa core	*Water:* 160 gals.
Spars: Aluminum	*Rating:* D-PN 79.4 suspect; PHRF 99
	Designer: John G. Alden

Straight bow. Note porthole and ventilator arrangement. Cutter rig. Counter and reverse transom.

The Alden is designed for IOR competition but has many cruising amenities. The hull is moderate displacement. She is claimed to be fast, dry, stiff, and close-winded.

There are two companionways, and the owner's stateroom is entered aft. Layouts vary. The one shown indicates two berths and the chart table, lockers, and a bureau. There is a hatch to port. The head, to port, and the galley, to starboard, are slightly behind the main companionway. The galley has hot and cold water, six drawers, and two lockers. There is a six-cubic-foot refrigerator and a four-foot freezer. The head is large and has access from both the aft stateroom and the main cabin. The main cabin has berths for two or, with a pilot berth, three. The table is drop leaf. Storage includes a hanging locker, bookshelves, and two storage lockers. Like the other ceilings, the main cabin ceiling is detailed with ash battens. The forward cabin has two berths, a hanging locker, and a chest of drawers. Ventilation includes seven opening ports and five translucent hatches.

Most winches are self-tailing. There are two for the main halyard, two for the genoa, two for the spinnaker, one for the Cunningham, one for the outhaul, two for the staysail halyard, two primary, two secondary, two for the mainsheet, two for the genoa sheets, and two for spinnaker sheets. There is a topping lift. A club-footed staysail is available. For racing, the staysail stay is removed.

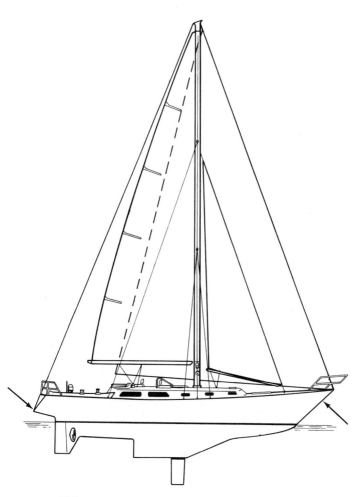

Alden 44

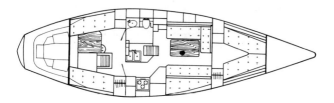

Bayfield 40

Length: 45 ft. 6 in. LOA;
   30 ft. 6 in. LWL
Beam: 12 ft.
Draft: 4 ft. 11 in.
Displacement: 21,000 lbs.
Sail area: Topsail, staysail, main,
   and mizzen: 1109 sq. ft. total
Hull: FRP
Spars: Aluminum

Berths: 6
Engine: Westerbeke 52 HP
Fuel: Not stated
Head: Standard
Galley: 2-burner propane
Water: 100 gals.
Rating: None
Designer: Ted Gozzard

Ketch. Note counter. Clipper bow and bowsprit. Double head-sails.

The lines of the hull are traditional. The foresail rig is unusual in a big ketch. Cabin layout, with a midships galley and no vee berths, is distinctly different.

The companionway lands at two aft berths, which may be converted to small staterooms. Both are identical, with top hatch, opening port, drawers, and a hanging locker. Both have double berths. Privacy is afforded by bulkhead panels that may be raised, and by sliding doors. Forward to starboard is a large dining area that converts to a double berth. The table has swing-out seats midships. To port is a full navigation station. There is a swivel chair, and the table will take a full-sized chart. The galley has electric refrigeration and two opening ports. A large hanging locker is opposite. Forward, the shower is separate from the rest of the head. Two hatches and two ports open. The forepeak stowage for sails and anchors is reached from the deck.

The 40 is a big boat with a lot of standard equipment. Sails (top, stay, main, and mizzen) are included. There are 10 opening ports and 4 opening hatches. The large skylight just aft of the mainmast also opens. There are 11 winches. Steering is wheel.

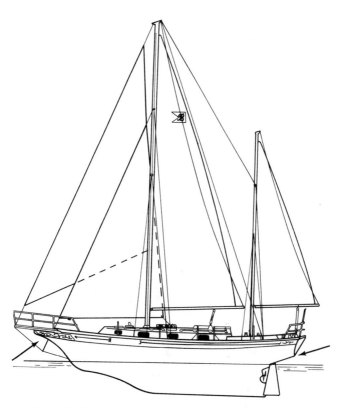

Bayfield 40

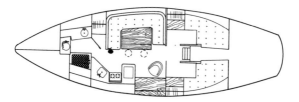

Appendix
Glossary
Index

One-Design Class Associations

National A Scow Class
  Association
Jim Smith
P. O. Box 311
Fontana, WI 53125

Int'l Abbott 33 Class
  Association
Harold Hoffman
4325 Elmway Dr.
Toledo, OH 43614

U.S. Albacore Association
Daphne Byron
13701 Beauwick Ct.
Silver Spring, MD 20906

Atlantic Class Association
Wilma Lauricella
255 Milbank Ave.
Greenwich, CT 06830

Baum Cat 3-Meter Sailing
  Association
Lawrence Baum
6619 132 Ave. NE, Ste. 200
Kirkland, WA 98033

New England Beetle Cat Boat
  Association
Dorothy M. Davis
195 Rosemary St. # 4
Needham, MA 02194

Blue Jay Class Association
Julie A. Dunbar
937 Lagoon Ln.
Mantoloking, NJ 08738

Buccaneer Class Association
Ursuala Brinkmann
31 Old Trolley Way
Rowayton, CT 06853

Bullseye Class Association
Emily L. Wick
37 Atlantic Ave.
Rockport, MA 01966

Byte Class Association
Janet Holland
65 Allan Pt.
Dorval, PQ Canada H9S2Z3

National C Scow Class
  Association
Jim Smith
P. O. Box 311
Fontana, WI 53125

National C Scow Sailing
  Association
David B. Bohl
835 The Pines
Hinsdale, IL 60521

Cal 20 Class Association
Jennifer Ellis
5901 Warner Ave. Ste. 149
Huntington Beach, CA 92649

Cape Cod Frosty Class
  Association
Jennifer Kano
P. O. Box 652
Cataumet, MA 02534

Capri 14.2 National
Association
David Dodell
10250 N. 92nd St., Ste. 210
Scottsdale, AR 85258

Capril 22 National
Association
Mike Gardiner
3337 W. Overbrook Dr.
Peoria, IL 61604

Catalina 22 Nat'l Sailing
Association
Joyce Seale
P. O. Box 30368
Phoenix, AZ 85046

Catalina 25 National
Association
Christy Morgan
5011 Revere Ave. NW
Massillon, OH 44646

Catalina 27 Association
Steve Reinhart
1450 Oakland R. SP66
San Jose, CA 95112

Catalina 30 Class Association
Doris Goodale
9141 Mahalo Dr.
Huntington Beach, CA 92646

Catalina 34 National
Association
Richard Barck
23041 Tiagua
Mission Viejo, CA 92692

Catalina 36 Association
Ed Hoffman
10710 Montgomery Dr.
Manassas, VA 22111

Celebrity Class YRA
Theodore B. Conklin
Box 1408
Westhampton Beach, NY
11978

Christmas Cove One-Design
Association
Neal Prescott
RR2, Box 413C
Yarmouth, ME 04096

Comet Class YRA
Larry Lefczik
43 S. Lakeside Dr. W
Medford, NJ 08055

Int'l Contender Class
Association
Jerry White
P. O. Box 831
Summerland, CA 93067

Coronado 15 Class Racing
Association
Ted Stoker
45157 El Roble St.
Long Beach, CA 90815

Crescent Sloop Class
Association
John Houston
1370 Nicolet
Detroit, MI 48207

Crusing One-Design Division
CBYRA, Ste. 201
Annapolis, MD 21403

Day Sailer Association
Patricia Skeen
1936 Danebo
Eugene, OR 97402

D.C. 10 Class Association
Carol Newman
Box 498
Woods Hole, MA 02543

American Int'l Dragon
Association
David Washatka
2244 Kilbirnie Dr.
Germantown, TN 38139

National Class E Scow
Association
Sherri Campbell
122 Laurel Ave.
Toms River, NJ 08753

El Toro International YRA
Helga Wolff
39673 Catamaban Ct.
Freemont, CA 94538

Ensign Class Association
Robin Durrschmidt
22 Locust Cir.
Rocky Hill, CT 06067

Int'l Etchells Class
Association
Pamela P. Smith
Box 30 Rte. 102A
Bass Harbor, ME 04653

U. S. Int'l Europe Class
Association
U. S. Sailing
P. O. Box 209
Newport, RI 02840

Express 27 National Class
Association
Bill Schwager
3350 Brittan Ave. #1
San Carlos, CA 94070

F-24 One-Design Class
Association
David Hahn
2917½ Havasupai Ave.
San Diego, CA 92117

U.S. Int'l Finn Class
Association
Gus Miller
600 Bristol Ferry Rd.
Portsmouth, RI 02871

U.S. Int'l Fireball Association
Scott Rovanpera
P. O. Box 3973
Walnut Creek, CA 94598

Int'l 505 Class Yacht Racing
Association
Ellen Ablow
22 Ridge Ct.
Woodside, CA 94062

Int'l Flying Dutchman
Class Org.
Dennis Anderson
215 Redcliffe Rd.
Greenville, SC 29615

FJ U.S.
Bruce Reichart
4032 W. 158th St.
Cleveland, OH 44135

Flying Scot Sailing
Association
Maryann Eubanks
3008 Millwood Ave.
Columbia, SC 29205

San Francisco Bay Folkboat
Association
Bill Madison
744 Funston Ave.
San Francisco, CA 94118

Force 5 Class Association
Clarence Mayott
238 Horizon Dr.
Edison, NJ 08817

Formula 500 Class
Association
Serge Pond
110 Esplande
Capitola Beach, CA 95010

Int'l 470 Association
James Appel
38 Arundel Rd.
Annapolis, MD 21401

U.S. Int'l 420 Class
Association
Elisabeth Wadsworth
66 Elmwood Ave.
Rye, NY 10580

One-Design 14 Class
   Association
Marshall Safffer
P. O. Box 176
Armonk, NY 10504

U.S. Int'l 14 Association
Dennis Williams
P. O. Box 30831
Seattle, WA 98103

Frers 33 Class Association
Paul Zabetakis
130 E. 77th St.
New York, NY 10021

Geary 18 Int'l YRA
Colin Jenkins
P. O. Box 101
North Bend, OR 97459

GP-14 Class Association
   of North America
Sandra Swenson
1734 Green St.
Philadelphia, PA 19130

H Class Association
William G. Harding
Box 1
Cataumet, MA 02534

Hampton One-Design
   Association
Scott D. Wolff
3385 Kings Neck Dr.
Virginia Beach, VA 23452

Hawkfarm One-Design Class
   Association
John Siegel
115 C. Southhampton Ln.
Santa Cruz, CA 95062

Highlander Class Association
Gordon Stafford
1674-A S. Elm St.
W. Carrolton, OH 45449

N.A. Hobie Class Association
Matt Bounds
31700 Middlebelt Rd.,
   Ste. 100
Farmington Hills, MI 48334

Int'l Hobie Class Association
P. O. Box 2855
Capistrano Beach, CA 92624

Ideal 18 Class Association
Frank R. Shumway, Jr.
100 Pattonwood Dr.
Rochester, NY 14617

U.S. Illusion 12 Class
   Association
David R. Forsman
212 Fox Hollow Ln.
Erie, PA 16511

Impulse 21 Class Association
Belinda Bates Owens
10610 Metric Dr. #145
Dallas, TX 75243

Interlake Sailing Class
   Association
Hans Haupt, Jr.
4738 N. Pennsylvania
Indianapolis, IN 46205

Int'l One-Design Class
   Association
Anthony Leggett
28 Old Fulton St., #5F
Brooklyn, NY 11201

J/22 Class Association
Carolyn Freeman
P. O. Box 843, 1st. & Main
Franklin, TN 37064

Int'l J/24 Class Association
Steve Podlich
612 Third St., Ste.4A
Annapolis, MD 21403

J/27 Class Association
Fred Hartner
656 Elliot Ct.
Somerville, NJ 08876

J/29 Class Association
Joel Hamburger
95 Penn Hill Dr.
Schnecksville, PA 18078

J/30 Class Association
Terry Rapp
P. O. Box 247
Riverside, NJ 08075

J/35 Class Association
David Nickerson
P. O. Box 227
Woodville, MA 01784

J/44 Class Association
Bob Johnstone
30 Walnut St.
Newport, RI 02840

Javelin Class Association
Gary Coryer
30 Central St.
Essex Junction, VT 05452

Jet 14 Class Association
Mary Ungemach
26 Pontiac Dr.
Wayne, NJ 07470

JY 15 Class Association
David Eck
1223 Pequoit Tr.
Stonington, CT 06378

San Francisco Bay Knarr
  Association
P. O. Box 2125
San Francisco, CA 94126

Int'l Laser Class Association
Allan Broadribb
8466 N. Lockwood Ridge Rd.
  328
Sarasota, FL 34243

U.S. Lechner Class
Lynn Hornosky-Lestock
P. O. Box 1412
Newport, RI 02840

Lido 14 Int'l Class
  Association
Anne Land
7435 Ashford Pl.
San Diego, CA 92111

Int'l Lightning Class
  Association
Donna Foote
808 High St.
Worthington, OH 43085

National M Scow Class
  Association
Jim Smith
P. O. Box 311
Fontana WI 53125

M-20 Sailing Association
Robert B. Witt
2881 Meritt Terr.
Port St. Lucie, FL 34952

U.S. Mariner Class
  Association
Rita Paleschuck
140 Redwood Dr.
East Hills, NY 11576

Mercury Class YRA
Jim Bradley
54 Lakewood Ave.
San Francisco, CA 94127

Milimeter Class Racing
  Association
Paaxton Davis
29 Oak Creek Ln.
San Carlos, CA 94070

U.S. Mirror Class Association
John M. Borthwick
5305 Marian Dr.
Lyndhurst, OH 44124

Mistral Class Association
Scott Steele
7222 Parkway Dr.
Dorsey, MD 21076

Mobjack Class Association
James Rice
206 Tabbs Ln.
Newport News, VA 23602

Int'l Nacra Class Association
Jack Young
1810 E. Borchard St.
Santa Ana, CA 92705

Narrasketuck One-Design
  Association
Donna Johnson
81 Jean Rd.
West Islip, NY 11795

National One-Design Class
  Association
Jolly Booth
1225 E. Bronson St.
South Bend, IN 46615

Int'l Nonsuch Association
Johnathan Ayers
317 Bay Ave.
Huntington, NY 11743

North American 40
  Association
John Martin
112 Vendome Rd.
Grosse Pte. Fams, MI 48236

Olson 25 Class Association
Bill Riess
6144 Wood Dr.
Oakland, CA 94611

Olson 30 Class Association
Jay Bennett
317 Bay Ave.
Huntington, NY 11743

Int'l 110 Class YRA
Will Craig
49 Vautrinot Ave.
Hull, MA 02045

U.S. Optimist Dinghy
  Association
Rick Bischoff
6500 Riviera Dr.
Coral Gables, FL 33146

Penguin Class Dinghy
  Association
Mark Kastel
1215 West George
Chicago, IL 60657

Prindle Class Association
Todd Smith
10965 Rochester Ave. #303
Los Angeles, CA 90024

Raner 23 Class Association
Ed Marks
3 Conservation Way
Scituate, MA 02066

National Rebel Class
  Association
Peggy Quiniff
421 Amherst Ave.
Des Plaines, IL 60016

Rhodes 19 Class Association
Arthur Mann
1100 Podras St., Ste. 2150
New Orleans, LA 70163

Rhodes Bantam Class
  Association
Kathy Burlitch
806 Hanshaw Rd.
Ithaca, NY 14850

S2 7.9 Class Association
David Grover
28988 Lake Park Dr.
Farmington Hills, MI 48331

Int'l Naples Sabot Association
Peggy Lenhart
690 Senate St.
Costa Mesa, CA 92627

San Juan 21 Class Association
Rick Ashworth
1204 Perry Loop
Kennewick, WA 99336

San Juan 24 Class Association
Ken Johnson
P. O. Box 70163
Seattle, WA 98107

Santana 20 Class Association
Chris Winnard
2841 Canon St.
San Diego, CA 97405

Schock 35 Class Association
Richard Schmidt
510 Cashmere Terr.
Los Angeles, CA 90049

National Shields Class
    Association
Ralph Walker
87 Nanepashemet St.
Marblehead, MA 01945

Snipe Class Int' Racing Assoc.
Thomas Payne
4096 Chestnut Dr.
Flowery Branch, GA 30542

U.S. Soling Association
Rose A. Hoeksema
1615 N. Cleveland #3N
Chicago, IL 60614

Sonar Class Association
Mike Rudnick
1 Possum Ln.
Rowayton, CT 06854

SR Max Class Association
Glenn Henderson
1150 19th St. N
St. Petersburg, FL 33713

SR 27 Class Association
Glenn Henderson
1150 19th St. N
St. Petersburg, FL 33713

Int'l Star Class YRA
Shery Hughes
1545 Waukegan Rd. #8
Glenview, IL 60025

U.S. Sunfish Class Association
Terry Beadle
P. O. Box 128
Drayton Plains, MI 48330

Sweet 16 Sailing Association
Bob Fink
5817 Seminole Ct.
Oaklahoma City, OK 73132

Tanzer 16 Class Association
Donnie Holmer
P. O. Box 26003
Raleigh, NC 27611

Tanzer 22 Class Association
Barbara Charters
P. O. Box 22
St. Anne Bellevue, PQ
Canada
H9X3L4

Tartan 10 Class Association
Paul Lady
35 Lakecrest Ln.
Grosse Pte. Farms, MI 48236

U.S. Int'l Tempest Association
David Duke
P. O. Box 483
Newport, RI 02840

Thistle Class Association
Honey Abramson
1811 Cavell Ave.
Highland Park, IL 60035

Int'l Three Meter Association
David Vinson
Box 70413 Ballard Station
Seattle, WA 98107

Thunderbird Class
    Association
Don Nutter
P. O. Box 1033
Mercer Island, WA 98040

U. S. Tornado Association
David R. Swope
11331 Lazy Lake Dr.
Baton Rouge, LA 70718

National Triton Association
Dot Stevens
300 Spencer Ave.
E. Greenwich, RI 02818

U. S. 2.4 Meter Class
  Association
David J. Schroeder
711 Fifth St. #310
Miami Beach, FL 33139

Int'l 210 Class Association
James R. Robinson
38 Fearing Rd.
Hingham, MA 02043

Udell Class Association
Robert B. Christie
141 W. Jackson Rm. 1325
Chicago, IL 60604

U.S. Wayfarer Association
Robert Frick
4765 Crescent Point
Waterford, MI 48327

Wianno Senior Class
  Association
Carter S. Bacon, Jr.
6 Curve St.
Sherborn, MA 01770

Windmill Class Association
Don Malpas
417 Golf Dr.
Hoover, AL 35226

National X Boat Class
  Association
Jim Smith
P. O. Box 311
Fontana, WI 53125

American X-Flyer YRA
Paul C. White
7349 Scarborough Blvd. E.
  Dr.
Indianapolis, IN 46256

North American Yngling
  Association
Brad Jones
P. O. Box 4047
Spencer, IA 51301

Glossary

Basic definitions of terms are given according to their use in the text. No attempt is made to give a complete definition.

Backstay A wire support for the mast, usually running from the stern to the head of the mast.

Bale A fitting on the end of a spar, such as the boom, to which a line may be led.

Ballast Weight, usually metal, placed low in a boat to provide stability.

Barber hauler A line, attached to the jib or jib sheet, used to adjust the angle of sheeting by pulling the sheet toward the centerline of the boat.

Battens Flexible strips of wood or plastic, most commonly used in the mainsail to support the aft portion, or roach, so that it will not curl.

Bilge A rounding of the hull along the length of the boat where the bottom meets the side.

Bilgeboards Similar to centerboards, and used to prevent lee way. Bilgeboards are located on either side of the centerline at the bilges.

Binnacle A support for the compass, raising it to a convenient position.

Board boat A small boat, usually mono rig. May have a shall low cockpit well. Typically has almost no freeboard.

Bobstay Wire stay underneath the bowsprit; helps to counteract the upward pull exerted by the forestay.

Boom crutch Support for the boom, holding it up and out of the way when the boat is anchored or moored. Unlike a gallows frame, a crutch is stowed when boat is sailing.

Boom vang A system used to hold the boom down, particularly when boat is sailing downwind, so that the mainsail area facing the wind is kept to a maximum. Frequently extends from the boom to a location near the base of the mast. Usually tackle- or lever-operated.

Boomkin (bumpkin) Short spar extending aft from the transom. Used to anchor the backstay or the sheets from the mizzen on a yawl or ketch.

Boot top A stripe near the waterline.

Bowsprit A short spar extending forward from the bow. Normally used to anchor the forestay.

Bridge deck The transverse partition between the cockpit and the cabin.

Bridle A short length of wire with a line attached at the midpoint. A bridle is used to distribute the load of the attached line. Often used as boom travelers and for spinnaker downhauls.

Bulkhead An interior partition, commonly used to stiffen the hull. May be watertight.

Bullseye A round eye through which a line is led, usually in order to change the direction of pull.

Bulwark A vertical extension above the deck designed to keep water out and to assist in keeping people in.

Cap A piece of trim, usually wood, used to cover and often decorate a portion of the boat, i.e., caprail.

Centerboard A board lowered through a slot in the centerline of he hull to reduce sideways skidding or leeway. Unlike a daggerboard, which lifts vertically, a centerboard pivots around a pin, usually located in the forward top corner, and swings up and aft.

Chain plate The fitting used to attach stays to the hull.

Chine A line, running along the side of the boat, where the bottom forms an angle to the side. Not found on round-bottom boats.

Clew For a triangular sail, the aftmost corner.

Coach roof Also trunk. The cabin roof, raised above the deck to provide headroom in the cabin.

Coaming A vertical extension above the deck to prevent water from entering the cockpit. May be broadened to provide a base for winches.

Companionway The main entrance to the cabin, usually including the steps down into the cabin.

Counter At the stern of the boat, that portion of the hull emerging from below the water, and extending to the transom. Apt to be long in older designs, and short in more recent boats.

Cunningham A mainsail control device, using a line to pull down the mainsail a short distance from the luff to the tack. Flattens the sail.

Daggerboard A board dropped vertically through the hull to prevent leeway. May be completely removed for beaching or for sailing downwind.

Deadlight Either a cover clamped over a porthole to protect it in heavy weather, or a fixed light set into the deck or cabin roof to provide light below.

Dodger A screen, usually fabric, erected to protect the cockpit from spray and wind.

Downhaul A line used to pull a spar, such as the spinnaker pole, or a sail, particularly the mainsail, down.

Dry sailing When boats, especially smaller racers, are kept on shore instead of being left anchored or moored, they are dry sailed. The practice prevents marine growth on the hull and the absorption of moisture into it.

Fairlead A fitting used to alter the direction of a working line, such as a bullseye, turning block, or anchor chock.

Fo'c'sle An abbreviation of forecastle. Refers to that portion of the cabin which is farthest forward. In square riggers often used as quarters for the crew.

Foot For a triangular sail, the bottom edge.

Forepeak The compartment farthest forward in the bow of the boat. Often used for anchor or sail stowage.

Forestay Wire, sometimes rod, support for the mast, running from the bowsprit or foredeck to a point at or near the top of the mast.

Foretriangle The triangle formed by the forestay, mast, and fore deck.

Fractional rig A design in which the forestay does not go to the very top of the mast, but instead to a point $\frac{3}{4}$, $\frac{7}{8}$, etc., of the way up the mast.

Freeboard The distance between the deck and the waterline. Most often it will vary along the length of the boat.

Garboard Used in conjunction with strake. Refers to the planks, or strakes, on either side of and adjacent to the keel.

Gollywobbler A full, quadrilateral sail used in light air on schooners. It is flown high, between the fore and main mast, and is also known as a fisherman's staysail.

Gooseneck The fitting that connects the boom to the mast.

Gunter rig Similar to a gaff rig, except that the spar forming the "gaff" is hoisted to an almost vertical position, extending well above the mast.

Gunwale Most generally, the upper edge of the side of a boat.

Guy A line used to control the end of a spar. A spinnaker pole, for example, has one end attached to the mast, while the free end is moved back and forth with a guy.

Halyard Line, usually of wire, that is used to pull up or hoist a sail.

Head For a triangular sail, the top corner. Also a marine toilet.

Head knocker A block with a jam cleat, located on the boom and used to control the main sheet on small boats.

Headfoil A grooved, streamline rod, often aluminum, fitted over the forestay. The primary purpose is to provide continuous support of the luff of the sail, but it may also help support the forestay.

Hiking stick An extension of the tiller that enables the helms man to sit at a distance from it.

Inspection port A watertight covering, usually small, that may be removed so the interior of the hull can be inspected or water removed.

IOR International Offshore Rating

Jiffy reefing A fast method of reefing. Lines pull down the luff and the leech of the sail, reducing its area.

Jumper stay A short stay supporting the top forward portion of the mast. The stay runs from the top of the mast forward over a short jumper strut, then down to the mast, usually at the level of the spreaders.

Keelson A structural member above and parallel to the keel.

Kick-up Describes a rudder or centerboard that rotates back and up when an obstacle is encountered. Useful when a boat is to be beached.

Lapper A foresail which extends back of and overlapping the mast, such as a 110% genoa jib.

Lazarette A stowage compartment at the stern.

Lazy jack Light lines from the topping lift to the boom, forming a cradle into which the mainsail may be lowered.

Lead Refers to the direction in which a line goes. A boom vang, for example, may "lead to the cockpit."

Lee boards Pivoting boards on either side of a boat which serve the same function as a centerboard. The board to leeward is dropped, the board to windward is kept up.

Leech The aft edge of a triangular sail.

Leech line A line running through the leech of the sail, used to tighten it.

Loose-footed Describes a mainsail attached to the boom at the tack and clew, but not along the foot.

Luff The forward edge of a triangular sail. In a mainsail the luff is that portion that is closest to the mast.

Mast step Fitting or construction into which the base of the mast is placed.

Masthead rig A design in which the forestay runs to the peak of the mast.

Mechanical advantage (or purchase) A mechanical method of increasing an applied force. Disregarding the effects of friction, if a force of 100 pounds applied to a tackle is magnified to a force of 400 pounds, the purchase or mechanical advantage is said to be four to one, or 4: 1.

Mizzen A fore and aft sail flown on the mizzenmast.

MORC Midget Ocean Racing Fleet

150 percent genoa For rating purposes, the length of a line drawn perpendicular to the luff and intersecting the clew is divided by the length of the base of the foretriangle. For instance, if the former is 30 feet and the latter 20 feet, the genoa is rated at 30/20 = 1.5, or 150 percent.

Outhaul Usually a line or tackle, an outhaul is used to pull the clew of the mainsail towards the end of the boom, thus tightening the foot of the sail.

Pedestal A vertical post in the cockpit used to elevate the steering wheel into a convenient position.

PHRF Performance Handicap Racing Fleet

Pulpit A metal framework on deck at the bow or stern. Provides a safety railing and serves as an attachment for the lifelines.

Pushpit Colloquial, a pulpit located on the stern.

Rake The fore or aft angle of the mast. Can be deliberately induced (by adjustment of the standing rigging) to flatten sails, balance steering, etc. Normally slightly aft.

Reef points A horizontal line of light lines on a sail which may be tied to the boom, reducing the area of the sail during heavy winds.

Roach The curved portion of a sail extending past a straight line drawn between two corners. In a mainsail, the roach extends past the line of the leech between the head and the clew and is often supported by battens.

Rocker The upward curvature of the keel towards the bow and stern.

Roller reefing Reduces the area of a sail by rolling it around a stay, the mast, or the boom. Most common on headsails.

Rub-rail Also rubbing strake or rub strake. An applied or thickened member at the rail, running the length of the boat; serves to protect the hull when alongside a pier or another boat.

Running backstay Also runner, or preventive backstay. A stay that supports the mast from aft, usually from the quarter rather than the stern. When the boat is sailing downwind, the runner on the leeward side of the mainsail must be released so as not to interfere with the sail.

Running rigging The adjustable portion of the rigging, used to control sails and equipment.

Sandwich construction Layered materials such as FRP-foam-FRP. Usually adhesively bonded. Typically strong and light. Often used in hulls; very widely used in decks.

Scupper Drain in cockpit, coaming, or toe-rail allowing water to drain out and overboard.

Scuttle A round window in the side or deck of a boat that may be opened to admit light and air, and closed tightly when required.

Seat locker A storage locker located under a cockpit seat.

Self-bailing cockpit A watertight cockpit with scuppers, drains, or bailers that remove water.

Self-tacking Normally applied to a sail that requires no adjustment other than sheeting when the boat is tacked.

Sheer The line of the upper deck when viewed from the side. Normal sheer curves up towards the bow and stern, reverse sheer curves down towards the bow and stern. Compound sheer, curving up at the front of the boat and down at the stern, and straight sheer are uncommon.

Sheer strake The topmost planking in the sides, often thicker than other planking.

Sheets Lines used to control the position of a sail.

Shrouds Lateral supports for the mast, usually of wire or metal rod.

Skeg For sailboats, usually refers to a structural support to which the rudder is fastened.

Slab reefing Also points reefing, and sometimes jiffy reefing. Reduces the area of the mainsail by partially lowering the sail and resecuring the new foot by tying it to the boom with points, or light lines attached to the sail.

Sole The flloor of the cockpit or cabin.

Spar Poles, most often of wood, aluminum or carbon fiber, used as supports, such as the mast, boom, or spinnaker pole.

Spinnaker A large, triangular sail, most often symmetrical, flown from the mast in front of all other sails and the forestay. Used sailing downwind.

Spirit The spar that supports the peak of a spritsail.

Splashboard A raised portion of the hull forward of the cockpit intended to prevent water entering.

Spreaders Also crosstrees. Short horizontal struts extending from the mast to the sides of the boat, changing the upward angle of the shrouds.

Spritsail A four-sided fore and aft sail set on the mast, and supported by a spar from the mast diagonally to the peak of the sail.

Standing rigging Permanent rigging used to support the spars. May be adjusted during racing, in some classes.

Staysail A sail that is set on a stay, and not on a yard or a mast.

Stem The most forward structural member in the bow.

Strake On wooden boats, a line of planking running from the bow to the stern along the hull.

Tabernacle A hinged mast step located on deck. Since it is hinged, the mast may be lowered easily.

Tack On a triangular sail, the bottom forward corner. Also, to turn the boat so that the wind exerts pressure on the opposite side of the sail.

Taffrail The rail at the stern of the boat.

Tang A fitting, often of sheet metal, used to attach standing rigging to a spar, or to the hull.

Thwart A transverse structural member in the cockpit. In small boats, often used as a seat.

Toe-rail A low rail, often slotted, along the side of the boat. Slots allow drainage and the attachment of blocks.

Topping lift A line or wire rope used to support the boom when a boat is anchored or moored.

Trampoline The fabric support that serves for seating between the hulls of a catamaran.

Transom The flat, or sometimes curved terminating structure of the hull at the stern of a boat.

Trapeze Wire gear enabling a crew member to place all of his weight outboard of the hull, thus helping to keep the boat level.

Traveler A fitting across the boat to which sheets are led. In many boats the traveler may be adjusted from side to side so that the angle of the sheets can be changed to suit conditions.

Twing Similar to a Barber hauler, a twing adjusts the angle of sheeting.

Vang A device, usually with mechanical advantage, used to pull the boom down, flattening the sail.

Ventilator Construction designed to lead air below decks. May have a cowl, which can be angled into or away from the wind; and may be constructed with baffles, so that water is not allowed below, as in Dorade ventilator.

Warp Heavier lines (rope or wire) used for mooring, anchoring and towing. May also be used to indicate moving (warping) a boat into position by pulling on a warp.

Whisker pole A short spar, normally kept stowed, which may be used to push the clew of a jib away from the boat when the boat is running downwind.

Window A transparent portion of a jib or mainsail.

Wishbone A boom composed of two separate curved pieces, one on either side of the sail. With this rig, sails are usually self-tending and loose-footed.

Index

Small Boats/ One Designs *Continued*				
Flying Scot	Force 5	420	470	
G-Cat	GP-14	Geary 18	Gryphon	Hampton One-Design
Herreshoff	Highlander	Hobie 14	Howmar Twelve	Impulse
Interlake	(International) 210	Invitation	Isotope	J/24
Javelin	Jet 14	JY	Laser	Lido 14
Lightning	MC	Mariner	Mercury	Moth
Nacra 5.2	One Design 14	110	Penguin	Phantom
Precision 16	Prindle 18	Puffer	Ranger 23	Rascal

Small Boats/ One Designs *Continued*	Raven	Rhodes 19	Sandpiper 100	Santana
	Shields	Shrimp	Siren	Sirius	Skipjack
	Skunk	Snipe	Soling	Sonar	Spindrift
	Star	Sundancer	Sunfish	Tanzer	Tech Dinghy
	Tempest	Thistle	Thunderbird	Tornado	Typhoon
	US 1	Vagabond	Victoria	Wayfarer	West Wight Potter
	Widgeon	Windmill	Windrose 5.5	Y Flyer	Yngling
Cruisers/ Auxiliaries	Achilles 24	Alajuela	Annapolis	Bahama

Cruisers/ Auxiliaries *Continued*	Bayfield	Beachcomber	Bristol	Cal
Cape Dory	Capri	Catalina 22	Catalina 38	Clark
Columbia	Contest	Corbin	Crealock	Dickerson
Dockrell	Dufour	Edel	Endeavour	Ericson
F3	FD 12M	Falmouth Cutter	Freedom	Gougeon
Hans Christian	Herreshoff 31	Hinckley 40	Hotfoot	Irwin
Irwin 41	Island Packet	Legend 40.5	Morgan	Nautical
Newport	Nordic	O'Day	Pearson	Pilot 35